Dragon De-mystified: Understanding People's Republic of China

Dragon De-mystified: Understanding People's Republic of China

Editor

Lieutenant General PK Singh, PVSM, AVSM (Retd)

(Established 1870)

United Service Institution of India

New Delhi

Vij Books India Pvt Ltd

New Delhi (India)

Published by

Vij Books India Pvt Ltd
(Publishers, Distributors & Importers)
2/19, Ansari Road
Delhi – 110 002
Phones: 91-11-43596460, 91-11-47340674
Fax: 91-11-47340674
e-mail: vijbooks@rediffmail.com

Copyright © 2018, United Service Institution of India, New Delhi

ISBN: 978-93-86457-78-3 (Hardback)
ISBN: 978-93-86457-79-0 (ebook)

Contents

Preface

The United Service Institution of India (USI) has been publishing its quarterly Journal since 1872. The Journal publishes articles on National Security, Military History and Defence related issues. To provide readers an insight into India's evolving national interests, geopolitical developments in the strategic neighbourhood, conflict spectrum, measures for developing comprehensive national power and defence capability, the USI decided to bring out its Annual Strategic Year Book in 2016. The articles for the Journal and the Strategic Year Book are contributed by eminent research scholars who have expertise on the subject. With the fast changing Security environment, some of the issues which have undergone rapid changes are covered in subsequent issues, at times without any linkage to the previous issues on the subject.

It was therefore consciously thought that if these articles on similar themes are brought together in an edited book form, it will provide an opportunity for the readers to link the previous articles as a background on the subject and how the things shaped with times. It will also provide the readers to get to know the mindset of different authors on the same subject and provide a different line of thinking.

To commence with this series, this book covers articles on China, its Strategic issues and its effect on India. There are a total of nineteen articles selected from previous issues of *USI Journals* and *USI Strategic Year Book* published between 2015 to 2017. These articles cover Economies of China and India, China Pakistan Economic Corridor, China's Energy Diplomacy, Chinese Military Reforms and Evolution of Chinese Armed Forces, China's Military Strategy and Mindset, One Belt One Road and the Shanghai Cooperation organisation. The book also has a chapter covering the talk delivered by His Excellency Mr Luo Zhaohui, Ambassador of the People's Republic of China in India at the USI.

I am sanguine that this book will provide a good platform for those who are pursuing this subject for further research work.

– Editor

Comparing the Economies of China and India and its Impact on India's Strategic and Security Interests[*][†]

Shri Sanjaya Baru

Introduction

One of the most influential research projects undertaken in the past quarter century was the study commissioned by the Paris-based Organisation for Economic Cooperation and Development (OECD) on structural changes in the world economy. British economic historian Angus Maddison led the study and gathered statistical data that shows, among other things, changes in the structure of world income and trade over the past millennium. The most striking result of the study was that in 1700 China and India accounted for nearly half of world income, with the two Asian neighbours having roughly equal shares (around 23.0 per cent each) and that their shares declined sharply to close to around 5.0 each by the middle of the 20th Century. Over two centuries of colonial rule and the fact that Asia missed out on the industrial and maritime revolutions were largely responsible for this. From 1950, both China and India have improved their shares of world income and even as recently as 1980 the two economies were more or less around the same level of development. It is now well known that in the post-Mao Dengist era, during the 1980s and 1990s, the Chinese economy took off and rapidly marched ahead of India. There was a further acceleration of China's growth

* This article was first published in the *Journal of the United Service Institution of India*, Vol. CXLVII, No. 607, January-March 2017.

† This is an abridged version of the talk delivered by Shri Sanjaya Baru on "Comparing the Economies of China and India and its Impact on India's Strategic and Security Interests" at USI on 21 March 2017 with Lieutenant General PK Singh, PVSM, AVSM (Retd), Director USI, in the Chair.

and its share of world trade after the year 2000.

Consequently, by 2016 the Chinese economy was over four times the size of the Indian economy (please refer Table 1 below). India's nominal gross domestic product, in terms of US Dollars, was USD 2.5 trillion in 2016, while China's was USD 11.2 trillion. This gap is expected to persist over the short to medium term. China's recent economic slowdown (see graph of China real GDP growth below) and India's improved economic performance may help reduce the gap provided these extant trends persist.

However, in the foreseeable future, next five years, India has to live with the reality of this wide national income differential. Clearly, one consequence of the income gap would be a potential power gap, with China having the economic capacity to sustain larger defence budgets.

China's real GDP growth
Annual % growth, quarterly

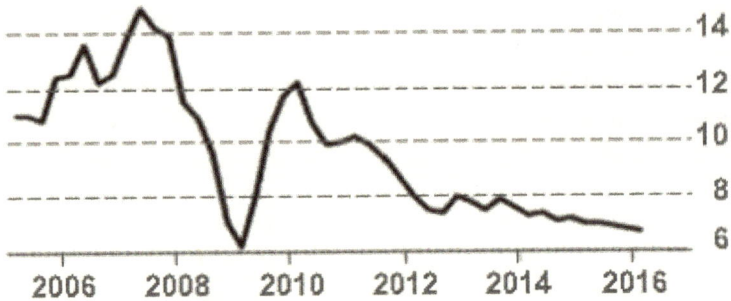

Source : CEIC Generate. 15 Apr 2016

Table 1 : China – India – Size of the Economy & Per Capita Income, 2016-2020

	India		China	
	2016	2020	2016	2020
Nominal GDP (Trillion USD)	2.5	3.6	11.2	16.2
PPP GDP USD	8.7	12.7	20.4	28.2
Nominal GDP Per Capita USD	1,942.0	2,672.0	8,659.0	11,449.0
PPP GDP Per Capita USD	6,746.0	9,328.0	14,813.0	20,004.0

China's Economic Slowdown

China's economic growth rate has slowed since 2012. A report on the economy presented to the National People's Congress states that the 'target rate of growth' set by the country's economic policy makers for the period 2016-2020 is 6.5 per cent. This is way below the double digit levels that China recorded over the past quarter century. Several China-watchers, however believe that the 6.5 per cent target is perhaps an ambitious one because the real rate of growth recorded last year and this could be closer to 4.0 to 5.0 per cent. Whatever the numbers, the fact is that the Chinese economy is slowing down. One reason for this is the slowdown of the world economy. China has been increasingly dependent on the world economy for sustaining its income growth and so the global economic slowdown after 2008 has hurt China more than a country like India that has been less dependent on the global economy for its own economic growth.

In response to this slowdown macro-economic authorities in China have sought to rebalance the economy by shifting the earlier emphasis on investment-led growth to consumption-led growth. However, this has not been an easy switch to engineer. Chinese consumers continue to be frugal consumers, opting to save over 40 per cent of their income. The slow growth of domestic consumption along with the rapid decline in export demand and investment demand remains a major challenge for China.

One consequence of the slowdown in exports has been that China's current account surplus has reduced sharply from 10 per cent of GDP in 2007 to 2 per cent of GDP in 2014. Along with the sharp fall in the current account surplus there has been a rise in the fiscal deficit. The attempt to sustain growth through some investment even when demand has been constrained has contributed to a decline in the rate of return on investment and a sharp escalation of internal debt, which has risen from 150 per cent of GDP in 2010 to 250 per cent by 2016.

China's growth has been sustained by its emergence as a global trading power. Its total foreign trade in 2015 was estimated to be USD 4 trillion, compared to India's USD 0.5 trillion. China is the largest trading partner for 130 countries. More than its exporting power, what has contributed to rising Chinese geo-economic power is the fact that it has emerged as a major importing power, especially with respect to its Asian neighbours and Africa.

China-India Bilateral Economic Relations

While China has emerged as one of India's major trading partners, the persistently high trade deficit that favours China (please refer Table 2 below). This has become a major political issue. In 2015, total bilateral trade between India and China stood at USD 70 billion, but the trade deficit (favouring China) was as high as USD 53 billion. India's trade deficit with China was almost half of India's total trade deficit.

Table 2 : China – India : 'Importing' Power

	Total Trade/ GDP 1960	Total Trade/ GDP 2015	Imports/GDP 1960	Imports/GDP 2015
China	9.0	41.0	4.4	18.7
India	11.0	42.0	6.7	22.6

Given these trends and concerns, where are India-China trade relations headed, and how can the problem of the trade deficit be tackled? First, it is important to recognise that the mounting trade deficit has become political mainly on account of persisting concerns about lack of transparency in China's domestic policies and the larger problem of a trust deficit between the two countries. Absence of credible data enables critics to speculate about intentions, including charges that China is out to 'subvert' India's manufacturing sector. In fact, both China and India have levelled anti-dumping charges against each other. According to the Indian Ministry of Commerce, out of a total of 290 anti-dumping investigations initiated by the Directorate General of

Anti-Dumping and Allied Duties between 1992, when the WTO system came into being, and 2013, as many as 159 cases involved imports from China. Hence, China must address the issue at a political and administrative level to gain India's trust. Establishing trust is the first major challenge.

Second, Indian exporters must do more to win brand recognition and the trust of Chinese consumers. India's overall image has to improve before ordinary consumer resistance can be overcome. China has been trying to overcome such consumer resistance around the world, including in India. If a select number of Indian brands emulate Lenovo's strategy in India, they may be able to overcome consumer resistance and widen the market for Indian goods in China.

Finally, China will have to graduate from exporting products to India to making India a part of its global supply chain and manufacturing some of these products in India. This is the only way in which the problem of the trade deficit can be tackled.

China's Financial Power

One consequence of the build-up of current account surpluses by China has been that it has begun to deploy these dollar reserves in pursuit of its geopolitical objectives. China's overseas development assistance (ODA) budget now exceeds that of the World Bank. The China Development Bank is now bigger than the World Bank in terms of its asset base and lending profile. China has created the Asian Investment and Infrastructure Bank (AIIB) in order to invest in overseas infrastructure and industrial development projects through tied aid that helps push Chinese investment and trade. China has acquired a stake in the European, African and Asian regional development banks, thereby, deploying its reserves to acquire voting power in almost all major development financing institutions globally.

Going beyond such unilateral initiatives, China has emerged as a major shareholder in the BRICS New Development Bank, headquartered in Shanghai, and has increased its vote share in the International Monetary Fund (IMF). The Chinese RMB is now one of the reserve currencies of the IMF, along with the US Dollar, the Euro and the Japanese Yen. Taken together all of this has given China enormous clout in the global financial system, enhancing China's geo-economic power.

Geo-economics of China's Rise

The fact is that even before China's emergence as a geopolitical power it has already become a major geo-economic power. It has been able to deploy its 'trading power' – especially its 'importing power' to reward and punish countries. Thus, after Mongolia hosted a visit by the Dalai Lama, China threatened punitive economic action, including blocking IMF aid to Mongolia, and secured an apology and an assurance from Mongolia that it would not host another visit by the Dalai Lama. China has threatened or taken such economic action against several countries establishing its geo-economic clout.

India has to take cognisance of the fact that China is today the largest trade partner, a source of increasing investment and even defence supplies to several of its South Asian neighbours. Notwithstanding the deceleration in economic growth, China has funded a sustained increase in its defence budget, reminding us of Kautilya's aphorism in the Artha Shastra, "from the strength of the treasury, the army is born." China has emerged as a "strategic economic partner" with respect to many of India's neighbours, investing in port, power and other infrastructure projects that enable China to extend its power projection into the Indian Ocean region.

It is worth noting the fact that while the US's so-called 'pivot to Asia', in terms of deployment of troops in the Indo-Pacific, has not been matched by an economic commitment to the region (with President Donald Trump abandoning the Trans Pacific Partnership (TPP) project), China remains in play on the economic front bilaterally as well as multilaterally, with the Regional Comprehensive Economic Partnership (RCEP) negotiations. China has evolved from being a Trading Power to becoming an Investing Power and the launch of the One-Belt-One-Road (OBOR) project is a manifestation of this new phase in China's geo-economic power projection.

Conclusion

China is presently dealing with a loss of competitiveness, rising debt burden, and excess capacity, all of which have combined to slow down its rate of growth. China has been hurt both by a decline in domestic investment, inadequate consumption demand and the global economic crisis. But, China has the capacity – both economic and political – to deal with the challenges posed by these factors. We must assume that China will come out of this and retain its geo-economic and geopolitical clout. If China's ruling class cannot manage the domestic political consequences of an economic slowdown, there could be changes in the way China manages itself. For example, the Communist Party of China (CPC) may yield political space to the Peoples' Liberation Army (PLA). But, one must assume that between the two they would be able to manage the domestic political situation, the economic situation and their external implications.

From India's view point the major challenge in China-India relations will remain the current imbalance in the relative geo-economic power of the two countries. It will take more than a decade for India to be able to bridge the economic gap with China. This economic gap is fast converting into an overall national power potential gap. Dealing with this challenge will remain India's principal strategic challenge in the near term.

Shri Sanjaya Baru is an eminent academic in economic affairs and was Media Adviser to the Prime Minister from 2004-08 as also a member of the National Security Advisory Board. He is also Visiting Fellow of School of Economic Studies, University of East Anglia, UK and East-West Centre, Hawaii. He has authored a number of books, the latest being 1991: How PV Narasimha Rao Made History.

China Pakistan Economic Corridor – Current Status with Focus on Energy Sector[*]

Commander MH Rajesh@

Introduction

The China Pakistan Economic Corridor (CPEC) is a flagship project of One Belt One Road (OBOR). It was one of the earliest initiatives under its ambit, announced in 2013 for a trusted ally and with a large budgetary outlay of USD 40-50 bn.[1] It deploys idle capital and infrastructure capacities of China in the neighbourhood in a Sinocentric fashion. It rebrands Chinese economic and foreign policy under one umbrella giving it a recall value and synergy, as a strategy for growth. CPEC lays an economic 'weft' over existing strategic 'warp' on China-Pakistan relationship.

CPEC includes mines, generation and transmission projects in energy segment, fibre optics, and sea and land ports spread across Pakistan. It has a prominent transportation spine; albeit not a continuous one, with road, rail and seaport projects in separate segments. At the sea ward end, it originates from Gwadar in Baluchistan, winds through a yet undecided trajectory, enhances certain sections of existing roads that lead up to the Karakoram Highway which thence leads to Kashgar in Xinjiang, China. It aspires to integrate Pakistan's economy with China, in turn connecting China to Indian Ocean bypassing the Malacca. President Xi Jinping's words sum it up as '(Pakistan and China)' need to form a "1+4" cooperation structure with the Economic Corridor at the centre and the Gwadar Port, energy, infrastructure and industrial cooperation being the four key areas to drive development across Pakistan and deliver tangible benefits to its people".[2]

---

[*]   This article was first published in the *Journal of the United Service Institution of India*, Vol. CXLVII, No. 607, January-March 2017.

This article uses data available on Pakistan Government's websites to examine the CPEC addressing spatial distribution of projects, budgetary outlays, and focusses on energy sector which doesn't get the attention it deserves.

Types of CPEC Projects

For the purpose of this article, only those projects which have been budgeted as per Pakistan Government websites at the time of writing this article have been considered for study. Unbudgeted projects have been listed but not used for calculations. It has been observed that the list of projects has varied over time due to political pressures. Present investment amounts to about USD 41.7 bn (refer to Annexure 1). The comparative share is depicted in the Figure 1 below.

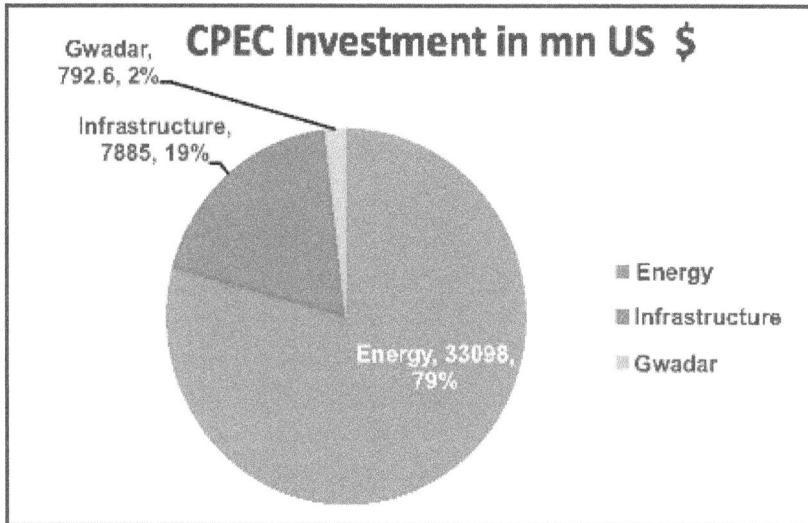

Figure 1 : Investments in the CPEC (road, rail, dry port and fibre optics is shown as infrastructure)

The Transportation Network

The central spine of the corridor involves the following:-

(a) **Roads.** The CPEC presently invests only in two specific road segments.

9

(i)   The Karakoram Highway (KKH) between Havelian and Thakot (USD 1.3 bn).

(ii) Sukkur-Multan Section (USD 2.8 bn).

(iii) CPEC in its initial tranche had no investments in western alignment in Baluchistan. However, there is now a plan of a network of roads in western regions with unbudgeted work in Roads Khuzdar-Basima and DI Khan-Zhob. The Thakot-Raikot section in KKH inside PoK has also recently emerged as an unbudgeted CPEC project. These have been included after the 6th Joint Coordination Committee (JCC) meet in December 2016 in Beijing and made public in early 2017.

(b) **Rail.** In rail connectivity, focus of investments has been on the main railway line (ML1) of Pakistan which carries 70 per cent of the national traffic. This line will be improved for higher speeds. The original investment of USD 3,650 mn has been enhanced with a second tranche after 6th JCC meeting. In connection with the rail investment, CPEC envisages a dry port at northern most railhead, at Havelian.

(c) **Port.** The main investment is in Gwadar Port. Though, less than two per cent of the total CPEC investment, it is the geographic spot in OBOR where the land and maritime networks converge. There is a gamut of investments here including port works, airport, projects to deal with water shortage and projects as listed in Annexure 1. Gwadar's commercial viability is suspect, considering its distance from circumequatorial navigation route and lack of rail connectivity with hinterdand. There are plans to include Keti Bandar port in the CPEC projects.

(d) **Fibre Optic Link.** A key project is Pakistan-China Fibre Optic Project at a cost of USD 44 mn. This will enhance telecommunication through the Gilgit Baltistan Region and is handled by Strategic Communication Organisation. This will connect Rawalpindi with Kashgar.

Focus on Energy- Pakistan Power Sector

Focus area of this article is energy projects in CPEC which constitute 79 per cent of the total investments. The reason for this is the dismal energy situation in Pakistan. Given that energy is central to any economy, issues in energy affects industries with cascading effects on investor sentiments, growth and employment etc. Estimates reveal that power shortage results in a loss of GDP of 2-2.5 per cent annually to Pakistan. Pakistan's power sector presently faces multiple problems as enumerated below :-

The power sector in that country has following problems:-

(a) **Shortage.** Pakistan's installed energy capacity is 25 GW. While demand for energy is 17 GW, production hovers around 12-15 GW. They have a power shortage of about 5 GW.[3] There is also a shortage in transmission capacity, which was around 16,300 MW in 2015[4] whereby, even if all the shortages in generation were resolved, the transmission capacity would limit its distribution. CPEC, therefore, includes generation and transmission projects.

(b) **Cost of Electricity.** Pakistan has very high electricity production cost. Pakistan charges the consumer an average of PKR 16.95 for a unit of electricity whereas in India it is PKR 7.36, Bangladesh PKR 5.47, and US PKR 8.59.[5] This high cost also results in non-payment of bills.

(c) **Use of Costly Fuel.** The primary cause of this high production cost of electricity is present mix of fuel that it used for generation of electricity. Pakistan produces electricity using oil (35 per cent), natural gas (29 per cent), hydroelectricity (30 per cent) and nuclear (five per cent) energy and imports from Iran (one per cent). This mix avoids coal. Though coal is considered a polluting fuel, it is cheap. India uses 60 per cent Coal and China uses 70 per cent coal in production of electricity. However, Pakistan energy sector evolved differently avoiding the use of coal. This contrasts pattern of developing nations and has resulted in the present high cost of electricity.

(d) **Subsidy and Circular Debt.** High cost results in subsidies from the government, which in turn affects economy. Despite the subsidy, the cost to the consumer is high; resulting in non-payment and power theft which triggers a 'circular debt'. This describes the vicious cycle where consumer doesn't pay the distribution company, affecting payments to transmission, generation and fuel companies. This results in debts, stoppage of production and power cuts. Currently the overall debt in power sector is around USD 5 bn.

(e) **High Import Bill.** Pakistan imports far more goods than it exports resulting in an unfavourable balance of payment situation. The oil and gas used for electricity generation in Pakistan is imported and constitutes 35 per cent of the import bill. It has forex reserves of only USD 20 bn. Its economy is under an extended fund facility by IMF who has already issued a warning pertaining to energy sector as well as CPEC payments. The GDP of Pakistan is USD 290 bn whereas the present external debt is USD 79 bn, or 30 per cent of GDP which is large as compared to other similar economies. If fuel import bill and low exports grow unchecked, the balance of payment and debt situation will only worsen.

CPEC Solutions in Energy Sector – Problems and Prospects

The CPEC promises several solutions in its fold. Firstly, it increases power capacity- bringing in three times the current shortage. Secondly, it infuses coal and renewables into the current energy mix reducing overall cost, since coal is cheaper than oil and gas. It is expected that this will reduce the foreign exchange requirements to some degree, though not all. Pakistan's oil import bill was USD 14.77 bn in 2014 and was down to USD 7 bn in 2016. This reduction was primarily due to low oil prices.[6] A cheaper fuel like coal will indeed decrease cost of imports further and provides options to Pakistan making its electricity generation cost far less vulnerable to price shocks driven by a single commodity in a volatile market.

In case the Chinese want to undertake any investment or industrial cooperation in Pakistan as President Xi Jinping has indicated, the power situation in Pakistan must improve in these multiple areas in a comprehensive manner. It is with this aim of preparing the ground for further investments that energy appears a core focus area in CPEC. A total of 16000 mw of energy projects are being launched under CPEC in which 10,400 mw are priority early harvest projects. Therefore, presently the planned investment is roughly three times the shortfall. This indicates that some legacy high cost plants may be shut down in the future. Of these new 16000 mw projects being created, 12000 mw constitute coal based energy projects. Rest of the projects are renewables. Notably oil is totally avoided in CPEC projects. What this high coal infusion will do to energy mix is that from near zero coal use in overall electricity generation pre-CPEC, Pakistan will produce 30 per cent of its energy using coal and renewables. Please refer to Figures 2, 3 and 4 for the transition infused by CPEC. This is one core attribute of CPEC.

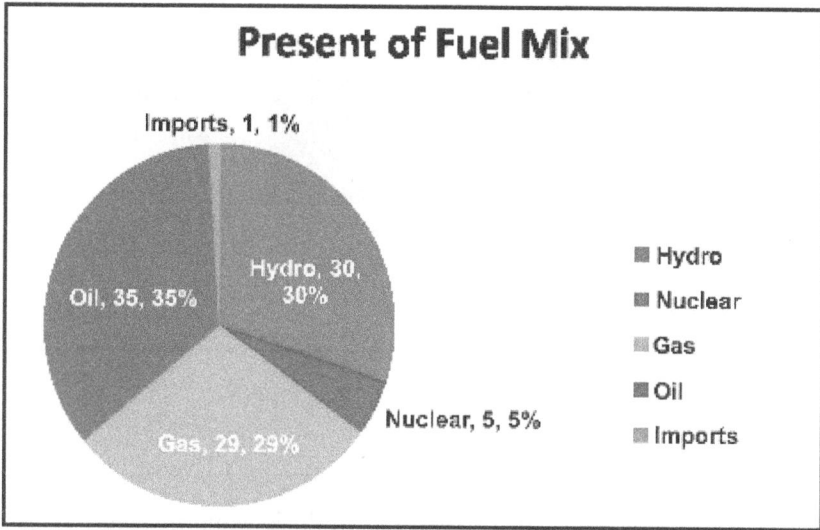

Figure 2 : Type of Fuel presently Used in Pakistan

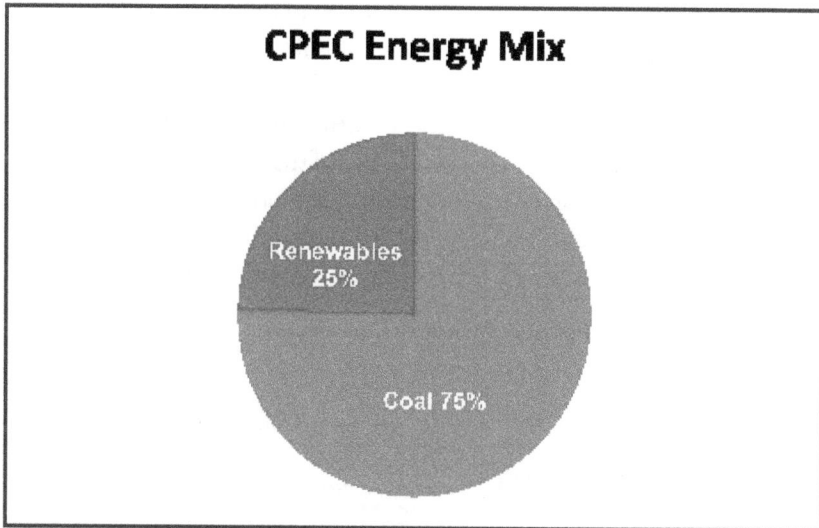

Figure 3 : Type of Fuel Mix CPEC

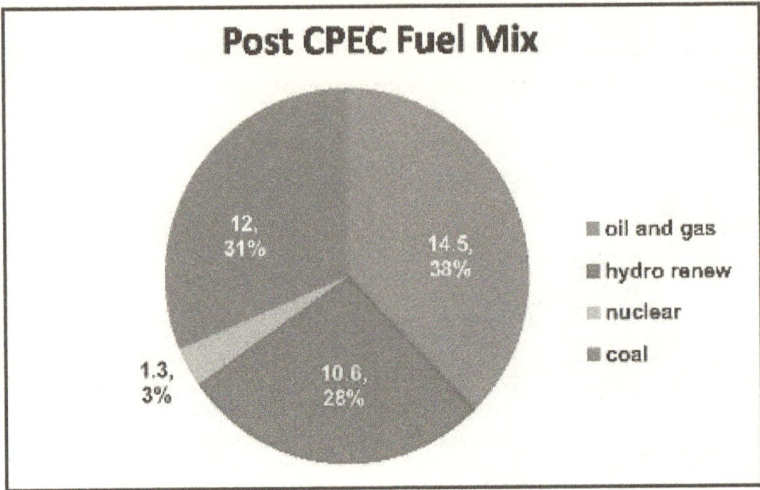

Figure 4 : Type of Fuel Post CPEC

Will Coal Solve the problem?

Since transition to coal, when rest of the world is weaning from coal, is a major element of CPEC, more analysis on coal is necessary. A vast majority of the coal based power plants coming up in CPEC are supercritical plants which are capable of working at higher temperatures. They also use imported high calorific coal. Pakistan doesn't have reserves of this variety of bituminous coal. Its reserves are mostly lignite, or low calorific coal (Please refer to Table 1). Hence barring power plants like Thar and Engro which are co-located with coal mines; high grade coal will be imported from abroad and, therefore, does not solve external dependency or balance of trade and payment problems which legacy energy sources had imposed. Coal based power will also add to climate change which a country like Pakistan, which has borne extreme weather calamities in recent years has to be concerned about.[7]

Table 1: Pakistan's Coal situation

Type of Coal	Bitumen	lignite	Coke gas	Coking coal	Blast furnace
Production	2383	1168	81		733
Import	2645			115	

Source : International Energy Agency[8]

14

High Interest Rate of Energy

Unlike the infrastructure segment, where government is deeply involved, the energy field of CPEC mostly involves Sino-Pak private partnership. Chinese banks will finance these private investments at 5-6 per cent interest rate. The Government of Pakistan will be contractually obliged to purchase electricity from those firms at pre-negotiated rates and provide a sovereign guarantee. This is at a high rate of PKR 18 per unit. Pakistan already has a consumer rate of PKR 16.95, which is the highest in the SAARC region. This high rate in CPEC according an analyst 'is a classical colony-making exercise by China, which Pakistan establishment and the Army is quite excited with'.[9] Chinese firms seek a revolving fund backed by sovereign, amounting to 22 per cent of power tariffs,[10] which could amount to USD 700 mn annually for all projects if local firms default.[11] This could be unfavourable to Pakistan in the long term. However, Pakistan's energy and economic scenario being where it is today, it has little choice but to take this bitter pill. The debt equity ratio of energy projects are to the order of 25 per cent equity: 75 per cent debt. The loan in addition to interest carries insurance fees of 7 per cent with Sinosure, the Chinese insurance arm. The returns on equity for these projects is at a very high rate of upto 34 per cent, which will eventually be borne by the consumer.[12]

Cost of Installation

The CPEC will eventually add a 16 GW capacity in energy generation at a cost of USD 34 bn which is at the rate of USD 2 bn per GW when all projects are considered. Power Plant installation estimations in CPEC varies from wind power installation at USD 2.5 bn /GW, solar USD 1.35 bn / GW, USD Hydro 1.9-2.68 bn /GW, Coal USD 0.8-1.5 bn /GW as per calculations by the author; whereas, India routinely builds its thermal power plants at a cost less than USD 01 bn /GW.[13] Hence, CPEC power plants are above normal costs. This will benefit the investors both in Pakistan and China. China also gets a near 100 per cent offset, benefitting Chinese firms, besides the sovereign guarantee and power purchase commitments.

Other Issues

Pakistan energy sector also suffers from load management problem, poor technology, theft, subsidies, free power and overstaffing etc.[14] Electricity transmission is also a problem in Pakistan. Except Punjab, all other provinces, especially Khyber Pakhtunkhwa and Balochistan have a suboptimal power distribution system and lack the capacity to take the additional load and deliver it to the consumers.[15]

Specifics of Thermal Plants and Coal

As far as new coal power plants being built under CPEC are concerned, they mostly use supercritical technology. A supercritical power plant operates with higher thermal efficiency compared to normal plants. Therefore, it can extract more heat out of coal. These plants demand superior metallurgy in its construction. The new set of power plants barring the Sino Sindh (SSRL) mine mouth water plant and Thar Engro, use imported coal as well. Pakistan doesn't have high calorific coal reserves too, which needs to be imported. The coal reserves of Pakistan are concentrated in Thar and Salt Range area where only lignite, a low calorific coal is available. Lignite is not an economical fuel when transported to distant location. The lower the quality of coal, the higher the transport cost as a percentage of overall coal cost. Both these mines have subcritical plants integral to them in CPEC plans considering advantages of co-location. Since a majority of coal plants will use imported, high calorific coal, which Pakistan doesn't possess, they will continue to impact the import bill albeit lesser in value than oil. This will be, in all likelihood, sourced from Australia or Indonesia opening new sea-lanes of communications and resource politics.

Regional Spread of Projects

Regionally, the power projects are more in Sindh, Baluchistan and Punjab with two projects namely the Karot and Kohala Hydel Project planned in PoK. However, the locations of major projects of Balochistan are adjacent to Karachi in Gaddani leaving vast swathes of rest of Balochistan devoid of any energy project. Only less than 2 per cent gets invested there considering Gaddani could be cancelled as per some reports. If one were to connect the dots representing energy projects, the notional eastern alignment becomes more prominent avoiding most of Baluchistan. The road between Multan and Sukkur is also on the Eastern side. Hence, one must conclude that the Western alignment remains aspirational with projects mostly along the eastern portion of Pakistan (Please refer to Figure 6, stars indicate projects which have been budgeted).

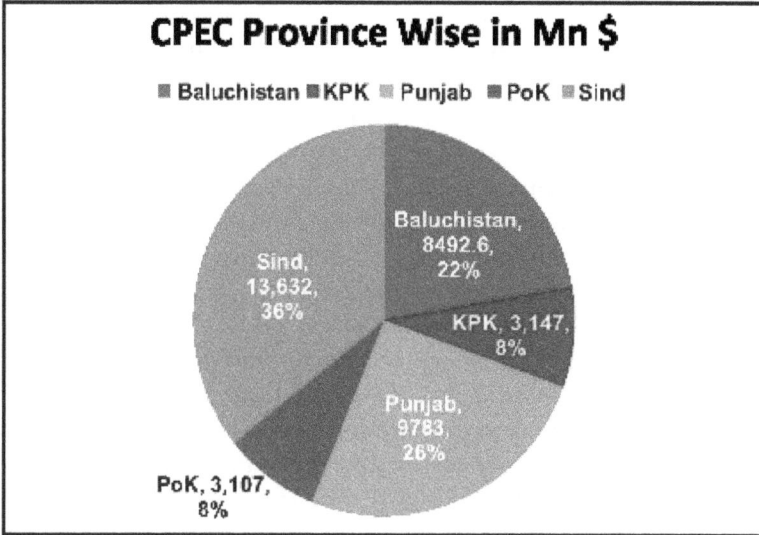

Figure 5 : CPEC projects based on Provinces (except rail)

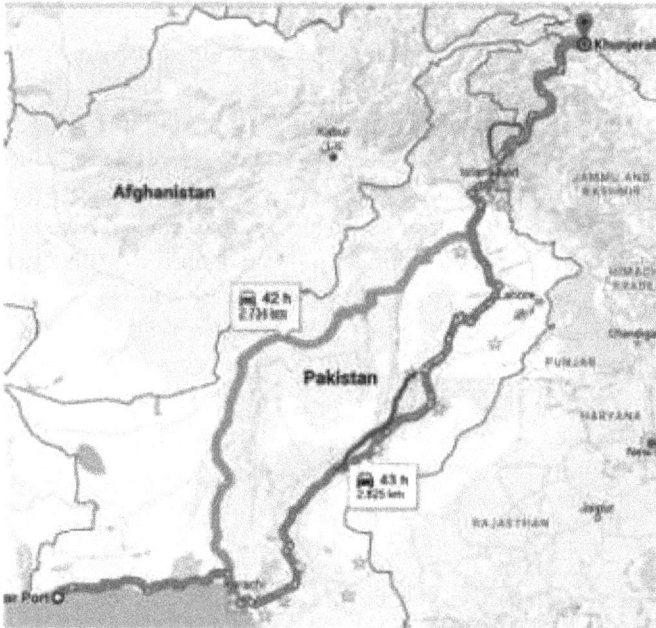

Figure 6 : Power projects of CPEC (denoted by stars) and approximate road segments in red showing the eastern bias[16]

Conclusion

CPEC is more about energy projects and less about corridor. On blueprint it is a plan addressing some core concerns of economy where corridor is a metaphor that will deepen the relation with strategic implications to the region. There is no 'one' continuous road or even an alignment in CPEC as etched in most mental maps. Contrary to official positions there is a noticeable bias in projects to the prosperous eastern provinces ignoring Baluchistan. This short shrift can accentuate current fissures. Only by easing the deep energy crisis within Pakistan can it be of any use to China for OBOR. In energy domain CPEC is a bitter pill of coal infusion in energy mix. However, only deep reforms can turn Pakistan's energy and economic situation around. CPEC will give rise to new resource politics for coal. China's Malacca Dilemma may also not be mitigated through this corridor, even as Pakistan portrays it to be. Cost of transportation simply doesn't serve economic logic hauling energy to Xinjiang which is not only oil rich, but also the terminus of Central Asian pipelines coming to China. The ability of Pakistan to absorb the investments in given period and thereafter pay back is also suspect considering historic trends. Hence, these debts could eventually become strategic equities for China, especially the Gwadar Port, which can worsen security in South Asia.

As far as India is concerned, CPEC has added a layer of complexity with more projects in PoK being drawn into its ambit without taking Indian concerns on board. That makes projects in contested areas politically vulnerable. If CPEC and OBOR are actually about regional economic growth, as the lending nation, China should rethink about investment in PoK and roll them back. Currently, it appears that the narrative is driven by Pakistan only with very little Chinese statements in the open. After all, it is not easy for any nation to grow ignoring the security and possibilities on the cards held by a rising India. This is especially relevant at a time of weak cues from global economy and western fatigue about globalisation. A stable and peaceful South Asia is crucial for Asia led growth. Investments in contested areas, does not augur well for that purpose, it will distance India further from any China led initiatives like OBOR.

Endnotes

1   "With a New Chinese Loan, CPEC Is Now Worth $51.5bn," DAWN.COM, September 30, 2016, http://www.dawn.com/news/1287040.

2   "Important Documents," accessed August 29, 2016, http://pk.chineseembassy.org/eng/zbgx/importantdocuments/.2015/04/20 Chin-Pak Dosti Zindabad HE Xi Jinping President of the People's Republic of China

3   To provide a comparative perspective, India generates 300Gw and Delhi's peak consumption is 6Gw.

4   Power transmission capacity surges to 16,300 MW, http://www.dawn.com/news/1192470, accessed October 4, 2016.

5   "Electricity Shock: 'Pakistanis Paying Highest Tariffs in Region,'" The Express Tribune, January 31, 2014, http://tribune.com.pk/story/665548/electricity-shock-pakistanis-paying-highest-tariffs-in-region/.

6   "Pakistan Saved $4.5bn on Oil Imports in FY16," DAWN.COM, July 24, 2016, http://www.dawn.com/news/1272751.

7   The dangers of Pakistan's coal revival, http://www.dawn.com/news/1242279, accessed October 4, 2016

8   "IEA - Report," accessed October 18, 2016, http://www.iea.org/statistics/statisticssearch/report/?year=2014&country=PAKISTAN&product=Coal.

9   China-Pak Economic Corridor: Why Gwadar Is An Overrated Port, http://swarajyamag.com/world/china-pak-economic-corridor-why-gwadar-is-an-overrated-port, accessed September 26, 2016

10   "ECC Approves Plan to Set up Special Funds for CPEC Projects."

11   Pal, "The China-Pakistan Corridor Is All About Power. Not Electricity, but the Real Thing."

12   "China-Pak Economic Corridor: Why Gwadar Is An Overrated Port," accessed September 26, 2016, http://swarajyamag.com/world/china-pak-economic-corridor-why-gwadar-is-an-overrated-port.

13   "Windfall for Chinese on Coal Fired Projects," The Express Tribune, February 15, 2017, https://tribune.com.pk/story/1327172/windfall-chinese-coal-fired-projects/.

14   Roberts and Sattar, "Pakistan's Economic Disarray and How to Fix It." http://www.heritage.org/research/reports/2015/06/pakistans-economic-disarray-and-how-to-fix-it accessed October 4, 2016,

15   Government fails to satisfy opposition over CPEC issues, http://www.dawn.com/news/1292529/government-fails-to-satisfy-opposition-over-cpec-issues, accessed October 27, 2016

16   Prepared by author using Google Map, road sections in red are approximate. Non-budgeted projects not shown.

17   "CPEC | China-Pakistan Economic Corridor (CPEC) Official Website," accessed February 17, 2017, http://cpec.gov.pk/#.

Overall Status of CPEC Projects[17]

Project	Quant	Cost ($ mn)	Technology	Location	Province
Energy Coal (Priority)					
Port Qasim Electric Company Coal Fired, 2 x 660	1320 mw	1,980	Super-critical	Port Qasim	Sindh
Sahiwal 2 x 660 MW Coal-Fired Plant	1320	1,600	Super-critical	Sahiwal	Punjab
Engra thar 4 x330 MW Coal-fired	1320	2,000	Sub Critical	Thar Block - II	Sindh
Surface mine in Blook II of Thar Coal Field, 6.5 metric ton per annum (mtpa)		1.470	Open Pit	Thar Block - II	Sindh
Gwadar Coal/LNG / Oil PowerProject	300	600	Not decided	Gwadar	Balochistan
HUBCO coal power plant 1 x 660 MW	660	970	Super-critical	Hub	Baluchistan
Rahimyar Khan Coal Power Project	1320	1,600	Super-critical	Rahimyar Khan	Punjab
SSRL Thar Coal Block I - 6.5 metric ton per annum (mtpa)		1,300	Open pit	Thar Block-I	Sindh
SSRL 2 x 660 MW Mine Mouth Power Plant			Subcritical	Thar Block-I	Sindh
Energy Coal (Actively Promoted)					
Gaddani Power Park Project (2 x 660 MW)	1320	3,960		Gaddani	Baluchistan
HUBCO Coal Power plant 1 x 660 MW	660	970	Super-critical	Hub	Baluchistan
Thar mine mouth oracle, Thar Sindh	1320	1,300		Thar	Sindh
Muzaffargarh Coal Power Project, Punjab	1320	1,600	Subcritical	Muzzafargarh	Punjab

Project	Quant	Cost ($ mn)	Technology	Location	Province
Energy Renewables (Priority)					
Quaid-e-Azam 1000 MW Solar Park	1000	1,350	PV	Bahawalpur	Punjab
Dawood 50 MW wind Farm	50	125	Wind Turbine	Bhambore Sindh	Bhambore Sindh
UEP 100MW wind Farm	100	250	Wind Turbine	Jhimpir Sindh	Jhimpir Sindh
Sachal 50MW Wind Farm	50	134	Wind Turbine	Jhimpir Sindh	Jhimpir Sindh
Suki Kinari Hydropower Station	870	1,802	Hydel	Suki Kinari	KPK
Karot Hydropower Station	720	1,420	Hydel	Karot	POK & Punjab
Energy Renewables (Priority)					
Kohala Hydel Project	1100	2,307	Hydel	Kohala	POK
Pakistan Wind Farm II 2 x 50 MW	100	150	Wind Turbine	Jhimpir	Sindh
Energy transmission Infrastructure (Priority)					
Matiari to Lahore Transmission Line		1,500			Sindh & Punjab
Matiari to Faisalabad Transmission Line		1,420			Sindh & Punjab
Energy Infrastructure (Actively Promoted)					
Gaddani Power Park Project (Jetty + infrastructure)		1,200		Gaddani	Baluchistan
Road					
KKH Phase II (Thakot -Havelian Section)	120 Km	1,366			KPK
Peshawar-Karachi Motorway (Multan-Sukkur Section)	392	2,980			Punjab Sindh

Project	Quant	Cost ($ mn)	Technology	Location	Province
Khuzdar-Basima Road N-30 (110 km)	110	NA			Baluchistan
Upgradation of D.I.Khan (Yarik) - Zhob, N-50 Phase-I (210 km)	210	NA			KPK Baluchistan
KKH Thakot-Raikot N35 remaining portion (136 Km)	136				KPK PoK
Rail					
Expansion and reconstruction of existing Line ML-1	1736	3,650			
Havelian Dry port (450 M. Twenty-Foot Equivalent Units)		40			KPK
Capacity Development of Pakistan Railways		NA			
Gwadar					
Gwadar East-Bay Expressway		140.6		Gwadar	Baluchistan
New Gwadar International Airport		230		Gwadar	Baluchistan
Construction of Breakwaters		123		Gwadar	Baluchistan
Dredging of berthing areas & channels		27		Gwadar	Baluchistan
Development of Free Zone		32		Gwadar	Baluchistan
Necessary facilities of fresh water treatment, water supply and distribution		130		Gwadar	Baluchistan
Pak China Friendship Hospital		100		Gwadar	Baluchistan
Technical and Vocational Institute at Gwadar		10		Gwadar	Baluchistan
Bao Steel Park, petrochemicals, stainless steel and other industries in Gwadar		NA		Gwadar	Baluchistan

Project	Quant	Cost ($ mn)	Technology	Location	Province
Gwadar Smart Port City Master Plan		NA		Gwadar	Baluchistan
Development of Gwadar University (Social Sector Development)		NA		Gwadar	Baluchistan
Upgradation and development of fishing, boat making and maintenance services to protect and promote livelihoods of local population					
Digital Connectivity					
Cross Border Optical Fiber Cable		44			
Pilot Project of Digital Terrestrial Multimedia Broadcast (DTMB)		NA			
Urban Transit					
Karachi Circular Railway				Karachi	Sindh
Greater Peshawar Region Mass Transit				Peshawar	KPK
Quetta Mass Transit				Quetta	Baluchistan
Orange Line - Lahore				Lahore	Punjab
Provincial Projects					
Keti Bunder Sea Port Development Project		NA		Keti Bunder	Sindh
Naukundi-Mashkhel-Panjgur Road Project connecting with M-8 & N-85		NA			Baluchistan
Chitral CPEC link road from Gilgit, Shandor, Chitral to Chakdara		NA			Gilgit KPK
Mirpur – Muzaffarabad - Mansehra Road Construction for connectivity with CPEC route		NA			PoK KPK Punjab

Project	Quant	Cost ($ mn)	Technology	Location	Province
Quetta Water Supply Scheme from Pat feeder Canal, Balochistan		NA		Quetta	Baluchistan
Iron Ore Mining, Processing & Steel Mills complex at Chiniot, Punjab		NA		Chiniot	Punjab
Economic Zones					
Rashakai Economic Zone , M-1, Nowshera		NA		Rashakai	KPK
Special Economic Zone Dhabeji		NA		Dhabeji	Sindh
Bostan Industrial Zone		NA		Bostan	Baluchistan
Punjab China Economic Zone M-2		NA		Shekhupura	Punjab
ICT Model Industrial Zone, Islamabad		NA		Islamabad	
Development of Industrial Park on Pakistan Steel Mills Land at Port Qasim near Karachi		NA		Port Qasim	Sindh
Bhimber Industrial Zone		NA		Bhimber	Pok
Mohmand Marble City		NA		Mohmand	KPK
Moqpondass SEZ Gilgit-Baltistan		NA		Moqpondass	GB PoK

---

* Commander MH Rajesh was commissioned into the Indian Navy on 01 Jan 1994 and served in the Submarine Arm. Currently, he is Research Fellow at USI of India.

The Chinese Military's Mindset[*]

Colonel Iqbal Singh Samyal

Introduction

The Chinese military figures preeminently in President Xi Jinping's "Chinese Dream" *(zhong guo meng)* as the "Strong Army Dream" *(qiang jun meng)*. China's rise and the PLA's growing capability are redefining global and regional power equations. Understanding the Chinese military's mindset has become even more important in this milieu. Rather than dwelling on an academic interpretation of strategic culture which continues to be theorised[1,] this article aims to look at the Chinese mindset in the framework of traditional strategic culture, which is focused outwards, and organisational culture, which is focused inwards. The primary aspects analysed are the traditional Chinese military strategic culture, the formative influences on the PLA and the contemporary developments to provide the practitioner with a framework to better discern the Chinese military's mindset.

The Traditional Chinese Military Strategic Culture

Traditional Chinese military culture has two strands viz. the civilisational attributes and the strategic culture. History and exclusiveness of the Chinese culture have led to certain deep rooted civilisational attributes. China saw early consolidation of political power under the imperial court of the Qin and Han dynasties after a violent and tumultuous ancient period. Imperial contiguity under subsequent dynasties, the strength of the Chinese culture and a strong 'Han' identity manifested into the 'Middle Kingdom' syndrome and the *Tianxia* concept. Overtime grew a self-perception as a superior, self-

---

[*]   This article was first published in the *Journal of the United Service Institution of India*, Vol. CXLVI, No. 605, July-September 2016.

contained, pacifist and defensive civilisation. There is also a strong belief in the strong correlation between internal stability and external threat. The constant threat from the northern nomads engendered a continental outlook towards strategy and led to the concept of frontier defence and peripheral buffers to protect the Han motherland.[2] The peripheral buffers to the Han motherland namely; Xinjiang, Inner Mongolia and subsequently Tibet have been controlled or lost depending on the strength of the ruling dynasty and this has been a cyclic process through most of Chinese imperial history.

The traditional strategic culture is evident from the ancient texts. The Chinese were the first to formally collate their ancient military texts including *The Seven Military Classics of Ancient China*.[3] Five of the Seven Classics including *The Art of War* were written during the 'Spring and Autumn' (722 - 481 BC) and the 'Warring States' period (approx 403 to 221 BC).[4] This era is termed as a period of basic establishment of Chinese strategic theory.[5] During the Warring States period seven major states on the North China plains[6] struggled in a long drawn political and military contest to become the hegemon (*ba*), with emphasis on statecraft, detailed assessment of relative state power, strategic alliances, deception, long term planning and preparation for war which permeated the subsequent Chinese strategic culture. The salience of the Seven Military Classics is that from the Song Dynasty (960-1126 AD) onwards, these were used as official texts for martial related examinations having a lasting impact on generations of military and political leaders.[7]

The PLA's *Science of Strategy (2005)* divides the content of ancient Chinese strategy into "Theory of Victory in Advance" (war preparation to include knowledge and war build up), "Theory of Complete Victory" (victory by safe and varied means including attacking the enemy's strategy and alliances, using psychological, coalition and economic warfare) and "Theory of Victory through Fighting" (actual war). The latter theory includes the use of dialectical terminologies to highlight the dynamic nature of war as characterised in *The Art of War*. These three theories were considered as an organic whole supporting each other to form a "strategic theoretical system" to conquer the enemy.[8] Much academic research has been carried out on the ancient and imperial Chinese military texts by both the Chinese and western scholars. Differing perceptions exist with one school of thought including the Chinese propounding that Chinese culture is essentially pacifist in nature preferring the use of nonviolent means to subdue or deal with adversaries and that this culture is rooted in Confucianism - Mencius principles.[9] Johnston (1995) claims that Chinese strategic culture is based on hard realpolitik considerations with emphasis on offensive action and on flexibility or *quanbian* (assessment of relative strengths and the situation). He bases this claim on an academic analysis of the contents of "The Seven Military Classics" and the military texts of the Ming Dynasty in dealing with the Mongols.[10]

The traditional Chinese military culture influenced many Chinese leaders including Mao Zedong, Zhu De who purportedly memorised "The Art of War" and Marshal Liu Baocheng who taught "The Art of War" at the PLA Academies.[11] Conservative "hawks" in the establishment, including the PLA, invoke this era and there are books written on the similarities between the Warring States period and the current multipolar world.[12] Thus the framework of the traditional Chinese military culture is important for understanding the military strategic culture.

The Formative Influences on the PLA

All organisations are shaped by their initial leadership and experiences. The PLA is no exception to this rule. Arbitrarily taking the period from 1927[13] to the Taiwan Straits Crisis of 1958 as the initial formative years of the PLA, the main formative influences can be summarised as the Marxist Strategic Theory, the towering leadership of Mao Zedong, the initial operational experiences and the Soviet influence. The importance of these formative influences is primarily in the organisational culture of the PLA.

Marxist Strategic Theory. The ideological fountainhead of communist ideology has been Marxism - Leninism. In addition to the ideological aspects, the PLA traces concepts related to People's War, Active Defence, advancement of science and technology and proletarian way of operations to Marxist Strategic theory.[14] Further, even today the PLA strives to align the contemporary situation to the ideological framework.

Mao Zedong's Military Strategy. Mao shaped the PLA and also produced a vast body of military writings which became a kind of scripture for the PLA. The most important aspects of Mao's strategy as per the PLA are his interpretations of Marxist-Leninist ideology as applicable to Chinese conditions, the primacy of politics in military strategy and the strategic guidance of People's War and Active Defence.[15] The PLA continues to abide by these principles showing Mao's enduring legacy in its discourse and Active

Defence suitably modified is the strategic guidance even today.[16]

The Operational Experience. During the formative years the PLA was constantly in conflict starting with the Revolutionary War (1920s to late 1940s; including the War against Japan (1937-45) and the Civil War (1946-49)) and continued after the establishment of the PRC with the Korean War and the Taiwan Strait Attacks (1954-55 and 58). Further during this period the PLA evolved across the entire spectrum of conflict from guerrilla warfare to conventional warfare. The PLA graduated to large scale manoeuvre and conventional warfare during the Civil War (1946-49) of which three important campaigns namely, the Liao Shen campaign, the Beijing Tianjin campaign and the Huai Hai campaign had major lessons for the PLA and are studied in the PLA Academies even now.[17] These initial operational experiences in conventional warfare shaped the operational and tactical level philosophy of the PLA.

The Soviet Influence. The Soviet influence, which had existed from the inception of the Communist Party of China (CPC), increased after the Korean War when it was decided to build a professional army modelled on the Soviet Red Army. Consequently the period between 1954-58 saw large scale 'Russianisation' covering all aspects including organisational changes, professional military education and doctrine, translation and dissemination of Red Army manuals (regulations, curricula, handbooks and research reports), weapons and equipment procurement and Soviet military advisers at practically every level.[18] Although the subsequent Sino-Soviet split impacted the relations, the PLA organisation was modelled on the Soviet Army and the PLA which for much of its existence due to necessity had been largely decentralised became centralised, hierarchical and rigid along horizontal and vertical organisational lines.

At the end of the formative period, the Chinese military had a nationalistic, ideological and operationally experienced mindset. Most Chinese military leaders had less or no formal military education and learned through practical experience. The CPC also saw enemies, both within and outside the country, posing an existential threat to it and reinforced the military's ultra-nationalistic outlook and sensitivity to territorial matters. On a broader note, the Chinese military mindset could be considered to be ultra-nationalistic with sensitivity to territorial integrity, realist by nature with reliance on assessment of relative military power (national power) and long term planning, laying emphasis on deception, offensive pre-emptive action and surprise at the operational level, dependent on Mao's military philosophy and drawing lessons from China's rich traditional strategic military culture. Some of these aspects are hard coded in the PLA mindset. However, contemporary changes in modern warfare have influenced the Chinese operational thought and the recent reorganisation will impact the organisational culture.

The Chinese military became highly politicised in the following years and became mired in the internal politics of the CPC. Deng Xiaoping's take over after Mao's death heralded a new era and the PLA's journey from becoming a combined arms force to the transformation for prosecuting integrated joint operations began in earnest.

Contemporary Developments

China has changed faster than any other country has in a short span of five decades. The Party has moved on from 'ideological purity' to 'economic development' as *raison d'être* and under the present leadership is drumming the nationalistic beat. Economic changes have created interests beyond the mainland. China has emerged from a regional power status to consider itself part of a triangle of big powers to include the USA, Russia and China.[19] In addition to these factors, the PLA has also been impacted with the changing nature of warfare and the expanding arc of PLA roles. Fortuitously the economic resources, leadership guidance and improving indigenous technological capabilities have been enablers for the PLA in its quest for the "Strong Army Dream". Given the opaqueness of China's real strategic goals, inferences have to be drawn from the important manifestations which are evident in the professionalism, modernisation and the changing priorities of the PLA.

Professionalism. The PLA's influence within the CPC has reduced in comparison to the past although it still stands as a powerful institution within the Chinese political structure. Heath (2015) contends that the PLA is evolving into a functional equivalent of a modern, national army while being organised along Leninist principles implying that the PLA is moving from a political first to becoming a professional political army.[20] It also implies that, like other State institutions in China today which have become more professional, the military is in tune with the strategic and ideological framework provided by the CPC and focused on the security domain. Consequently, it mostly retains major influence in the security and defence related issues including strategic arms, territorial disputes and policies with regard to countries like India, Japan, North Korea, Pakistan, Russia and the USA.[21]

Modernisation. The comprehensive modernisation process, aimed at being capable of winning wars under conditions of informationisation by mid-21st century, is largely on track with interim objectives being achieved. In consonance with the demands of integrated joint operations, the PLA has carried out reorganisation of higher and operational level defence organisations. A major driving force of the PLA modernisation is the large military research community including the PLA Academy of Military Science and other military education institutions. Comprehensive study on foreign armies, conflicts and concepts is carried out by this community and an important outcome has been the hybridisation of Chinese military thought with western war fighting concepts. It is common to see military texts using terminology like asymmetric, non-linearity, tempo of operations alongside phraseology straight from Mao Zedong's thought *(Mao Zedong Sixiang)*. Chinese war fighting concepts are aligning more with the West, though the change is more in nature of Michael Porter's definition of 'operational efficiency' rather than strategy.[22] The PLA graduated from combined arms operations *(hetong zuozhan)* in the 1980s to joint operations *(lianhe zuozhan)* in the 1990s to its current aspirational doctrine of integrated joint operations *(yitihua zuozhan)* with system of systems *(zuozhan tixi)* capability, akin to the western network centric warfare, under an overall vision of time bound "mechanisation *(jixiehua)* and informationisation *(xinxihua)*". The PLA has systematically carried out its modernisation to become a more capable and effective modern fighting force and a modicum of confidence is already evident in the unfolding events in the South and East China Seas.

Maritime Focus. The Chinese Defence White Paper 2015 titled "Military Strategy" clearly states that China has to build itself into a maritime power.[23] The PLA Navy (PLAN) has moved beyond Admiral Liu Huaqing's "Near Seas Active Defence Strategy" to "Far Seas Operations". While Chinese articulations are indicative of a defensive outlook towards Chinese economic maritime interests there are indications of the influence of Mahan on Chinese Strategists.[24] Contemporary Chinese maritime strategy is still being analysed based on the growing PLAN capability, Chinese publications and PLA texts with some scholars positing that China is making a layered developmental strategy with a combination of "Near Seas Defence, Far Seas Operations", as it projects power in an incremental manner outwards.[25]

Geopolitics. The PLA has always established a 'main strategic direction' for any given period. As mentioned in the *Science of Strategy*, its orientation in the 1950s was the South East Coast and in the 1960s post the Sino-Soviet split, became the Northern Areas[26]. The current reorganisation into five Theatre Commands clearly indicates its new orientation towards the maritime domain in the Asia-Pacific region. The geopolitical significance of Taiwan has grown because of the Chinese contest for geostrategic space with the US in the Asia-Pacific region. Further, though not clearly articulated, there is a clear perception of the East China Sea and the South China Sea being considered as the new maritime buffers akin to the peripheral buffers in the historical continental strategy. The developments in the South China Sea and East China Sea signal that the Chinese will use both coercive and non-coercive policies in this quest for regional dominance which can be considered a litmus test for China becoming a 'Big Power' in its own right. [27]

Conclusion

China's metamorphic and rapid change has created both prosperity and contradictions. Wealth has also created inequality; capitalism flourishes in the cloak of modified communist ideology, and growing societal aspirations co-exist with and challenge authoritarianism. Metaphorically, the PLA also reflects this reality and despite the projection of rapid development, the PLA will absorb the changes desired in a much longer time frame than is being projected, especially in the organisational culture. In order to comprehend the Chinese military's mindset, all the frames of reference including the traditional and formative influences as also the contemporary developments need to be appreciated.

The Chinese military has a realist and nationalistic outlook with both hard-line and moderate factions within its ranks. The maritime outlook of the military is coming to the forefront and the Chinese are aiming to contest the maritime space in the Asia-Pacific from the US. The important question in the future will be – if the Chinese, and by corollary the military, be successful in applying an essentially continental strategy in the maritime domain where the connotations are different and zero sum outlook cannot be applied. Further, will China continue to view the world through the insular lens of the 'Middle Kingdom' and the outlook of 'Warring States' period in a bid for world pre-eminence or adopt a more mellow outlook to limit the military buildup and work out a regional security architecture which is based on mutual trust and accommodation?

Endnotes

1   Alastair Iain Johnston. *Thinking about Strategic Culture.* International Security, Vol. 19, No.4 (Autumn, 1995), pp. 32-64.

2   Michael D Swaine & Ashley J Tellis. *Interpreting China's Grand Strategy : Past, Present, And Future.* 2000. California: Rand Corporation.

3   The Seven Military Classics of Ancient China are *The Art of War (Sun Zi Bing Fa), Wu Zi Bing Fa, The Methods of the Si Ma (Si Ma Fa), Wei Liao Zi, Tai Gong's Six Secret Teachings (Tai Gong Liu Tao), Three Strategies of Huang Shi Gong (Huang Shi Gong San Lue) and Tang Tai Zong Li Wei Gong Wen dui.*

4   Ralph D Sawyer & Mei Chun Sawyer. *The Seven Military Classics of Ancient China.* Westview Press, Boulder, Colorado.1993.

5   Peng Guangqian & Yao Youzhi. Eds. *The Science of Military Strategy.* Military Science Publishing House, Academy of Military Science of the People's Liberation Army, Beijing. 2005.p.88.

6   John K Fairbanks & Merle Goldman. *China : A New History (Second Enlarged Edition).* Harvard University Press, Cambridge .2006. p.49.

7   Alastair Ian Johnston. *Cultural Realism : Strategic Culture and Grand Strategy in Chinese History.* Princeton University Press, New Jersey. 1995. p.46.

8   Peng Guangqian, et.al. *op. cit.* pp.90-91.

9   Address at United States War College by Lt Gen Li Jijun, Vice President of Academy of Military Sciences, Aug 1997 Letort Paper No 1.

10 Alastair Ian Johnston, *Op. cit.*

11 Li Xiaoping. *A History of the Modern Chinese Army.* The University Press of Kentucky. 2007. pp 48, 68 & 121.

12 Michael Pillsbury. *The Hundred Year Marathon : China's Secret Strategy to Replace America as the Global Superpower.* Henry Holt and Company, New York. 2015. pp. 51-58.

13 The Red Army traces itself to the Nanchang Uprising of 01 Aug 1927.

14 Peng Guangqian, et.al. *op. cit.* p.102.

15 *Ibid.* p.104.

16 Information Office of the State Council, The People's Republic of China. *China's Military Strategy (National Defense White Paper) 2015.* Accessed from http://eng.mod.gov.cn/Database/WhitePapers/ on 08 Aug 2015.

17 Mark A. Ryan, David M. Finkelstein & Michael A. McDevitt. Eds. *Chinese*

Warfighting : The PLA Experience Since 1949. M E Sharpe, Reprinted by KW Publishers, New Delhi. 2010, p.56.

18 Li Xiaobing, *Op. cit.* pp.122-123.

19 Fu Ying. *How China Sees Russia, Beijing and Moscow are Close, but not Allies.* Foreign Affairs. January/February 2016, p.104.

20 Timothy R. Heath. *China's New Governing Party Paradigm: Political Renewal and the Pursuit of National Rejuvenation (Rethinking Asia and International Relations).* Ashgate Publishing Company.2014. pp. 85-86.

21 Linda Jakobson and Dean Knox. *New Foreign Policy Actors in China.* SIPRI Policy Paper No 26. p.13. Accessed at http://books.sipri.org/product_info?c_product_id=410 on 08 Aug 2015.

22 Michael E Porter. *What is Strategy?* Harvard Business Review, On Strategy. November- December 1996. pp.4-22.

23 Information Office of the State Council, The People's Republic of China. *China's Military Strategy (National Defense White Paper)* 2015 . op. cit.

24 James R Holmes & Toshi Yoshihara. *The Influence of Mahan upon China's Maritime Strategy.* Comparative Strategy, Volume 24, Issue 1, 2005. Pp.23-51; *Chinese Naval Strategy in 21st Century: The Turn to Mahan (Cass Series: Naval Policy and History).* Routledge, 2007.

25 Andrew S. Erickson. *China's Blueprint for Sea Power.* China Brief Volume 16 Issue 11, July 06, 2016.

26 Peng Guangqian, et.al. *op. cit.* pp. 231-234.

27 SL Narasimhan. *China's Strategy : History to Contemporary.* Journal of the United Service Institution of India, Vol CXLIV, No. 597, July-September 2014.pp. 386-394.

---

† **Colonel Iqbal Singh Samyal** was commissioned into the KUMAON Regiment in Dec 1990. He served as the Defence Attaché in the Embassy of India, Beijing from Oct 2011 to Nov 2014. Presently, he is posted as the Deputy Commander of an infantry brigade in the Eastern Theatre.

South China Sea in Retrospect: Post Tribunal Verdict*

Commander MH Rajesh

Introduction

In July 2016 a tribunal in Hague delivered its award over several features and an ambiguous line over water in the South China Sea (SCS) – an issue that has been brewing for several years between China and her maritime neighbours. The appellant to the arbitral tribunal – a redressal forum of the United Nations Conventions on the Laws of the Sea (UNCLOS) – was the Philippines. The award went against China and in favour of the Philippines. However, the heat and dust over SCS is unlikely to settle anytime soon, considering the hard, *historical* (emphasis added) line adopted by China. This article tries to place some relevant aspects of that case in retrospect and gauges some of its impacts.

The South China Sea

The SCS is a marginal sea in the Pacific Ocean, littoral to the South East Asian Nations and China (**Figure 1**). It has several reefs and shoals, which make it rich in fish and other resources. Nations that abut that sea – China and the ASEAN nations – are also significant engines of global growth. They are also deeply into trade, 90 per cent of which happens via the oceans. This is especially true of China, which is the most trading nation in the world.[1] The SCS is also an important maritime conduit that connects the Indian and Pacific Ocean Economic Systems which has markets at one end and resources at the other. Any disturbance to this Indo-Pacific system can upset global economy.

---

*   This article was first published in the *Journal of the United Service Institution of India*, Vol. CXLVI, No. 605, July-September 2016.

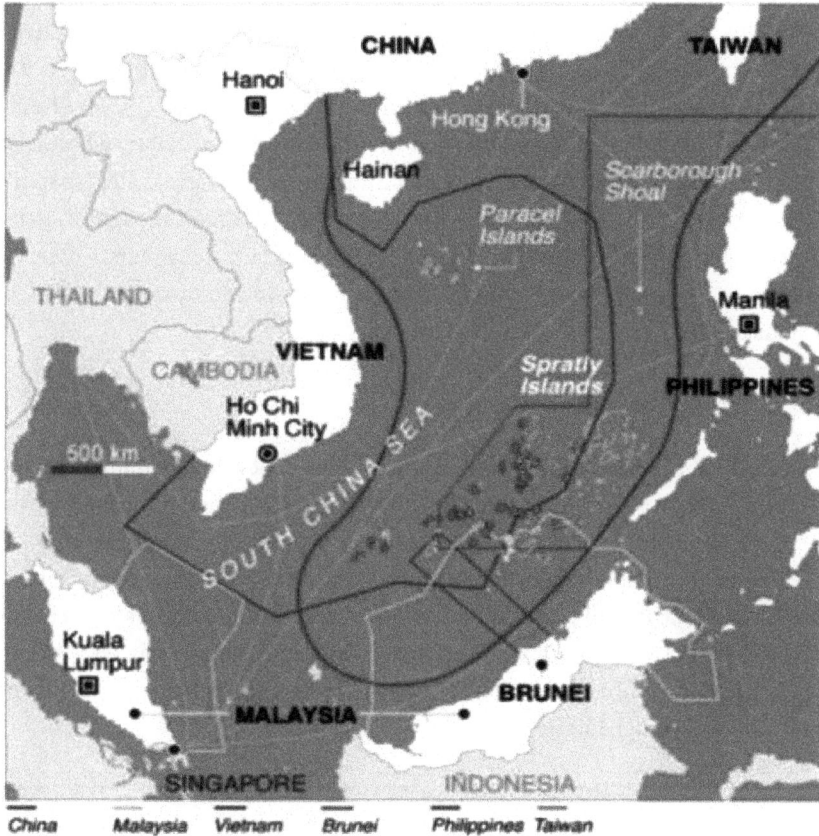

Figure 1 : The Map of SCS

source http://blogs.voanews.com/state-department-news/2012/07/31/challenging-beijing-in-the-south-china-sea/)

The Disputes over SCS

The SCS has over two hundred land features in separate groups, many of which are presently contested. Of all the disputes, the Spratlys involve the most number of claimants including China, Malaysia, the Philippines, Taiwan and Vietnam. Over and above these contests, there is a unique claim over these small features by China known as the 'nine dash line'. This is a Chinese cartographic expression which dates back to a 1947 map produced during the Nationalist rule. This makes matters complex with hardening positions taken by Communist China and Nationalist Taiwan.[2] The modern version of this nine dash line surfaced in 2009. That year, China in its *note verbale* to the UN in response to the continental shelf claim by Vietnam and Philippines, placed the present version of the nine dash line.[3] Over the years the dashes have varied both in numbers and positions.[4] Two dashes in Tonkin bay vanished, as China settled that portion of the claim, whereas an additional dash got added near Taiwan. China since 2012 also issues passports with a map showing this nine dash line. UNCLOS does not recognise such a line over water. Hence, the SCS disputes have two main arguments – national ownership of land features as well as legality and meaning of the infamous nine dash line.

The Laws of the Sea

UNCLOS is the modern law of the ocean, first articulated as *mare liberum,* meaning open seas. The concept got refined over a period, resulting in the three mile *cannon shot* law. Rising marine activities demanded adapting the UNCLOS, a process that commenced in 1958, which finally came into force in 1994. China and all parties involved in SCS disputes are signatories to the UNCLOS. The most notable non-party is the USA, which has reservations with its Seabed Convention. Some relevant UNCLOS tenets of the dispute are as follows (Refer **Figure 2**) :-

(a) A country's entitlements over sea stem from its ownership of adjacent land. This is the doctrine of *"la terre domine la mer"* or land dominates the sea.

(b) The extent and rights of entitlement from 12 nm territorial rights to 350 nm economic rights for a continental shelf claim.

(c) Waters landwards of 'baseline' are *internal waters,* where sovereign rights can be exercised.

(d) Land features such as drying heights, rocks, and islands may confer some entitlements as under:-

   (i) Small features that are visible only during low water (Low Tide Elevations (LTE)) do not provide entitlement over sea, nor can they be appropriated by occupation, but they become part of baseline points.

   (ii) Rocks accrue only a 12nm territorial sea (TS) around them.

(iii) To qualify as Islands, features in their natural condition, must be able to sustain habitation and have capacity for non-extractive economic activity. Islands fetch territorial sea and 200 nm Exclusive Economic Zone (EEZ).

(e) UNCLOS accounted for *historic claims* during its formulation. Pre-existing rights to resources were considered, but not adopted by the convention. Such rights were extinguished with provisions of EEZ / Continental Shelf (CS) in UNCLOS.

(f) The UNCLOS defines an archipelago regime exclusively for states that exist as a group of islands which entitles an archipelagic baseline and internal waters inside them (refer figure 2).

(g) The degree of freedom of passage varies, depending on nature of waters – i.e. straits, internal, territorial and high seas.

UNCLOS Maritime and Airspace Zones

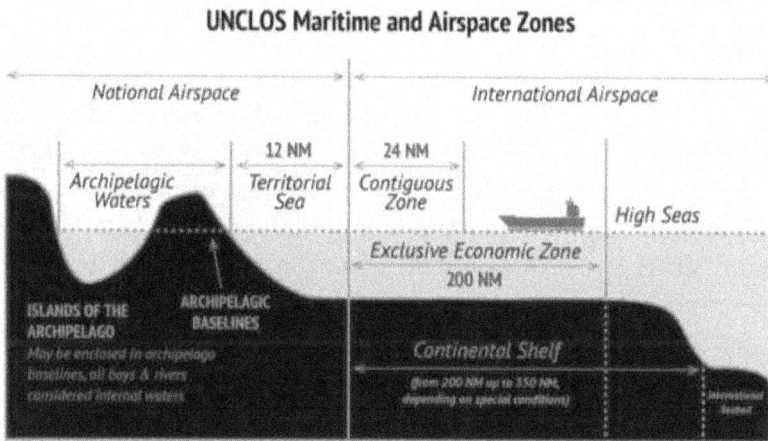

Source: Batongbacal and Baviera (2013).

Figure 2 : Maritime and Air Space Zones

Along with UNCLOS came a dispute resolution mechanism. States could choose one or more designated organisations for settling disputes including the International Tribunal for the Law of the Sea (ITLOS), International Court of Justice or Arbitral tribunals.

A Brief History of Disputes

There are several reasons behind onset of SCS disputes. National maritime capacities and awareness expanded simultaneously with UNCLOS negotiations. One trigger point was discovery of oil in Spratlys in 1970s. The presence of reefs and shoals also made the area abundant in fish, a significant source of protein. The East Asian economies and China grew phenomenally, relying on trade as well as energy flows through the SCS. As significance of SCS grew, disputes too became bitter. China and Vietnam fought naval battles over the Paracel group in 1974 and a Spratlys reef in 1988. The coming in to force of UNCLOS in 1994, accentuated the disputes. By 2002, diplomacy yielded a declaration of conduct between parties in SCS which provided some mitigating mechanisms. Nations had also commenced building and reclamation on the features in their possession. Some of it was with a military perspective to improve habitability and status as per UNCLOS. This altered natural state of the features reclaiming approximately 3300 acres, majority being Chinese efforts.

The Arbitration

The territorial disputes kept simmering till early 2013 when the Philippines chose the arbitration route, through the Permanent Court of Arbitration at The Hague as per UNCLOS provisions. Instead of raising sovereignty, the Philippines, pivoted the case on interpretation of UNCLOS.[5] This was an astute strategy, primarily since the tribunal has no mandate to award on sovereignty or delineation but can interpret legalities based on UNCLOS. Two core questions from the Philippines comprised the legality as per UNCLOS of *'Historic Rights and the 'Nine-Dash Line' and 'Status of Features'* in Spratlys. From these two core questions emerged *lawfulness of Chinese actions.* It also raised *aggravation of dispute and harm to environment* also in its submission.

China abstained from the arbitration, but pronounced its views and non-acceptance of arbitration through position papers. Yet, the hearing proceeded since *'absence of a party or failure of a party to defend its case shall not constitute a bar to the proceedings'* according to UNCLOS. The tribunal initially decided on admissibility and jurisdiction and awarded the final verdict in Jul 2016 against China.

The Award

The salient points of the award along with comments are given in the succeeding paras :-[6]

Historic Rights and the 'Nine-Dash Line'

(a) **Nine-Dash Line.** Award stated that scope of entitlement is defined by UNCLOS. Claims in excess by China are invalid regarding nine dash line.

Comments. An entitlement over sea originates from ownership of land. The waters in contest are more than 350 miles away from Chinese mainland, beyond maximum zone of entitlement (i.e. extended Continental Shelf). Therefore, Chinese entitlement around Spratlys if any, would emerge from the ownership of features within it and not the 'nine dash line' over water. It is here, that historical aspect of the claim becomes relevant.

(b) **History and UNCLOS.** It stated that UNCLOS during the formulation had considered historic rights but were not adopted and deemed subsumed and extinguished in EEZ rules. The award stated that though Chinese mariners historically made use of the islands, there was no evidence that it historically exercised exclusive control over water or their resources. Tribunal, therefore, concluded that there is no legal basis for China to claim historic rights, to resources within sea areas of the nine dash line.

Comments. UNCLOS considers historic claims in two instances. They are articulated as historic *bays* and historic *titles*. Both pertain to sovereignty over a sea area close to land, with certain quantifiable as well as subjective criteria, treating them as 'internal waters'. In these cases claimant has to prove propriety, continuous effective control, besides acquiescence of foreign states in exercise of that authority.[7] In distinguishing between historic water, title and rights, there is an interpretation that historic 'water' or historic 'title' are about sovereignty whereas historic 'rights' are lesser set of rights.[8]

Status of Features. The tribunal considered the features. As described earlier, an island, rock or an LTE accrued different entitlements over water. Tribunal concluded from the present and historical evidence that none of the Spratlys features was an island.

Implications and Comments. This meant that none of it generated an EEZ or a CS irrespective of ownership by any nation freeing up a very large area for global commons. To illustrate, merely a spot on island would generate 125600 sq nm of EEZ, whereas 'rocks' reduced entitlement to 452 sq nm of territorial sea.[9] The verdict implied that certain seas were part of the Philippines EEZ since they were not in any 'possible' entitlement of China. Additionally, EEZ entitlement also has a navigational implication considering China's views on freedom of navigation in EEZ.

Other Awards. The other awards, of relevance are:-

(a) China violated the Philippines' sovereign rights in its EEZ and created a serious risk of collision with Philippine vessels.

(b) China caused severe harm to environment and violated its obligation to preserve ecosystems.

(c) China had aggravated the dispute, by land reclamations and construction during dispute resolution.

Responses

International responses were along expected lines, mostly measured and diplomatic. Even domestic responses within affected nations were muted and controlled. A few of these are highlighted below:-

(a) The Chinese response to the Tribunal award was that it was *'a political farce under the pretext of law',* and declaring the award *null and void* with no *binding force.* It reiterated China had neither accepted nor recognised the same. It had crafted a response, one alluding to existence of internal waters in SCS taking the archipelagic/historic route for legitimising what was within the nine dashes.[10] A White Paper was also released with copious historic details reinforcing its historic claim. The response fails to challenge the logic of the verdict apart from hardening the historical route to the claim. In an attempt to gain support, China has also incorrectly interpreted the joint Russia-India-China statement as a measure of Indian and Russian support.[11] Pakistan and Taiwan were notable supporters of China.

(b) Indian statement mentioned the following :-[12]

(i) Expressed support to freedom of navigation, overflight and unimpeded commerce.

(ii) Ushered respect to International law and UNCLOS.

(iii) Sought resolution of disputes using peaceful means without use of force and threats.

(iv) Sought self-restraint in not complicating disputes.

(c) The dynamics in the Philippines have also undergone a change. New President Duterte is busy with extra-legal crackdowns and has even risked falling out with its ally, the USA. It seems to be mending fences with China with ex-President Fidel Ramos as the chief interlocutor. The official reactions have also been with restraint.[13] Hanoi, too has clamped down anti-China protests.[14]

A Geopolitical Perspective

China's late maritime resurgence, geography and its historical actions in the continent partly answer why it is undertaking contrarian positions after signing UNCLOS in 1996. It appears, just as it had created a continental buffer around a coastal Han core by annexing Xinjiang, Tibet and Inner Mongolia in initial days of PRC, it is in the process of creating a maritime buffer zone in the SCS. It is called a *core*,[15] albeit in unofficial parlance, due to following reasons :-

(a) SCS is vital to its maritime commerce and energy needs especially with the *'new normal'* of slow economic growth. Even a minor disturbance to trade flows can cause severe imbalance, with a political price to pay. This is also closely linked to their Malacca Dilemma.[16]

(b) SCS holds reasonable reserves of oil and gas.

(c) As the largest consumers of fish in the world with the depleting fish stock in Chinese EEZ, SCS is a source of food and livelihood for China.

(d) SCS is the vital area leading to Malacca Straits critical to a two ocean strategy. Kaplan argues that SCS is key to China's two ocean strategy just as Caribbean Sea was key to the US's two Ocean presence with the making of Panama Canal.[17]

(e) The US Pivot to East Asia accentuates that insecurity.

Steps to Control that Buffer

China's aim appears converting SCS into zones where it has higher control. According to UNCLOS the legal nature of waters, whether internal, territorial, EEZ or high seas, decides degree of freedom of navigation through those waters.[18] Since land dominates the sea, a line over water has no *locus standi* and only a feature in the sea can give a nation control over water. That must explain the scramble for features and island building. Among maritime zones of control within the ambit of UNCLOS 'internal *waters*', offer highest navigational control.[19] They are usually landwards of 'baseline' or within boundaries of an archipelago.[20] The geography of contested waters in SCS legally cannot become internal waters to China because :-

(a) It is not landwards of any Chinese baseline.

(b) Creation of archipelagic base line is an exclusive privilege of an *archipelagic* state which China isn't with a continental mainland.[21]

(c) The tribunal has also ruled that Spratlys do not fulfil the archipelago criterion as per UNCLOS on its own, even if features were deemed as a single entity.

Yet, the three post tribunal Chinese responses on *sovereignty* and *arbitration*, by Foreign Minister Wang Yi, the Government and the White paper mention *internal* waters in the SCS![22,23,24]

Whilst, creation or claim over features provides measurable methods of control, there is another route – of history which in very rare, well defined cases provides internal waters and rights. In a peculiar position of Marxist Leninist state over history, Chinese statements hinge on the *historic* claim[25] in an effort to give a fillip to its 'rights' over these waters. In fact, the Chinese post tribunal response invokes history over twenty times, whereas UNCLOS mentions history just twice, that too in a text ten times as voluminous. This desire to turn the clock back into a historic era with incipient law will do China and the world more harm. The SCS issue is back to where it started with such a stand, albeit with greater public clarity over UNCLOS.

Implications of the Award

The most significant implication of the award is that it clarified several UNCLOS aspects hitherto not available from a legal perspective to a wider audience; such as:-

(a) This offers a legal respite to affected parties.

(b) By awarding that the subject features are not islands but rocks and low tide elevations, it has freed large water space for use by global commons.

(c) It has awarded that historic rights were considered and deemed extinguished when EEZ's were decided.

This award serves as a precedence and reference to further resolutions of disputes in the region. However, it did not judge on sovereignty, leaving that question open for resolution. Here, China's insistence of a bilateral approach to resolution is a ploy considering the power differential between China and individual nations.

The verdict has affected China's claim to adherence to rule of law and peaceful development. Even though it abstained and rejected the verdict as a "farce", it reacted throughout the proceedings through position papers, public hearings across nations and newspaper advertisements.

As a cue for the road ahead, it is good to recall that power in global politics will remain diffused in the future.[26] This is also one reason why adherence to law becomes all the more important with lesser powers for the hegemon. Concepts like buffer zones have proven to be part of the problem than solutions, and could become redundant when rule based, equitable cooperative constructs emerge in a new order. It would be ideal and augur well for China as a responsible global power to scale down the actions and take lead in a cooperative, oceanic regime based on rule of law with all stake holders. That should assuage some of its own insecurities.

The award will positively affect rule of law for oceans. So far members of the Security Council including the USA have shown little respect to previous arbitrations.[27] Whereas middle powers have amicably settled issues by arbitration irrespective of sizes of countries involved like India-Bangladesh Settlement.[28] China has portrayed the Philippine action as a proxy initiative by the USA; whereas the USA, a non-party to the convention was not allowed to be a part of the Tribunal hearings. The USA becoming a party to UNCLOS will strengthen the regime in a world which is becoming increasingly multipolar. Bill Hayton highlights the irony that China has ratified UNCLOS but doesn't adhere to it, whereas the US has not ratified but adheres to most of its provisions!

Chinese internal situation is presently marked by a powerful President, an anti-corruption campaign which has shaken its polity, triggered an economic slowdown and a transition of its economic model. Such a transition makes any nationalist spark, a sensitive issue. Despite etching the 'nine dash line' on public consciousness, China has so far clamped down on public response.[29] It can ill afford any popular uprisings as previous experiences indicate that such events quickly spin out of control and attain a different tone and tenor.

The SCS has so far not been elevated to a core status, unlike Taiwan, Tibet and Xinjiang.[30] Yet, it's response evoking *internal* waters and historical rights are signs that the issue is far from over. The 'verdict' is one window, to tone down the rhetoric as a first step to an eventual settlement. It remains to be seen how far China would push the envelope in the matter, as 'nine dash line' has been tattooed. However, it can alter interpretations to suit the verdict for non-exclusive rights such as those over Scarborough Shoals or the joint development route that it seeks as per UNCLOS. Whatever be its choice, it appears that the issue is far from over considering the stakes involved. India and the world must encourage parties to resolve disputes through peaceful means without use of force and exercise self-restraint based on the principles of UNCLOS. Law must remain above politics.

Endnotes

1   "WTO | 2015 Press Releases. Accessed September 8, 2016, https://www.wto. org/english/news_e/pres15_e/pr739_e.htm.

2   Bill Hayton, *The South China Sea: The Struggle for Power in Asia* (Yale University Press, 2014).

3   "Full Text: China Adheres to the Position of Settling Through Negotiation the Relevant Disputes Between China and the Philippines in the South China Sea - Xinhua | English.news.cn," accessed September 9, 2016, http://news.xinhuanet. com/english/china/2016-07/13/c_135509153.htm.

4   Limits in the Seas, No. 143 China: Maritime Claims in the South China Sea, United States Department of State Bureau of Oceans and International Environmental and Scientific Affairs

5   Hayton, *The South China Sea.*

6   "PCA Case No 2013-19 In The Matter Of The South China Sea Arbitration

Before An Arbitral Tribunal Constituted Under Annex VII To The 1982 United Nations Convention On The Law Of The Sea Between The Republic Of The Philippines And The People's Republic Of China Registry: Permanent Court of Arbitration PH-CN-20160712-Award.pdf," accessed July 18, 2016, https://pca-cpa.org/wp-content/uploads/sites/175/2016/07/PH-CN-20160712-Award.pdf.

7   Juridical regime of historic waters, including historic bays, Extract from the Yearbook of the International Law Commission 1962 , vol. II

8   For detailed discussion read Limits of the Seas, No 143 ibid

9   Hayton, *The South China Sea.*

10 "Statement of the Government of the People's Republic of China on China's Territorial Sovereignty and Maritime Rights and Interests in the South China Sea," accessed July 17, 2016, http://www.fmprc.gov.cn/mfa_eng/zxxx_662805/t1379493.shtml.

11 "India with Us on Verdict, Says China - The Hindu," accessed July 17, 2016, http://www.thehindu.com/news/national/india-with-us-on-verdict-says-china/article8850469.ece.

12 Statement on Award of Arbitral Tribunal on South China Sea Under Annexure VII of UNCLOS http://www.mea.gov.in/pressreleases.htm?dtl/27019/Statement+on+Award+of+Arbitral+Tribunal+on+South+China+Sea+Under+Annexure+VII+of+UNCLOS

13 "Philippines Urges 'restraint and Sobriety' after South China Sea Ruling - The Economic Times," accessed July 20, 2016, http://economictimes.indiatimes.com/default-subsec/defence/philippines-urges-restraint-and-sobriety-after-south-china-sea-ruling/articleshow/53172579.cms.

14 "Hanoi Clamps down on Protests against China after Ruling - Taipei Times," accessed July 20, 2016, http://www.taipeitimes.com/News/front/archives/2016/07/18/2003651263.

15 China's Assertive Behaviour Part One: On "Core Interests" Michael D. Swaine

16 "China's 'Malacca Dilemma,'" *The Jamestown Foundation,* accessed August 2, 2015, http://www.jamestown.org/single/?no_cache=1&tx_ttnews% 5Btt_news%5D=3943.

17 Robert D Kaplan, *Asia's Cauldron: The South China Sea and the End of a Stable Pacific* (Random House Publishing Group, 2014).

18 As per China's interpretation.

19 Internal waters are landwards of Base line. Archipelagic states, which are only five in the world, can have internal waters depending upon their archipelagic

baseline.

20   Article 47(1)UNCLOS

21   Article 47(1)UNCLOS

22   "Full Text: China Adheres to the Position of Settling Through Negotiation the Relevant Disputes Between China and the Philippines in the South China Sea - Xinhua | English.news.cn."

23   "Remarks by Chinese Foreign Minister Wang Yi on the Award of the So-Called Arbitral Tribunal in the South China Sea Arbitration," accessed September 9, 2016, http://www.fmprc.gov.cn/mfa_eng/zxxx_662805/t1380003.shtml.

24   "Full Text of Chinese Govt' Statement on China's Territorial Sovereignty and Maritime Rights and Interests in S. China Sea - Xinhua | English.news. cn," accessed September 9, 2016, http://news.xinhuanet.com/english/2016-07/12/c_135507754.htm.

25   "Infographics: White Paper on Settling Disputes with Philippines - Xinhua | English.news.cn," accessed July 17, 2016, http://news.xinhuanet.com/english/photo/2016-07/13/c_135509723.htm.

26   "Global Trends 2030," accessed November 12, 2015, http://www.dni.gov/index.php/about/organization/global-trends-2030.

27   Graham Allison Diplomat The, "Of Course China, Like All Great Powers, Will Ignore an International Legal Verdict," *The Diplomat,* accessed July 17, 2016, http://thediplomat.com/2016/07/of-course-china-like-all-great-powers-will-ignore-an-international-legal-verdict/.

28   "Kerry Praises India's Approach to Solve Maritime Disputes, Says No Military Solution to S China Sea Issue | Latest News & Updates at Daily News & Analysis," *Dna,* August 31, 2016, http://www.dnaindia.com/world/report-kerry-praises-india-s-approach-to-solve-maritime-disputes-says-no-military-solution-to-s-china-sea-issue-2250702.

29   Lucy Hornby, "Beijing Censors South China Sea Protest," *Financial Times,* July 18, 2016, http://www.ft.com/cms/s/0/2e3ec4fe-4c8c-11e6-8172-e39ecd3b86fc.html#axzz4EuVQQHL0.

30   ibid

†   **Commander MH Rajesh** was commissioned into the Submarine Arm of the Indian Navy on 01 Jan 1994. Currently, he is a Research Fellow at USI of India.

China, Japan and the Evolving Risks in the East China Sea: Implications and Policies to Avert Risks*

Ms Amrita Jash

Introduction

With much of the attention being paid to the South China Sea dispute, it becomes imperative to note that the constant militarisation of the East China Sea signals greater risks of an accidental military confrontation between the two Asian powers, China and Japan. At the outset, although the potential costs involved discourage any such intended move either by China or Japan but the increasing trends of escalation and constant militarisation of the East China Sea has seemingly increased the likelihood of an unintended confrontation between China and Japan, if not deterred. In this view, the alarming trends call for immediate de-escalation policies to be adopted by both China and Japan in order to quell the dangers of an imminent confrontation. Thus, the latent emergency needs to be acted upon by precautions to avert an unwarranted calamity imposed with heavy costs. Given this perspective, the paper examines the building tensions between China and Japan in the East China Sea. The paper argues that the increasing trends of military escalation between China and Japan reflect unwarranted risks. In this view, the paper examines the potential risks involved and therefore, recommends some policies in order to avert any form of miscalculated tragedy.

Background

On July 12, 2012, The Hague based Arbitral Tribunal's verdict on the South China Sea arbitration rejected China's historic claims to the South China

---

* This article was first published in the *Journal of the United Service Institution of India*, Vol. CXLVI, No. 605, July-September 2016.

Sea and declared the "nine-dash lines" as illegal, causing serious legitimacy crisis for China to its disputed sovereignty claims.[1] At the same time, one of the most contested sovereignty stakes is rested in the East China Sea, where China faces a challenge from Japan over the territoriality of Diaoyu/Senkaku islands and the surrounding maritime waters. In its act of rejection of the South China Sea verdict, Beijing executed a strong showdown of force in the East China Sea. As on August 1, 2016, China carried out live-fire navy drills in the East China Sea, sending strong signals of its sovereignty claims and reflecting an uncompromising attitude.[2]

China's naval activism in East China Sea has heightened in the recent times. On June 9, 2016, China flexed its military muscles in the East China Sea by deploying a Chinese Navy frigate, identified as PLA-N Type 054 *A Jiankai-class* frigate,[3] into the 24-nautical mile contiguous zone around the disputed Diaoyu/Senkaku islands in the East China Sea. This act of intrusion was further compounded by China's June 15, dispatch of a Chinese navy reconnaissance vessel - a PLA-N Type 815 Dongdiao-class spy ship[4] into Japanese territorial waters of Kuchinoerabushima Island south of Kyushu. What makes this Chinese act important is that until now only China's coast guard ships patrolled the disputed waters but the frigate's deployment marked the first military ship that transited into the contiguous waters. This signifies *upping the ante* in China's militarisation of the East China Sea. Making matters worse, on June 17, two Japanese Air Self Defence Force (JASDF) *Mitsubishi F-15J Eagles* intercepted two Chinese *Sukhoi Su-30* fighters over the East China Sea in the Beijing declared Air Defence Identification Zone (ADIZ) near the Japanese-controlled Diaoyu/Senkaku Islands.[5] Besides, in 2015 Chinese incursions into Japan's airspace prompted a record-high 571 fighter scrambles,[6] elevating Japanese concerns. In this regard, with China's growing naval activism through increased incursions by coast guard vessels and jet fighters in surrounding waters and airspace, Japan too has upped its defensive posture.

In counter response, Japan has recently switched on a radar station in the East China Sea,[7] giving it a permanent intelligence gathering post close to Taiwan and the disputed islands, and has also, increased its fleet presence by deploying 12 coast guard vessels.[8] Tokyo also plans to develop and deploy by 2023 a new land-to-sea missile, which reportedly will have a range of 300 km, on islands such as the Miyako in Okinawa prefecture. The range will cover the disputed island chain.[9]

This continuous spiralling of tensions has caused the new low in China-Japan relations, making East China Sea take the centrestage in their security concerns. These actions imply little more than just causing diplomatic 'cold' in the relations. Even the recent diplomatic talks between China and Japan have failed to de-escalate the tensions. Following a temporary thaw in China-Japan relations after the 2015 Security Talks, maritime territorial tensions have ramped up again in the East China Sea. In the recent talks between Premier Li Keqiang and Prime Minister Shinzo Abe on the sidelines of the Asia-Europe summit meeting (ASEM) in Mongolia, Abe raised concerns over China's expanding military activity in the East China Sea.[9]

Given the above perspective, whatever the significance, the chain of events has raised the fundamental question on the likelihood of a potential conflict between China and Japan. With the heightened pressure of an inflated risk, an unwarranted military casualty is of central concern. With the envelope being pushed to extremes and no quick fix solution to avert an uncalled tragedy, both China and Japan need to rethink their military postures in order to practically reason whether the costs of a confrontation are in their best national interest. Therefore, pragmatism lies in acting proactive rather than reactive in this dilemma of accidental risks.

China and Japan's East China Sea Dispute: Contested Interests

The dispute between China and Japan in the East China Sea is multifaceted. The contestations mainly revolve around legal claims and material interests. These are discussed in the succeeding paras.

Clash of Legal Claims

On legal grounds the dispute is two-fold, which concerns: (a) the sovereignty over the Diaoyu/Senkaku Islands and (b) the way the maritime border between China and Japan in the East China Sea should be drawn.

First, it concerns the contested sovereignty over the territoriality of Diaoyu/Senkaku Islands which comprises five uninhabited islands and three rocks. The islands are currently administered by Japan but claimed by China based on historical records. Here, the clash of interest lies in the competing claims made by China and Japan over the territoriality based on differing international laws. Japan claims that the Diaoyu/Senkaku Islands were *terra nullius* (or land without owner) at the time they were formally incorporated into Japanese territory in 1895. Thus, the fundamental Japanese claim is that the disputed islands were acquired by virtue of "discovery occupation," one of the established modes of territorial acquisition under international law, whereby valid title under a piece of territory can be acquired through occupation if it was recognised as *terra nullius*.[10] Hence, for Japan there exists no dispute on the sovereignty of the islands as they belong to Japan.

On the other hand, China makes its claims based on historical records, arguing that the islands have been Chinese territory as they were "first discovered, named and used by the Chinese as early as the 14th century".[11] Based on this, China negates Japan's claims based on the principle of "discovery occupation" as the islands were not *terra nullius*. In this view, China's 2012 White Paper on "Diaoyu Dao" strongly claims:

> *"Diaoyu Dao and its affiliated islands are an inseparable part of the Chinese territory. Diaoyu Dao is China's inherent territory in all historical, geographical and legal terms, and China enjoys indisputable sovereignty over Diaoyu Dao."*[12]

With this view, China firmly opposes Japan's sovereignty over the islands as Beijing argues that Japan's occupation of the islands as part of the Treaty of Shimonoseki of the First Sino-Japanese War in 1895 is "illegal and invalid"[13] and thereby, asserts that the islands should have been returned to China under the Cairo (1943) and Potsdam (1945) Declarations, which stated that Japan must return all territories stolen from China.[14] Unlike Japan, Beijing acknowledges the presence of a sovereignty dispute in the islands and thus, wants to establish its own jurisdiction in the East China Sea by challenging Japan's administrative control over the islands and the surrounding waters.[15]

Secondly, the dispute revolves around the demarcation of the sea boundary and different interpretations by of the UNCLOS in the East China Sea, which stipulates the 200-nautical-mile maritime border claim over Exclusive Economic Zones (EEZs). Here the conflict lies in the overlapping of the EEZs between China and Japan. China in using the UNCLOS principle of the natural extension of its continental shelf delimits at the Okinawa trough just west of the Ryukyu Island chain, while Japan draws it halfway between the Ryukyu and the Chinese mainland.[16] This has created overlapping claims of nearly 81,000 square miles.[17]

Clash over Material Interests

The dispute also involves both China and Japan's competing national interests in the East China Sea. The Diaoyu/Senkaku Islands are not only strategically located but also their adjacent waters are rich in economic value given the abundance of hydrocarbon resources and rich fisheries stock, both vitally important for China and Japan, given their heavy dependence on oil and gas, and their rich appetite for fish. The untapped oil reserves are estimated at 100 to 160 billion barrels, according to the US Energy Information Administration.[18]

According to the relevant prospecting data, it is estimated that the oil and natural gas reserves in the East China Sea will be enough to meet China's needs for at least 80 years. While the abundance of manganese in the waters near the Diaoyu/Senkaku Islands will meet Japan's needs for 320 years, enough cobalt for 1,300 years, enough nickel for 100 years, and enough natural gas for 100 years, not to mention other mineral resources and plentiful fish.[19]

Hence, based on the contested claims and interests, the main maritime security concerns relating to China and Japan in the East China Sea are: (*a*) disputes over islands (*b*) disputes over maritime rights and interests (*c*) the Chinese Navy passing through international waters, through the Japanese archipelago into the Western Pacific and (*d*) overlapping ADIZs.[20]

Escalating Risks and Policies for Crisis Management

Since the normalisation of relation in 1972, the East China Sea issue was just a minor irritant in China-Japan ties until becoming one of the potential flashpoints. The latest escalation of tensions in the East China Sea has renewed the attention to foresee the possibility of there being a military clash between China and Japan in the contested maritime region. The accelerated trend with which the East China Sea is getting increasingly militarised by China and Japan, has pushed the maritime security index to dangerous levels. This has heightened the possibility of a latent clash between China and Japan and has therefore, become a matter of concern as the chances of accidents remain high.

Given the inflated dimension of the maritime tension, the potential risks that call for precautionary actions are mainly three-fold:[21]

Firstly, the risk of accidental and unintended military confrontation between China and Japan given the heightened emotions and the operational activities at close proximity. To cite an example, the June 17 incident when two Japanese fighter planes intercepted two Chinese fighters over the China's ADIZ, in the East China Sea could have resulted in a serious incident.

Secondly, the risk involves political miscalculation in an effort to demonstrate sovereign control which can lead to an armed conflict. This can be caused by misperceptions of the other's motives and actions. The patrolling activities carried by China and Japan as well as their strong military postures in terms of deployment of frigates (China) or installing radar stations (Japan) does pose concerns of a military clash based on perception gaps. Additionally, in this miscalculation the US factor looms large given Washington's commitment to safeguard Japan against any aggression. There are high chances of Beijing's miscalculation of US intentions in the dispute.

Thirdly, the risk involves a deliberate action to forcibly establish control over the islands, which largely remains unlikely for either China or Japan to enact, but the possibilities cannot be overlooked. The activities, such as the Japanese Government's purchase of the Diaoyu/Senkaku islands in 2012 and similarly, China's unilateral establishment of ADIZ in 2013 does imply the potential risks. Given these prominent conceivable risks, although both China and Japan do not seem to make use of force to guarantee their positions, but there is still some catalysts which can foster the two actors to do so. One of the critical factors is the increasing nationalist sentiments in both countries that largely narrow down the room for any form of settlement of the dispute. Additionally, both China and Japan are equally strong actors who can counter-weigh each other at any level of an armed escalation. In this scenario, the best policy for both countries lies in adopting proactive measures to manage an unwarranted military tragedy.

With the heightened risks of an armed conflict between China and Japan in the East China Sea, prevention remains the central question. With a failure in establishing a crisis management mechanism to meet the risks, it is important to note that any framework of management at the foremost will require a mutual understanding and trust of both the countries. To do so, first it requires to build diplomatic efforts to exchange information and negotiate in order to quell the risk of misperceptions. Second, both countries need to tone down their military postures to de-escalate the brimming tensions. Third, both China and Japan should build a crisis management mechanism as well as successfully implement it to thwart any form of emergency in the East China Sea.

In order to successfully establish and implement a crisis management mechanism in the East China Sea, both China and Japan need to do the following:-

(a) Make the 'security-talks' a regular phenomenon in the bilateral relations. This could help in building the trust and thereby, bridging the gap between misperceptions of intentions and actions.

(b) Both China and Japan can have joint naval exercises between PLAN and JMSDF and also exchange communications between each other to maintain the status-quo in the East China Sea.

(c) Both China and Japan can initiate third party intervention such as the United States to act as the mediator in times of emergency and hence, maintain the stability in the relationship.

Conclusion

The brimming tensions in the East China Sea call for serious attention. With the spiralling tensions between China and Japan as reflected in the increased militarisation, the risks of an unintended confrontation looms large. Any form of military confrontation will impose severe costs on both, China and Japan. Thus, to avert an uncalled tragedy both China and Japan should undertake passivity in controlling the military tensions. In doing so, the best policy lies in adopting a crisis management mechanism that acts as a strong impediment in neutralising any form of potential risks. Both China and japan need to act proactively in scaling down the tensions in the East China Sea, which if not controlled could result into an unwarranted tragedy.

Endnotes

1 See Permanent Court of Arbitration, "PCA Case No 2013-19 in the matter of the South China Sea Arbitration", 12 July 2016, https://pca-cpa.org/wp-content/uploads/sites/175/2016/07/PH-CN-20160712-Award.pdf

2 Jesse Johnson, "Chinese Navy holds live-fire drills in East China Sea", *The Japan Times,* 2 August 2016, http://www.japantimes.co.jp/news/2016/08/02/asia-pacific/chinese-navy-holds-live-fire-drills-in-east-china-sea/#.V6SOYmWO6gQ.

3 Katsuji Nakazawa, "China ups ante in East China Sea", Nikkei Asian Review, 17 June 2016, http://asia.nikkei.com/Politics-Economy/International-Relations/China-ups-ante-in-East-China-Sea.

4   "Dangerous Chinese Air and Sea Incursions in the East China Sea", *Submarine Matters,* 5 July 2016, http://gentleseas.blogspot.in/2016/07/dangerous-chinese-air-and-sea.html.

5   Sam LaGrone, "Chinese and Japanese Fighters Clash Over East China Sea", *USNI News,* 5 July 2016, https://news.usni.org/2016/07/05/chinese-japanese-fighters-clash-east-china-sea.

6   "Japan scrambled fighters against China a record 571 times in fiscal 2015", *The Japan Times,* 23 April 2016, http://www.japantimes.co.jp/news/2016/04/23/national/japan-scrambled-fighters-china-record-571-times-fiscal-2015/#.V6RVNWWO6gQ

7   Nobuhiro Kubo, "Japan opens radar station close to disputed isles, drawing angry China response", *Reuters,* 28 March 2016, http://www.reuters.com/article/us-japan-china-eastchinasea-idUSKCN0WT0QZ.

8   Vasudevan Sridharan, "Japan deploys a dozen coast guard vessels in East China Sea", *International Business Times,* 5 April 2016, http://www.ibtimes.co.uk/japan-deploys-dozen-coast-guard-vessels-east-china-sea-1553172.

9   The Hindustan Times, New Delhi, 15 Aug 2016.

10 Amrita Jash, "East China Sea Dispute is Getting Worse not Better", CogitASIA, 18 July 2016, http://cogitasia.com/east-china-sea-dispute-is-getting-worse-not-better/.

11 Han-yi Shaw, "The Diayutai/Senkaku Islands Diapute: Its History and an Analysis of Ownership Claims of the P.R.C., R.O.C. and Japan", Occasional Papers/Reprint Series in Contemporary Asian Studies, No. 3, School of Law, University of Maryland, 1999, p. 22.

12 *Ibid.,* p. 38.

13 "Diaoyu Dao, an Inherent Territory of China", White Paper, State Council Information Office of the People's Republic of China, 25 September 2012, http://english.gov.cn/archive/white_paper/2014/08/23/content_281474983043212.htm

14 *Ibid.*

15 Daqing Yang, "History: From Dispute to Dialogue", in Tatsushi Arai et.al (eds.) *Clash of national Identities: China, Japan, and the East China Sea Territorial Dispute,* Woodrow Wilson Center, p. 23.

16 "Competition and Confrontation in the East China Sea and the Implications for U.S. Policy", A Roundtable Report by Laura Schwartz, The National Bureau of Asian Research, February 2014, p. 3.

17 Ian Forsyth, "A Tale of Two Conflicts", p. 6.

18 Teshu Singh, "China & Japan: Tensions in the East China Sea", IPCS Issue Brief, No. 129.

19 Cary Huang, "Diaoyu Islands dispute about resources not land", *South China Morning Post,* 4 December 2012, http://www.scmp.com/news/china/article/1096774/diaoyu-islands-dispute-about-resources-not-land.

20 Ibid.

21 Zhang Tuosheng, "Building Trust between China and Japan: Lessons learned from Bilateral Interactions in the East China Sea", SIPRI Policy Brief, February 2015, p. 2.

22 Sheila A Smith, "A Sino-Japanese Clash in the East China Sea", Contingency Planning Memorandum No. 18, April 2013, http://www.cfr.org/japan/sino-japanese-clash-east-china-sea/p30504.

†   **Ms Amrita Jash** is a Doctoral Candidate in Chinese Studies at the Centre for East Asian Studies, School of International Studies, Jawaharlal Nehru University. She is also Editor-in-Chief at IndraStra Global, New York.

China's Policies – Their Regional and Global Impacts[*]

Major General Nguyen Hong Quan, PhD

Introduction

Over the last few decades, especially since the 18th National Congress of the Communist Party of China (CPC) convened in 2012, China has reoriented its domestic and foreign policies. Most importantly, the recently published document on 'Essentials of National Security, Defence and Military Strategies' in January 2015, reveals that the shift in China's policies and their activities are affecting regional defence and security. How this is impacting the global strategic balance is analysed in the succeeding paragraphs.

Adjustments in China's Foreign Policy, National Security, Defence and Military Strategies

Renovation of China's Foreign Policy. Some of the prominent features of China's foreign policy changes, since the 18th National Congress of the CPC, are as follows:–

(a) China is making considerable effort to develop its strategic capabilities to become a major power in the region and the world; enhancing its global reach; and step by step establishing new rules to change the current status quo. China's "two centenaries,"[1] the realisation of the concept of "China's Dream"[2] put forward for the first time by the CPC President, Xi Jinping in March 2013, and the transformation from "peaceful rise" to the "fostering of the new model of major-

---

[*] This article was first published in the *Journal of the United Service Institution of India*, Vol. CXLVI, No. 603, January-March 2016.

country relations," first and foremost with the United States (US), have further clarified China's ambition to become a superpower. Regarding new rules and the world order, China has accepted the current status quo temporarily but is beginning to seek and make changes in the existing international institutions and mechanisms from inside. China suggests that "Asian problems should be solved by Asian people," and it is gradually pushing the US out of East Asia for establishing a new order in the region, led by China.

(b) China is paying attention to the exploitation of opportunities by closely monitoring situations and proactively creating opportunities.

(c) China has become more proactive and assertive than ever before with a view to claiming a larger strategic domain, displaying pragmatism and self-confidence.

Essentials of Current National Security Strategy. China adopted the current 'Essentials of National Security Strategy' on 23 Jan 2015 which focussed mainly on dealing with domestic and internal security issues; such as, corruption, interest groups, the gap between the rich and poor and separatist movements. In addition, it reaffirmed China's viewpoint, set forth at the Conference on Interaction and Confidence Building Measures in Asia (CICA), the Shanghai Cooperation Organisation (SCO), Shangri-La Dialogue and the 2015 Xiangshan Forum, etc.

At present, China's foreign policy gives priority to enhancing relations with major powers and developed countries, especially China-US-Russia Axis; its neighbouring and developing countries. China has never brought forward urgent global security issues and emphasised that China is facing some unpredictable security threats.

China's Defence and Military Strategies. Later, on 26 May 2015, China released its 2015 Defence White Paper whose contents focus mainly on China's Military Strategy in the new era. The strategic guideline of "active defence" is set to enhance military modernisation and creating a firm foundation for realising "China's Dream". China's military is concentrating on four essential components of global power: namely, development of military capability in maritime domain, outer space, cyberspace and upgradation of nuclear weapon systems.

The People's Liberation Army Navy (PLAN) is gradually shifting its focus from "offshore waters defence" to the combination of "offshore waters defence" with "open seas protection." The PLA Air Force (PLAAF) is shifting its focus from territorial air defence to both defence and offence, and building an air-space defence force. The PLA Strategic Rocket Force [the PLA Second Artillery Force (PLASAF)] is strengthening its capabilities for strategic deterrence and nuclear counterattack, medium and long-range precision strikes. China will also enhance international cooperation and actively participate in regional and international security issues[3] and would foster the new model of "military relations" in line with the new model of "major-country relations" between China and the US.

This is the first time ever that China has publicly revealed its sovereign claims over the South China Sea (hereafter referred to as the East Sea); and the PLAN, for the first time, is playing a leading role in safeguarding China's sovereignty over seas and islands. China's "offensive" intent stands clearly exposed, indicating its preparation for resorting to threats or using force in order to gain step by step control of the whole of East Sea.

Impacts on the Region and the World

China is playing an increasingly important role in the world economy by making great contribution to global economic growth and trade. In recent years, China has contributed about 30 per cent to global GDP growth,[4] increased its control over the world economy, and sought to globalise the Chinese Renminbi.[5] These moves have helped to improve the world's competitive strength, increased other economies' dependence on China, and attracted the investment from most of the major multinational groups in the world.

At present, China is the world's second-largest economy after the US. Some experts have projected that before 2049, China's economy would surpass the US in terms of nominal GDP. However, the real living standards of the people in China remain well behind those in the US, Japan, Germany, and even Russia in terms of science and technology. China is still the world's biggest production base with an export-oriented economy and heavy dependence on the world economy. China's economy has witnessed slowdown recently. The need for institutional renovation and addressing social inequality has become more pressing than ever before. While developed nations' economy develops depth, China's economy develops width. The global financial crisis and economic recession in 2008 made China's major export markets shrink. It exposed "four nos" in its economic structure; namely, instability, lack of solidity, coordination and sustainability." Notably, not many countries are attracted by China's economic model despite its emergence as the world's biggest economy.[6]

Facilitating the Trend towards Multi-Polarisation

The development of China has contributed to maintaining a peaceful environment, enhancing the emergence of a multi-polar world order, creating a fairer and more equal "playground," and strengthening the voice of developing countries. China is giving increasingly diversified and active support to developing countries through debt relief, loans, economic assistance and military aid by making effective use of multilateral forums, especially the United Nations (UN).[7] In fact, China has gained the support of a number of developing countries, especially those in Africa. China is employing a flexible strategy to protect its economic and security interests at multilateral organisations, enhancing its prestige while reducing the US influence and; actively participating in the reformulation of the international laws and concluding many multilateral treaties.[8] So far China has taken part in most of the international and regional organisations and mechanisms which have culminated in negotiating over 300 multilateral treaties. Presently, China is holding the initiative in settling global economic and political issues, including the proposal for using the Special Drawing Rights (SDR) of the International Monetary Fund (IMF), and the proposal for replacement of the US dollar by a "new global currency."

China's economic diplomacy is based on enhancing and protecting its overseas investments with a view to serving its national interests. At the same time, China is gradually expanding its influence and strategic reach in other regions including Europe, Africa, Latin America and Australia. There will be fierce competition between China and other newly emerging countries for playing a lead role at the international fora and also in non-traditional security and financial issues, controlling the relationship among major powers and giving rise to interest groups.

China, however, is facing many challenges. China has not really succeeded in getting into a binding alliance with any country, not even with the US. In Asia, Chinese products are reputed to be of lower quality than the US items. America's soft power still prevails. Although China's soft power has recorded some notable achievements in recent years, China's assertiveness is viewed with suspicion by some of its neighbouring countries.

Impact on International Security

China has made positive contribution in prevention of conflicts and their settlement. It has also actively participated and taken the initiative in addressing issues related to international peace and security. In particular, China has cooperated with major powers and other relevant countries while dealing with "volatile" issues such as the nuclear programmes of Iran and North Korea, and international terrorism etc. China has also made positive contribution to development efforts, humanitarian assistance and provided more personnel than any other members of the UN Security Council for UN peacekeeping missions.

China's rapid military build-up, however, has caused great concern amongst a number of countries in the world. The US seeks to rebalance forces in the region to contain China. China also pays attention to involving other countries in order to expand its spheres of influence and to break the US stronghold. The moves made by China and the US have resulted in tension, conflicting interests and mistrust. China's recent assertiveness in neighbouring waters is of great concern to many countries – potentially leading to a new regional arms race.

The military build-up, procurement of weapons and equipment, and escalation of disputes, from between China and its neighbouring countries to between China and other major powers, especially the US, would gradually enable China to succeed in its plot to divide the world into two blocs. At the same time, China's activities in the East China Sea and the East Sea have provided an opportunity to the US to set up an "anti-China front."

Potential Impact on the Region

China's moves have undermined trust amongst neighbouring countries, and increased suspicion which does more harm than good to China. As for the region; China's development strategy not only creates favourable conditions for development but it also results in manifestation of new threats.

Potential Threats to Safety and Security in the East Sea

China's military build-up and naval activities in the East Sea, including military manoeuvres; enlargement or construction of military bases in the Paracel Islands; renovation and construction of artificial islands in the Spratly Islands for turning these islands into military outposts in the East Sea, are posing serious threats to security and safety of maritime navigation and overflight in the region.

China's release of its Defence White Paper in 2015 has implied that differences in international maritime domain tend to escalate conflicts of interest; and China is ready to resort to use of force to settle the disputes instead of using peaceful means.

Raising the Likelihood of Arms Race and Conflict

China's development of military capabilities and modernisation of PLAN have caused concern amongst its neighbouring countries, and are likely to lead to arms race in the region. China's Defence White Paper also signals a firm message on sovereignty related issues and warns regional countries to desist from enhancing their relations with the US and Japan.

Countries in the region must consider increasing their defence budgets and expedite acquisition of advanced weapon systems in order to defend their territorial sovereignty and national interests. These moves will, in turn, intensify the risk of arms race and regional conflict, if parties concerned do not abandon the rhetoric of military confrontation.

Creating Fierce Competition among Major Powers

The East China Sea and the East Sea are witnessing fierce competition between two great powers which would draw increasing attention of other powers. However, conflicts are not likely to occur in the short term. China and the US may, however, bring pressure to bear upon specific political issues.

Posing Threats to Countries in the Region

The modernisation of PLAN and China's physical activities at sea, including the holding of military exercises in order to demonstrate China's improving maritime prowess by securing the Sea Lanes of Communication (SLOCs), have worried China's neighbouring countries and enhanced their apprehension that China might resort to using military force to gain control over natural resources and to settle their bilateral disputes.

Conclusion

At present, China has emerged as the most dynamic actor in the great-power politics. China's domestic and foreign policies have never been more assertive and proactive than they are today. China's desire to become a major power in the region and the world, when compared to their posture in earlier decades and the realisation of "China's Dream", would not be so easy because the world is foreseeing a new era full of difficulties for China.

Given its geostrategic position in close proximity to China, and the rivalry among great powers, East Asia has and would continue to suffer unpredictable and serious challenges due to China's current assertive foreign policy and military strategy.

Endnotes

1 The "first centenary" is to complete the building of a moderately prosperous society in all respects by 2021 when the CPC celebrates its centenary. The second centenary is to complete the building of a modern socialist country that is prosperous, strong, democratic, culturally advanced and harmonious by 2049 when the People's Republic of China marks its centenary.

2 The concept of "the Chinese Dream" consists of four main aspects: Strong China (economically, politically, diplomatically, scientifically, and militarily); Civilized China (equity and fairness, rich culture, high morals); Harmonious China (amity among social classes); and Beautiful China (healthy environment, low pollution). "The Chinese Dream" is associated with the attainment of the above-mentioned ambitious "two centenaries."

3 According to the Defence White Paper, China's military needs to perform well on eight fundamental tasks: (i) to deal with a wide range of emergencies and military threats, and effectively safeguard the sovereignty and security of China's territorial land, air, and sea; (ii) to resolutely safeguard the unification of the motherland; (iii) to safeguard China's security and interests in new domains; (iv) to safeguard the security of China's oversea interests; (v) to maintain strategic deterrence and carry out nuclear counterattack; (vi) to participate in regional and international security cooperation and maintain regional and world peace; (vii) to strengthen efforts in operations against infiltration, separatism and terrorism so as to maintain China's political security and social stability; and

(viii) to perform such tasks as emergency rescue and disaster relief, rights and interests protection, guard duties, and support for national economic and social development.

4   Sheard Paul, China's contribution to the global GDP growth in 2012 is projected at 30%. http://finance.eastmoney.com/news/1585,20100915962248493.html.

5   Several research have projected that Chinese Reminbi would become an international currency by 2020.

6   People in the world still consider West as their "desired house." In addition, many people regard China's model as a transitory one which would finally enable them to achieve a democratic model with institutions similar to those of South Korea, etc.

7   The UN cooperated with China and Africa to establish China-Africa Enterprise Association, and China-Africa Business Council in 2005. The United Nations Development Programme (UNDP) supported the establishment of the International Poverty Reduction Centre in 2006 in Beijing, which aims to enable China to share its development experience with other developing countries.

8   Thai Cao Cuong, The Rise of Major Powers and Development of International Law, Journal of Tianjin University, July 2009, page 64.

---

†   **Major General Nguyen Hong Quan, PhD** of the Vietnamese Defence Forces is the Deputy Director General of the Insitute for Defence Strategy, Ministry of Defence of Vietnam.

China's Military Reforms: Strategic Perspectives[*]

Major General GG Dwivedi, SM, VSM and Bar, PhD (Retd)

Background

In People's Republic of China (PRC), Communist Party and Military enjoy a unique relationship. The origin of this bonding can be traced back to the Ninth Meeting of the Communist Party of China (CPC) convened in December 1929 at Gutian, a town in South West Fujian Province, for building Party and the Army. Significantly, this was the first meeting post Nanchang Uprising of 01 Aug 1927, which formally marked the formation of People's Liberation Army (PLA).

During the Gutian Conference, Mao Zedong addressed the men of Fourth Army to clarify the role of military. In the Congress Resolution, absolute leadership position of the CPC over the Red Army was entrenched; purpose of army "to chiefly serve the political ends".[1] Thereon, PLA has remained the military of Communist Party and not of the Country. It played a key role during the Revolution, as an armed component of the Communist Party. Mao, Deng and other first and second Generation CCP leaders served as the top commanders in the PLA.

Even after eight and a half decades, the above policy has remained sacrosanct, evident from President Xi Jinping's visit to Gutian on 30 Oct 2014, where he addressed 'Military Political Work Conference' of the PLA and reiterated the principle of 'Party leading Military'.[2] The President stated, "PLA still remains Party's Army and must uphold its revolutionary traditions and maintain absolute loyalty to the political masters".[3]

---

[*] This article was first published in the *Journal of the United Service Institution of India,* Vol. CXLVI, No. 603, January-March 2016.

Modernisation of the PLA was taken up in the right earnest, as a sequel to its poor performance during the 1979 Sino-Vietnam War. In fact, Defence was the last of the four modernisations enunciated by Deng Xiaoping to transform China. However, the approach lacked strategic direction. Critical reforms were long overdue; evident from the configuration of the military regions, which remained unaltered since 1950s.

Ever since President Xi Jinping assumed power as the fifth generation leader of PRC three years back, military reforms have been high on the agenda. The process commenced in 2013 during the Third Plenum of 18th Central Committee of CPC, with the establishment of National Security Commission. Primary reasons for the current phase of reforms are twofold: prepare the military to effectively safeguard China's expanding strategic interests and establish firm control of the CPC over armed forces, through Central Military Commission (CMC), the apex defence body headed by President Xi as the Chairman. The ongoing reforms process is deep rooted and not just confined to structural changes. Its impact is expected to be far and wide, having internal and external ramifications. The paper undertakes a holistic overview of China's current military reforms process, with specific focus on genesis, strategic cum doctrinal dimensions and structural architecture, to enable a balanced assessment of PLA's emerging profile.

Genesis

Sense of urgency in implementing military reforms can be attributed to multiple factors, geopolitical considerations being the key drivers. President Obama's Doctrine, 'Pivot to Asia' which aims to rebalance Asia-Pacific, by redeploying 60 per cent of US military assets in the region has lent impetus to China's military modernisation.[4] Defence planners in Beijing are well aware of the wide gap that exists between the military capabilities of China and the US, despite the former possessing credible nuclear deterrence and a formidable missile force. This fact was acknowledged recently by the 'Global Times', a state run Chinese daily, in its editorial.[5]

The Chinese are ardent protagonists of the concept of Comprehensive National Power (CNP), which includes both hard and soft power. Acquisition of hard power is seen as an imperative in enhancing China's CNP. As per President Xi, for realising the 'Chinese Dream", military reforms is the key.[6] This will also facilitate the implementation of 'One Belt One Road' initiative.

Core national objectives of the PRC are Stability, Sovereignty and Development. Stability implies unchallenged supremacy of the CPC and its continuation in power. PLA's absolute loyalty to the Communist Party is an essential prerequisite. On 01 Feb 2016, during the inaugural ceremony of the newly constituted theatre commands, President Xi stated, "Centralisation of military architecture is vital; all the theatre commands and PLA should unswervingly follow the absolute leadership of the Communist Party and the CMC to the letter".[7] Sovereignty, besides external non- interference implies unification of Taiwan with the motherland, wherein use of force remains an option. It includes control over South China Sea alongside diminution of US influence and containing Japan in the Asia-Pacific. Emergence of Nationalist Government in Taiwan is yet another driver in speeding up reforms. Development remains an essential prerequisite for survival of the Communist regime. To this end, strong central authority and peaceful periphery are considered vital to sustain the pace of progress.

Strategic and Doctrinal Dimensions

China's military strategic culture lays great emphasis on exploiting propensity of things – 'strategic configuration of power'; shi to achieve one's objectives.[8] Aim is not annihilation, but relative positioning of own resources to gain position of advantage. Strategy thus aims not to fight an adversary but to create a disposition of forces so favourable that fighting is unnecessary. As Sun Tzu famously wrote "To subdue the enemy without fighting is the acme of skill". The ongoing military reforms are oriented towards capability building and force projection.

Chinese White Papers on National Defence issued periodically since 1998 define the general trend of strategic thinking. The theme of the Ninth White Paper published in May 2015 titled "China's Military Strategy" was 'active defence'.[9] Focused on winning 'Local Wars under the conditions of modern technology', its thrust was on expounding maritime interest, priority being accorded to navy and air force over the ground forces. It also marked a shift in naval strategy from 'off shore waters defence' to a combined strategy of 'off shore waters defence and open sea protection'.

China's military Doctrine of "Local Wars under Informationalised Conditions" envisions short swift military engagements, to achieve the political objectives by leveraging technology. Joint operations and integrated logistics are inherent components of the new doctrine. President Xi has laid emphasis on the need for military to adapt to the information based wars, as informatisation is the core of military development.[10] Establishment of 'Air Defence Identification Zone' (ADIZ) in East China Sea is also part of the military reforms. It is significant both for geopolitical considerations and China's domestic scene.

Military Reforms – Thrust Areas

Main thrust of the ongoing military reforms is on revamping of systems and structures at the political, strategic and operational levels. Some of the salient facets which merit attention are summarised in the succeeding paras.

The major changes being instituted at the macro level are in consonance with the guidelines issued by the CMC on deepening national defence and military reforms with Chinese characteristics; the focus is on civil-military integration, jointness and optimisation. The composition of the CMC itself has been balanced out, obviating the erstwhile ground forces bias. As a sequel to the military reforms, CMC will be responsible for the policy formulation, controlling all the military assets and higher direction of war. PLA, People's Armed Police (PAP) and Theatre Commanders will directly report to the CMC.

The erstwhile PLA Headquarters had four key Departments – General Staff, General Political, General Logistics and General Armament. This structure was perceived to be cumbersome, army dominated, resistant to change and led to the creation of political fiefdom. These Departments have been reorganised and integrated into the enlarged CMC set up, to ensure centralised control at the highest level. In the new structure, there are 15 functional bodies. These include six departments and three commissions, besides, six affiliated institutions (Table 1 refers).[11] Integrated joint staff under the CMC will ensure streamlining of the decision making process.

Table 1

CENTRAL MILITARY COMMISSION

CMC General Office	CMC Joint General Staff	CMC Political Work Department	CMC Logistics Department
CMC Equipment Development Dept	CMC Training Management Dept	CMC Military Defense Mobilisation Dept	CMC Discipline Inspection Commission
CMC Political and Law Commission	CMC Science and Technology Commission	CMC Strategic Planning Office	CMC Reform and Establishment Office
CMC International Military Cooperation Office	CMC Auditing Administration Office	CMC Administration Affairs Management Office	

(**Source - Stratfor 2016, www.stratfor.com**)

Three new Service Headquarters have been created besides the existing PLA Navy (PLAN) and PLA Air Force (PLAAF) Headquarters. These are the 'Ground Forces Command' making it a separate service, 'Rocket Force' – an upgrade of erstwhile Second Artillery which operates strategic as well as conventional missile weapons, and 'Strategic Support Force' to control and secure the cyber and space assets; key elements to execute the doctrine of 'Local Wars under Informationised Conditions', as also to meet the challenges of new generation warfare.[12]

Formation of five theatre commands (Battle Zones) – Eastern, Western, Central, Northern and Southern by reorganising the earlier seven military regions is aimed to revamp the joint operations capability of the PLA (Map 1 refers). This will facilitate seamless synergy in deploying land, air, naval and strategic assets in a theatre. While presenting flags to the theatre commanders, President Xi exhorted "Each command must concentrate on studying modern warfare...... proactively seize initiative, enhance joint command, joint action, joint logistics and ensure troops are combat ready to complete the mission".[13]

Map 1

Theatre Commands – Battle Zones

Source: Economist.com, South China Morning Post

Planned reduction of 300,000 personnel, mostly from the ground forces and non combat positions is to make the PLA nimbler; right sized to around two million. This will be the tenth time that the reduction exercise is being implemented since 1951, when the strength of the armed forces had peaked to 6.27 million.[14]

Ramifications

The military reforms are in consonance with PRC's expanding role as an emerging global power. It is perhaps the biggest military shake-up in a generation. While the architecture does not follow any western model or template, yet is in sync with the mainstream developments in the modern warfare. Although the primary aim is to enhance national defence capability marked by Chinese characteristics, the process goes on to serve multiple objectives with wide ranging implications.

Internally, predominance of the Party over PLA stands further validated, with centralisation of power structure under the revamped CMC. By gaining absolute control over the Defence Forces, President Xi Jinping has emerged as an unquestionable leader. His enhanced stature as a 'paramount leader' puts him in the league with Deng Xiaoping and as 'core' – at par with former President Jiang Zemin.

Externally, PLA's exponential accretion in the capability is a cause for concern, especially in China's neighbourhood. Beijing is likely to be more assertive in pursuit of its national objectives, particularly with respect to its claims in South and East China Seas. Asia-Pacific region is set to be the scene of intense rivalry with the changing balance of power equations. The USA is expected to play greater role in protecting its interests and assuage the concerns of allies, given the emerging security dynamics in the region.

Specific to India, so far Lanzhou and Chengdu Military Regions were responsible for operations against India's Northern and Eastern Theatres. With the newly reorganised structures, facing the PLA's Western Battle Zone with integrated assets of the Army, Air Force and Rocket Force under a single commander will be own four Army Commands (Northern, Western, Central and Eastern) and three Air Force Commands (Eastern, Central and Western). Enormity of challenge by way of coordination and synergy in deployment of assets in a telescopic time frame merits serious attention. Even during the 1962 War, China had constituted a single Headquarters to control the operations in Ladakh and NEFA, while on the home side, battles were fought in isolation, even within the theatre. Lately, Arunachal Pradesh has been included in the list of issues which are of Beijing's core national interests. Further, China's forays into Indian Ocean have long term strategic implications for India (emphasis added).

In retrospect, the radical military reforms initiated under the stewardship of President Xi Jinping are indeed path breaking. The thrust of these reforms is on how best the PLA capabilities can be optimised to further China's aspirations as a rising global power. While sticking to the vision of founding fathers; 'Party rules the Gun', Xi has been able to gain firm control of the PLA, eliminate resistance by pulling down top Generals like Xu Caihou and Guo Boxiong, and cultivate his own team. The central theme of the reforms process in essence, is indicative of both continuity and change. The Chinese strategic community has drawn richly from the historical, strategic and recent doctrinal documents, simultaneously infusing new thinking in tune with the futuristic trends. They seem to have also drawn heavily from the American experience in recent conflicts across the globe. Rise in China's military capability will have serious ramifications, both in the regional and global perspective.

The ongoing military reforms are envisaged to be in place by 2020, well before the end of President Xi's term in 2022.[15] However, given the ambit and magnitude of the task, it may take decades before the PLA transforms into a modern force at par with the western counterparts. Above notwithstanding, PLA certainly is poised for a "Great Leap Forward"!

End Notes

1   David Shambaugh (1996), "The Soldier and the State in China" in Brain Hook "The Individual and State in China", Clarendon Press - Oxford, New York, p108.

2   China Military Online, (3 Nov 2014) 'Party Commands Gun'.

3   The Economist (16 Jan 2016) "Xi's New Model Army", Beijing.

4   Remarks by President Obama to the Australian Parliament (17 Nov 2012), Parliament House Canberra, Australia. https:// www. White house. gov/ the-press- office / 2011/11/17/ remarks-president - Obama - Australian parliament. Accessed on 20 Jan 2016, 11 AM.

5   Global Times (07 Feb 2014), "China to Match US Military Spending by 2030s, but Power will Lag"

6   The Hindu (03 Feb 2016) "China Revamps Military Command Structure"

7   Ibid.

8   Thomas G Mahnken (2011), "Secrecy and Stratagem: understanding Chinese Strategic Culture", The Lowy Institute of International Policy, Australia p18.

9   "White Paper on China's Military Strategy" (May 2015), The State Council Information office of People's Republic of China, Beijing.

10 Mu Chunshan (05 Dec 2015), "The Logic behind China's Military - Reforms" The Diplomat, http:// the diplomat.com/2015/12/ the logic. Accessed on 02 Feb 2016, 2 PM.

11 Business Insider (14 Jan 2016), "Chinas Latest Military Reform Reveals it's Rising Ambitions". http://www. Business insider. Com/ China's - latest military-reform-reveals its rising ambitions -2016-I? I R=T. Accessed on 05 Feb 2016, 6 PM.

12 Ibid.

13 Global Times, http:// www.global times.cn/content/ 961440. Shmtl. Accessed on 18 Jan 2016, 5 PM.

14 Minnie Chan (01 Sep 15), "The Radical Plan to Turn China's People's Liberation Army into a Modern Fighting Force" South China Morning Post.

15 Global Times, op. cit.

---

† **Major General GG Dwivedi, SM, VSM and Bar, PhD** retired as Assistant Chief Integrated Defence Staff in 2009. Commissioned into 14 JAT in November 1971, he commanded 16 JAT in Siachen, Brigade in J&K and Division in the North East. He served as Military Attaché in China, with concurrent accreditation to Mongolia and North Korea from 19 Jan 1997 to 19 Aug 1999. Currently, he is Professor and Chairperson, Faculty of International Studies, Aligarh Muslim University.

Continuing Evolution of Chinese Armed Forces – A Review of Recent Organisational Changes*

Commander MH Rajesh

Introduction

Change has been a constant in the Chinese military for the past three decades. This article places the recent changes announced in January 2016 in the People's Liberation Army (PLA) organisation within the larger context of transformation that is happening in the Chinese Military and Security Apparatus. The series of radical changes in the PLA can be traced back to Deng Xiaoping era where along with sweeping economic reforms, he utilised the vacuum left by Mao, the fount of PLA's military wisdom to commence a series of transformations. These changes were tailored to alter the PLA from a People's Army created for revolutionary purposes to a professional Western style defence force in form and function. Therefore, modernisation has been a recurring theme in the PLA affecting most facets of the PLA including force structure, training, strategy and manpower. The modernisation progressed albeit incrementally during the Jiang Zemin and Hu Jintao periods.

The changes seem to be gathering a unique pace now in the Xi Jinping era. After Deng, it is the present President Xi Jinping who has re-initiated such radical transformations. President Xi also personally heads the 'Leading Group for National Defence and Military Reform of the Central Military Commission'- an elite committee that steers the reforms. Even though Xi had indicated revamp of military upon taking reins, its rough contours started emerging a few months prior to the official announcements. Earlier in Sep

---

* This article was first published in the *Journal of the United Service Institution of India*, Vol. CXLVI, No. 603, January-March 2016.

2015 and later in Nov 2015 President Xi had declared deep reforms regarding organisational changes as well as troop cuts. [1] The reforms were reiterated in Xi's address at a meeting on reforming the armed forces in Beijing from 24 - 26 Nov 2015 aimed to establish a three-tier system where Central Military Commission (CMC) will serve as the first tier of structure, Battle Zone Commands/Troops Command system as the second functional tier and an Administrative System that runs from CMC through various services to the troops.[2]

January 2016 is certain to go down in history as a point of inflection in the transformation of PLA with the following changes:-

(a) On 31 Dec 2015, China instituted a Ground Forces (Army) Chief with separate Headquarters (HQ) and a PLA Strategic Support Force (likely, a Cyber Command?).

(b) The Second Artillery was renamed People's Liberation Army Rocket Force (PLARF) and also upgraded from a 'branch' to a 'service' the same day.

(c) This was followed by transforming the four departments in mid Jan 2016 into fifteen smaller departments under Central Military Commission.

(d) On 01 Feb 2016, the formation of the Theatre Commands completed the major changes that had been announced.

Since the changes appeared in three different instalments through the January of 2016, they are commented upon in that order. The article focuses more on the organisational changes and has not included recent material developments such as the first SSBN patrol and plans to build a second aircraft carrier.

First Set of Changes Announced on 31 Dec 2015

The first set of changes appears to revolve around organisational reforms. In a ceremony attended by President Xi on 31 Dec 2015, three new military organisations took shape within the Chinese military establishment as under:-

(a) Formation of a PLA Ground forces Headquarters with a separate Chief. Till now there was no Army Chief, since the Army was the basic organisation with other two services conceptually being a part of Army. Therefore, the Army's HQ function was dispersed in the 'four HQ' of a generic PLA, namely the General Staff Department, General Political Department, General Logistics Department and General Armaments Department.

(b) Formation of PLARF. The erstwhile Second Artillery has been renamed and has been upgraded as a service from being just a branch. Till now it was not given a service status and was deemed less than Air Force/Navy as a 'branch'. This 'strategic' organisation will report to the CMC directly.

(c) Formation of a new organisation, the PLA Strategic Support Force (PLASSF) which has been newly commissioned. Complete details regarding this organisation are not known yet. The South China Morning Post cites a source to state that the PLASSF would be responsible for hi-tech warfare in space and on the internet.[3] If that be the case, it could be a C3I, Cyber Command. This formation was a surprise indeed.

Formation of Army Headquarters

The creation of HQ for the army shows two separate trends as under:-

(a) Firstly it is to accommodate a long standing professional requirement of PLA ground forces. The Navy and Air force had separate HQ and their respective Chiefs for long, but the Army, despite being the premier service was left out in that professional progress. This change means that generic, diffused management of ground forces by the four departments could be replaced by an Army HQ with its own Chief.

(b) Secondly in a way, portends the larger role played by other services in the PLA. Army instituting a HQ also means PLA is not the preserve of the ground forces alone! Since 2005, the Air Force and Naval Chiefs have been members of the CMC predominantly consisting of Army officers. The present Vice Chairman of CMC is an Air Force General Xu Qiliang. That he retains his Air Force uniform unlike Admiral Liu Huaqing who was also a Vice Chairman, albeit as an Army General indicates the improving trend of joint outlook to military affairs.[4]

Like the PLA Naval and Air Force Chiefs, Army Chief could be in protocol equal to the five Theatre Commanders (equivalent to C-in-Cs). All current theatre commanders are Army officers and at the Military Region (MR) level, Naval and Air Forces serve under an Army hierarchy. Air Force or Naval officers occasionally served as Deputy Chief of Staff at MR level. The Service Chiefs, though ranked alongside MR leaders in protocol, are slightly more privileged to be members of CMC which is the highest military decision making body. This change could also mean new members in the CMC, about which no information is presently available.

The erstwhile Chengdu MR Chief, General Li Zuocheng has now been made the Army Chief, which means that the new office could be equal or ranked higher than the MR Chief. General Li, one of the youngest to achieve Army Commander's rank commanded the 41st Group Army, was promoted in Jul 2015 to the rank of full General along with ten others. The Army HQ also gets a Political Commissar in General Liu Lei, previously, the Political Commissar of the Lanzhou MR.

Formation of the Rocket Force

The Second Artillery, now as the PLA Rocket Force continues to be the same organisation in function, albeit with a change of name and upgradation of status, becoming par with Navy and Air Force.[5] This is a step to get the organisation at par with other four services, namely Army, Navy, Air Force and most likely the PLASSF directly under the control of CMC. Even though this organisation was under the CMC earlier, in the status conscious military, such an upgradation can elevate the significance of organisation and status of its leader. The composition of leadership remains same.

Formation of the Strategic Support Force

The newly created PLASSF is headed by General Gao Jin who was Director of the PLA Academy of Military Science (AMS), the apex research institute of the PLA and General Liu Fulian as the Political Commissar, previously the Political Commissar of the Beijing MR.[6] From the nature of its Chief's previous appointment this organisation could have high technology role. C3I systems, Information and Cyberwarfare could be its areas of responsibility (?). Being a new organisation very limited information is presently available.

Second Set of Changes – Mid-January 2016

Reformation of the Four Departments. A significant overlay to the entire scheme is increasing party's grip over the military apparatus. This has been partly achieved by breaking the existing four HQ, the behemoths that controlled PLA into fifteen lean organisations under CMC as announced on 10 Jan 2016. The four giants will now metamorphose into following CMC organs:[7]

(a) **CMC's Six Departments.** The Joint Staff, Political Work, Logistical Support, Equipment Development, Training and Administration Department, and National Defence Mobilisation Departments.

(b) **CMC's Three Commissions.** Discipline Inspection, Politics and Law, Science and Technology Commissions

(c) **CMC's Six Offices.** The General Office, Administration, Auditing, International Cooperation, Reform and Organisational Structure, and Strategic Planning Offices.

Third Set of Changes Declared on 01 Feb 2016

Theatre Commands. The reforms declared on 01 Feb 2016 were around the battle zones which replace the existing MR. This was a much anticipated change, in the air for the past several years. At a ceremony attended by CMC members, General Fan Changlong, Vice Chairman of the CMC, read out the CMC's order to establish the PLA's theatre commands.[8] President Xi officially inaugurated the five theatre commands with cardinal orientations of North, South, East, West and Central Commands giving their Commanders the ceremonial flags. The Commanders and Political Commissars of the Theatre Commands were also announced in the ceremony. Other than nomenclature of Commands, which reveals its orientation and names of leaders, no other concrete information is presently available, although there are reports regarding locations of the command HQ and their subordinate organisations. Available information is appended in Table 1 below.[9]

Table 1 : Details of the new Commanders and Commissars

Theatre	Designation	Name and Year of Birth	Previous Position	Rank And Seniority
Eastern	Commander	Liu Yuejun 1954	Commander, Lanzhou MR October 2012	General 31 July 2015,
	Commissar	Zheng Weiping, 1955	Political Commissar, Nanjing MR	31 July 2015, General
Southern	Commander	Wang Jiaocheng 1952	Commander, Shenyang MR 2012	General July 2014
	Commissar	Wei Liang 1953	Political Commissar, Guangzhou MR October 2012	NA
Western	Commander	Zhao Zongqi 1955	Commander, Jinan MR November 2012	General July 31, 2015,
	Commissar	Zhu Fuxi 1955	Political Commissar, Chengdu MR November 2012	Lieutenant General NA
Northern	Commander	Song Puxuan 1954	Commander, Beijing MR 2014	General 31 July 2015
	Commissar	Chu Yimin 1953	Political Commissar, Shenyang MR 2010.	General July 2014
Central	Commander	Han Weiguo 1956	Deputy Commander Beijing MR 2013	Lt Gen? 2013
	Commissar	Yin Fanglong 1953	Deputy Director of the General Political Department of the PLA October 2012	General 2015

Earlier reports had indicated that the new commands, called Battle Zones, could have a cardinal/inter cardinal focus under a joint structure within five years. The present announcement on

01 Feb 2016 not only advances that date but also lays some of those speculations to rest. The reorganisation is indeed cardinal based which in Xi's words is for 'responding to security threats from their strategic directions, maintaining peace, deterring wars and winning battles'. However, no official maps have been released yet.

These battle zones or theatre commands have been under consideration for long and have been reported by Dennis Blasko in his seminal work

'Chinese Army Today' published in 2008. He articulated them as 'War Zones' which will be activated as a temporary measure during crisis. Those warzones are now being translated as 'Battle Zones' or permanent theatre commands by official PLA websites.[10]

The number of MRs has periodically varied in history stabilising at present seven, which will now effectively be these five Theatre Commands. There simply is no news of what happens to the old MRs, but in a significant move in end January 2016, the seven PLA MR Newspapers were shut down, which portended what lay ahead for the MRs.[11]

Given the enormous clout that the MR leaders possess, it will be also relevant to note that all erstwhile MR leaders, except General Xu Fenlin, Chief of the Guangzhou MR have been accommodated in this change. The Chengdu MR leader was earlier appointed the Chief of the Ground Forces. General Cai Yingting is reportedly a confidant of the President and has been appointed the Chief of the Academy of Military Sciences.[12] The Beijing Deputy MR leader has been upgraded to a Theatre Commander, and is apparently the only Lieutenant General in this new structure indicating that the Central Command could have a slightly different role as a hinterland command. The reduction from seven to five definitely cuts some fat making PLA more nimble. It also gives a larger scope to deploy reserves. Most significant call is the consistent exhortation for 'jointness'. The Western Command will cover the largest area, absorbing both Chengdu and Lanzhou MRs, which cover almost half of China's land area and borders. The other four theatres occupy the other half of China, giving away some indications of the present threat perceptions as well as geographic compulsions of that country. The high density of commands in the Eastern half shows preoccupations in East Asia.

As suggested earlier the Theatre Command System for operations will run parallel to the service oriented administrative structure (Army, Navy, Air force, PLARF and now PLASSF) that ensures professional management of services. Xi stated whilst inaugurating the new Command Structure that this is 'a strategic decision made by the CPC Central Committee and the CMC with an eye to realising the Chinese Dream and the Dream of a Strong Military. The establishment of the five theatre commands and their joint operational institutions is of great and far-reaching significance in ensuring the PLA to be capable of fighting and winning battles and effectively safeguarding China's national security.'[13]

Certain other exhortations by President Xi reveal what is expected of theatre commands; he stated that the new commands must (emphasis by the author):-

(a) 'Focus on **combat readiness,** and the various military services pursue their own construction and development.

(b) Unswervingly follow the **absolute leadership of the CPC** over the military and carry out the orders and instructions of the CPC Central Committee and the CMC to the letter.

(c) Devote themselves to **studying how** to fight wars, research the principles of winning modern warfare, speed up the formulation of the theatre commands' strategies, perfect their combat plans, and focus on joint training, so as to obtain initiatives in future warfare.

(d) Strengthen joint command, **joint operations and joint support** within the theatre commands, and organise troops to complete daily (at all times) combat-readiness and military operations.

Other Recent Changes

In the backdrop of latest developments, it is relevant to recall the recent significant changes carried out or announced thus far by China during President Xi's period which has military or security implications. These are as under:-

(a) Intention of troop cuts to the tune of 40 per cent from the Army, 30 per cent from Air Force and only 10 per cent from the Navy. Such a change will eventually settle the overall PLA manpower including Peoples Armed Police (PAP) from 3 million to 2 million with a 30 per cent overall reduction.[14] There are reports about reservations in the State Owned Enterprises to absorb the demobilised soldiers.

(b) There is intra-army change of removing divisional structures to let brigades serve directly under Corps or Group Armies. This is expected to make the organisation more effective with optimal reserves. There are also unconfirmed reports on reduction in numbers of Group Armies.[15]

(c) The PAP has been renamed as National Guard. This is a law enforcement body primarily for civilian policing which provides support to the PLA during wartime. [16]

(d) There was also a formation of National Security Commission earlier which works under the political leadership to combat terrorism, separatism, and religious extremism.[17]

(e) China appointed its first Counter Terrorism Chief, Liu Yuejin, a key figure in China's crackdown on illegal narcotics.[18]

(f) China passed a new Terrorism law with wide ranging implications including power for the PAP/National Guard to operate abroad.[19]

(g) The five separate entities termed five dragons that dealt with Maritime Security have been united into a single body under the State Oceanic Administration.[20]

(h) Publication of new Defence White Paper that in essence makes the PLA far more mobile with high thrust on Navy providing PLA a global role.

Conclusion

Overall the recent changes lie on the long road to modernisation which commenced three decades ago. Considering the scale of this reform, they are by no means small. They appear aligned with domestic and global realities. This reform makes the Chinese armed forces leaner, improves command and control, and assimilates technological shifts in cyber domain into its command structures. The last comparable change in any military of a similar scope occurred in 1986, in the United States, through the Gold Water Nichols Act, wherein command structures were reorganised to improve warfighting. Just as PLA has improved its hardware through 'imitative, inspired innovations', this set of equally important organisational 'software' changes too, is inspired by western models and have definitely gathered steam under the present regime after prolonged incremental measures by previous regimes.

The change upgrading the individual services is congruent to the latest Defence White Paper which clearly weighs 'the maritime over land' in a China which is venturing out in an incremental manner. However, in reality, ground forces will continue to dominate through theatre commands and constitution of CMC which remain dominated by the Army. The upgradation of the status of Second Artillery to PLARF, an independent service, could accentuate its status and control of strategic forces by the CMC. That it occurred around the time the first Ballistic Missile Submarine (SSBN) patrol was reported does not seem a coincidence. [21] The break-up of the 'four departments' into fifteen manageable organs under the CMC, including a discipline section could also increase the party's grip of all matters military.

As a nation, China is in the midst of deep changes today under a transformational leadership. Its economic model is being revamped, as a corollary it has rolled out the 'One Belt One Road' construct with economic and strategic implications to the region. Its internal political structures are being shaken up with anti-corruption campaign, the internal security organs and laws have been reformed, it has become more assertive in its maritime claims, and there are far more frequent forays into the Indian Ocean including acquisition of a base in Djibouti. The central theme, at the grand strategy level, appears to be Xi's 'China Dream', of overall, time bound national rejuvenation.

At national level, changes appear to tread on a tight rope between increasing professionalism as much as the party's grip over the military. Therefore, it is to be noted that changes do not alter the basic nature of the PLA as the party's army. Barring that core tenet, change, it appears remains a constant in the Chinese Armed Forces. Since this is the early stage of the change, several gaps remain in the information that is available. Therefore, it remains for military analysts to observe how PLA assimilates these rapid and drastic changes, probably the largest in scope and scale by any military in the world in recent history.

Endnotes

1 "The Radical Plan to Turn China's People's Liberation Army into a Modern Fighting Force," South China Morning Post, accessed September 30, 2015, http://www.scmp.com/news/china/diplomacy-defence/article/1854534/radical-plan-turn-chinas-peoples-liberation-army.

2 "Xi Urges Breakthroughs in Military Structural Reform," accessed January 3, 2016, http://eng.mod.gov.cn/DefenseNews/2015-11/26/content_4630715.htm.

3 "Chinese Military Launches Two New Wings for Space and Cyber Age," South China Morning Post, accessed January 3, 2016, http://www.scmp.com/news/china/diplomacy-defence/article/1897356/chinese-military-launches-two-new-wings-space-and-cyber.

4 "PLA Succession: Trends and Surprises," The Jamestown Foundation, accessed January 3, 2016, http://www.jamestown.org/single/?tx_ttnews%5Btt_news%5D=40244&no_cache=1.

5 "PLA Forms Rocket Force and Strategic Support Force | SinoDefence," accessed January 3, 2016, http://sinodefence.com/2016/01/01/pla-forms-rocket-force-and-strategic-support-force/.

6 Ibid.

7 "China Reshuffles Military Headquarters - Xinhua | English.news.cn," accessed February 1, 2016, http://news.xinhuanet.com/english/2016-01/11/c_134999061.htm.

8 "President Xi Announces Establishment of PLA Theater Commands - China Military Online," accessed February 1, 2016, http://english.chinamil.com.cn/news-channels/2016-02/01/content_6884075.htm.

9 The details of newly appointed theatre commanders have been compiled from various sources such as Chinavitae and Wikipedia.

10 "Major Restructuring of PLA Military Regions?," The Jamestown Foundation, accessed January 4, 2016, http://www.jamestown.org/single/?no_cache=1&tx_ttnews%5Btt_news%5D=35368.

11 "Military Shuts down 7 Newspapers in Reshuffle - China Military Online," accessed February 1, 2016, http://english.chinamil.com.cn/news-channels/china-military-news/2016-01/22/content_ 6865663.htm.

12 "China's Army Keeps Grip on Top Military Jobs in 'compromise' Reshuffle," South China Morning Post, accessed February 4, 2016, http://www.scmp.com/news/china/diplomacy-defence/article/1898444/chinas-army-keeps-grip-top-military-jobs-compromise.

13 "President Xi Announces Establishment of PLA Theater Commands - China Military Online."

14 "The Radical Plan to Turn China's People's Liberation Army into a Modern Fighting Force."

15 For a detailed report read "PLA Organization," accessed January 3, 2016, http://www.globalsecurity.org/military/world/china/pla-org.htm.

16 "China to Drastically Overhaul Its People's Liberation Army in 'Ambitious' Plan to Build Modern Fighting Force on Par with West | South China Morning Post," accessed January 3, 2016, http://www.scmp.com/news/china/diplomacy-defence/article/1854607/china-aims-modern-fighting-force-overhaul-peoples?page=all.

17 "What Will China's National Security Commission Actually Do?," Foreign Policy,

accessed September 30, 2015, https://foreignpolicy.com/2014/05/08/what-will-chinas-national-security-commission-actually-do/.

18 "China Names First Counterterrorism Chief - China - Chinadaily.com.cn," accessed January 3, 2016, http://www.chinadaily.com.cn/china/2015-12/21/content_22757979.htm.

19 "China Approves Wide-Ranging Counter Terrorism Law - CNN.com," CNN, accessed January 3, 2016, http://www.cnn.com/2015/12/27/asia/china-terror-law-approved/index.html.

20 "Dragons Unite," The Economist, March 16, 2013, http://www.economist.com/news/china/21573607-protect-its-maritime-interests-china-setting-up-civilian-coastguard-dragons-unite.

21 "Inside the Ring: China's Nuclear Missile Submarine Patrols Give New Strike Capability," The Washingtion Times, accessed December 28, 2015, http://www.washingtontimes.com/news/2015/dec/9/inside-the-ring-chinas-nuclear-missile-submarine-p/.

---

† **Commander MH Rajesh** was commissioned into the Submarine Arm of the Indian Navy on 01 Jan 1994. Currently, he is Research Fellow at USI of India.

Shanghai Cooperation Organisation Expansion: Strategic Ramifications*

Major General GG Dwivedi, SM, VSM and Bar (Retd), PhD

Background

Expansion of the Shanghai Cooperation Organisation (SCO) at its recently concluded 15th Summit in Ufa, Russia on 9-10 Jul 2015 has far reaching ramifications. With larger representation and broadened base, SCO is bound to evolve into a significant player in the global politics, well beyond its current regional reach. Consequently, in the times ahead, it will pose a challenge to the US domination and lend impetus to shaping of a polycentric world order.

It was on 26 Apr 1996 that 'Shanghai Five' grouping was created with the signing of the "Treaty on Deepening Military Trust in Border Regions" in Shanghai by the leaders of China, Kazakhstan, Kyrgyzstan, Russia, and Tajikistan. The SCO was founded in Shanghai in 2001 with the inclusion of Uzbekistan. As a political, economic and military organisation, the six nation group accounted for 60 per cent of Eurasian land mass and a quarter of the world population. Since its inception, it has emerged as a regional force, acquiring significant importance in the Asian security dynamics, with two of its founding members Russia and China being permanent members of the United Nations Security Council.[1]

The activities of this Forum have gradually expanded over the last decade to include defence cooperation, intelligence sharing and counter terrorism. Energy security has gained pre-eminence since last few years. There exists

---

* This article was first published in the *Journal of the United Service Institution of India*, Vol. CXLV, No. 601, July-September 2015.

vast potential and excellent opportunity for the SCO nations to cooperate in linking the energy surplus Central Asia with energy deficient South Asia. The Organisation faces multifarious challenges due to the divergent interests of the member states and long standing territorial disputes. Situation in Afghanistan is also of serious concern for the SCO, post the US withdrawal.

Geographic separation notwithstanding, Central Asia is of immense strategic significance to India. With China and Pakistan controlling all the land access to the region, India's engagement with the Central Asian Republics (CARs) remained constrained. While China's trade with these countries is almost US $ 50 billion, India's is below 1 billion.[2] For better access to this region, since long, India has been on the lookout to set up an alternate route through Iranian Port of Chabahar and North-South Corridor connectivity that would connect Turkmenistan and Uzbekistan with Afghanistan. Due to the UN sanctions on Tehran, the progress on the above projects has been rather tardy. By gaining the membership of SCO coupled with the signing of Iran nuclear deal and consequent easing of sanctions, window has opened for India to play an important role in the region.

With India and Pakistan being granted full membership (the process is underway) the SCO will then stand enlarged to eight. It implies adding 1.5 billion people, as also South Asia and Indian Ocean Region. Expansion of the SCO well serves the strategic interests of its dominating members, China and Russia; yields tangible benefits for the other members as well. Projected to be more of a partnership, in the coming times it could act as a counter balance to the western alliance like the North Atlantic Treaty Organisation (NATO). This paper seeks to examine the strategic ramifications of the expansion of SCO, particularly with respect to its key players.

SCO Expansion-Strategic Ramifications

According to Brzezinski's theory, "control of the Eurasian landmass is key to the global domination and control of Central Asia is the key to control of the Eurasian landmass".[3] Both Russian and Chinese leaders have paid close attention to this theory since the formation of SCO in 2001. As per the western diplomats, SCO together with Brazil, Russia, India, China and South Africa (BRICS) is a way for China and Russia to cooperate with each other in creating stability in Central Asia as also challenge the western domination. However, lack of resources is seen as a major shortcoming.

The expanded membership implies greater legitimacy to SCO; adds to its credentials as a global institution with diverse architecture. Besides boost to its influence and appeal, there are numerous pay-offs that accrue to the SCO members, including integrated development of infrastructure, expanded cooperation in the economic arena and strengthening of cultural bonding. With four observer states (Afghanistan, Belarus, Iran and Mongolia) and six dialogue Partners (Armenia, Azerbaijan, Cambodia, Nepal, Sri Lanka and Turkey), the SCO is all set to make deep in roads into the Persian Gulf, South Asia and the Indian Ocean, which is bound to disturb the current balance of power equations in the region. As per Alexander Gabuev, head of Asia-Pacific Region programme of the Carnegie Moscow Centre, the SCO is changing quantitatively but not qualitatively and continues its search for a mission. He further argues that Russia supported India's membership primarily to counter balance growing Chinese influence.[4]

China

Originally, SCO was seen as a manifestation of China's ambition for regional leadership and forum for coordination of security mechanism. For China, the gains from the expanded SCO serve its strategic, security and economic objectives. It helps Beijing in realising its aspiration to emerge as an undisputed leader in the whole of Asia and not just Asia-Pacific. President Xi Jinping has stated that SCO members have created a new model of international relations-partnership instead of alliance.[5]

SCO is central to China's efforts to fight terrorism. During the SCO Foreign Ministers meeting held in Moscow last June, China's Foreign Minister Wang Yi had called for SCO to play a larger role in guaranteeing regional security and stability. He also called for greater economic integration through Eurasian Economic Union (EEU) comprising Armenia, Belarus, Kazakhstan and Russia with Silk Road Economic Belt.[6] Pakistan's inclusion in the SCO will prove valuable for China in allaying its concerns from the extremism emanating from Central Asia, Afghanistan and Pakistan itself. Cooperation from the SCO partners will help China in its efforts to effectively combat the threat posed by the members of Uighur terrorist groups in 'Xinjiang Uighur Autonomous Region' (XUAR), who are known to have links with East Turkestan Islamic Movement (ETIM).

From the economic perspective, enlarged SCO will enable China to expand the multilateral trade and investment opportunities as part of its 'One

Belt One Road' initiative. These include Central Asia-China Gas Pipeline, China-Pakistan Economic Corridor (CPEC) and Bangladesh-China-India-Myanmar (BCIM) Corridor. Besides the security concerns, Afghanistan is of immense importance for China, given its vast economic potential and Beijing's 'look West' policy.

Russia

Russia has been advocating the enlargement of the SCO since long. Hence its expansion comes as a victory for Moscow. It also eases Russian concern about Chinese dominance in the region. It gains significantly in terms of political stature and recognition as a global player through the SCO expansion.[7] In the wake of current rift with the West, post Crimea annexation alongside involvement in Ukraine and expulsion from the G8, SCO is the ideal forum for Moscow to scout for new partnerships beyond Europe.[8] Its pivot to East is a long term strategic move. SCO will have a significant role in facilitating Russia to be an important stake holder in the Asian Century.

Even Russia aspires to connect East European Union (EEU) with China's Silk Road Economic Belt as part of the economic vision for the region.[9] It has adopted a policy of accelerated economic integration. Moscow-Beijing US $ 400 billion gas deal is in the realm of its planned initiative. Russian economy ranks second among the SCO members and is the eighth largest in the world. Enlarged SCO opens fresh avenues for Russia in exploring new markets.

India

For India, assuming the full membership of the SCO has definite pay-offs.[10] As per Prime Minister Modi, "India's inclusion as full member of SCO mirrors the region's place in India's future". India's key interests in Central Asia are security, energy, trade and mutual cooperation in multiple arenas. Delhi can also address its security concerns more effectively in Afghanistan and Central Asia with increased stakes in the region, by scaling up the level of defence cooperation. Joint production of defence equipment, training and related fields offer vast scope. Cooperation in the area of Uranium extraction is in the offing with Kazakhstan, Uzbekistan and Tajikistan. It provides India a platform to effectively thwart any design which may be inimical to its national interests.[11]

Energy security is of utmost importance for India. Kazakhstan, Turkmenistan and Uzbekistan are endowed with large hydrocarbon reserves. India will get access to the vast energy resources of Central Asia and implementation of long pending Turkmenistan-Afghanistan-Pakistan-India (TAPI) project will also get impetus.

There is vast scope in enhancement of bilateral cooperation in the field of education, health, agriculture, pharmaceuticals, textiles, petrochemicals, mining, tourism and service sector. It provides India an opportunity to leverage potential and project itself as an important player, well beyond the confines of South Asia. It also helps Delhi to pursue multi aligned policy, negating the pro-USA bias.

In certain quarters, there is an apprehension that the SCO membership does not confer India much advantage. China may not permit India to gain significant benefits from the SCO membership. On the other hand, increased economic engagement between Delhi and Beijing could create more conducive environment and help narrow the prevailing trust deficit between the two neighbours.[12]

Pakistan

Since long, Pakistan had been making efforts to become a SCO member state. Islamabad perceives that as a member, it will be able play a more effective role in the stability of the region.[13] Therefore, Pakistan has a lot to gain as full SCO member with the enhancement of its stature in the region. It can exploit geo-strategic location to seek support from the SCO members to combat extremism and terrorism.

Beijing-Islamabad all weather relationship lends added advantage to Pakistan for diplomatic posturing in the expanded SCO. With the development of Gwadar Port, Pakistan can emerge as an energy and trade corridor for the SCO nations. It also offers Islamabad an avenue to seek SCO facilitation in finding solution towards settlement of the vexed Kashmir dispute.[14] Pakistan could make a strong case for China's entry into SAARC on Beijing's behest.

CARs

The CARs are located at the intersection of the Chinese and Russian interests. The largest and wealthiest Central Asian State, Kazakhstan has large mineral deposits. Closest to Russia, its participation in the SCO is in consonance with its multi vector policy, allowing it to pursue the national interests. It is India's largest trading partner in Central Asia with strong ties in the field of space and nuclear research.

As per Farkhod Tolipov, Director of "Knowledge Caravan" Centre, Tashkent, for Uzbekistan, the primary focus of the SCO's geopolitical agenda still remains Central Asia centric.[15] Because of the concerns about Taliban and Afghanistan, it wants stronger ties between the SCO nations and desires to be less dependent on China and Russia. It perceives that inclusion of South Asian agenda could overburden the organisation and complicate the issues. President Islam Karimov while speaking at Ufa drew attention to the fact that the SCO is about to be joined by two nuclear powers in a state of permanent conflict.[16] In the expanded SCO, Tashkent would be in the thick of multilateral agendas, something it has sought to avoid

Tajikistan which borders Afghanistan and Pakistan was embroiled in civil war from 1992 to 1997 and still remains unstable. Dushanbe seeks to pursue balanced policy in its dealing with Delhi and Islamabad; has worked closely with India over the years. It envisions that expanded SCO could facilitate in resolving the Afghanistan issue

Kyrgyzstan is the smallest yet most democratic among the Central Asian States. Sandwiched between Chinese and Russian interests, it continues to experience serious economic difficulties in raising capital for various developmental projects. It has active military cooperation with India. Turkmenistan has the world's fourth largest gas reserves. Since the death of strongman Saparmurat Niyazov in 2002, the country is slowly opening up.[17] When the TAPI pipeline comes up, India will have its first land connectivity to Central Asia.

In Retrospect

The SCO expansion is occurring at a time of rising tensions between US-EU and Russia. It is seen as a counter balance to NATO. An expanded membership will confer greater legitimacy to the SCO which will yield multiple benefits to its members, especially in the security and economic arena. Cumulative geopolitical clout of SCO is already impressive. Its geographic reach stretches across Asia-Pacific, to Caspian Sea, Arctic Region, Eastern Europe, Indian Ocean and the Persian Gulf. As part of the future growth process, SCO's influence and appeal is bound to grow in the international arena. Inclusion of India and Pakistan implies broader integration of Central and South Asia. India as the largest democracy and third largest economy (in PPP terms) lends international recognition to the SCO. On the other hand, Delhi can make deeper inroads into Central Asia by optimising the potential of the SCO. As a hub of terrorism, Pakistan could emerge as a key player in combating the menace, both in regional and global terms.

Currently, the SCO is facing both economic and systemic challenges. As per Joseph Dobbs, Research Fellow at European Leadership Network (ELN), since its establishment, the SCO has suffered from existential malaise.[18] Originally designed to maintain stability in Central Asia and counter US influence in the region, China has been constantly seeking to strengthen its hold in the SCO. Russia has been an impediment in checkmating Beijing's expansionist agenda.

While enlarged SCO offers numerous advantages to its members, there could be negative fallouts as well. It could dilute the current clout of the founding members in the organisation. With Moscow's genuine concern about the likelihood of its influence diminishing in the CAR, there are chances of tensions brewing up between Russia and China for the leadership role in the enlarged set up. India-Pak traditional rivalry could create a negative impact on the functioning and effectiveness of the SCO.

At the 2014 Conference on 'Interaction and Confidence Building' in Asia, President Xi Jinping has spoken about the new Asian Security Concept (Asia for Asians).[19] China aspires to be a leader in whole of Asia and not just Asia-Pacific. A factionalised or fractured SCO would be harmful to the Chinese strategic interests. In fact, there is scepticism in certain quarters that SCO may turn out to be another forum, high on symbolism and low on substance.

With the ongoing process of expansion, the SCO is set to transform from a purely regional grouping to a global entity. Although security dimension remains the core issue, enlarged ambit and charter of SCO encompassing numerous economic and social initiatives have long term strategic implications. In the emerging new world order, the SCO is destined to play a pivotal role in defining the course of the ensuing shift in 'centre of gravity' from West to East, in the times ahead.

Endnotes

1. Marcel De Hass (edt.) (2007). The Shanghai Cooperation Organisation -Towards a Full-Grown Security Alliance ? Netherlands: Netherlands Institute of International Relations Chingendael. Pp.5-10. Visit : www.clingendael.nl / sites/default/files/ 20071100 Accessed: 03/07/2015 Time: 1:15 PM

2. Harsh V Pant (July, 26, 2015) India and China Slug it out in Central Asia. The Japan Times-Opinion. http://www.japantimes.co.jp/opinion/2015/07/26/ commentary /world-commentary/india-and-china-slug-it-out-in-central-asia/#. VchU7fmqqko. Accessed 31/07/2015. Time: 11:30 AM

3. Zbigniew Brzezinski (1997) 'The Grand Chessboard-American Primary and its Geo-Strategic Imperatives'. New York: Basic Books Pp. 198-210.

4. Alexander Gabuer (May 29, 2015) Smiles and Waves 'What Xi Jinping Took away from Moscow' Carnegie Moscow Centre. Carnegin.ru/ eurasianoutlook/?fa=60248. Accessed 06/07/2015 Time: 10:20 AM

5. Ankit Panda (July 7, 2015) India and Pakistan Set to join the Shanghai Cooperation Organisation. So what? The Diplomat. Visit: http://thediplomat.com/2015/07/ india-and-pakistan-are-set-to-join-the-shanghai-cooperation-organization-so-what/ Accessed: 09/07/2015 Time: 10:15 AM

6. Shannon Tiezzi (June 05, 2015) China Urges Greater Security Role for the SCO. The Diplomat. http://thediplomat.com/2015/06/china-urges-greater-security-role-for-the-sco/Accessed: 06/08/2015. Time: 11:00

7. Mikhail Troitskiy (May, 2007) 'A Russian Perspective on the Shanghai Cooperation Organisation'. In the Shanghai Cooperation Organisation 'SIPRI Policy Paper', No. 17 Stock home P.30.

8. Bruno Waterfield, Peter Dominiczak and David Blair (March 2014). 'G8 suspends Russia for Annexation of Crimea' The Telegraph. Visit: www. Telegraph. co.uk/news /worldnews/europa/Russia/10720297/G8-suspends-Russia-forannexation-of-Crimea. html. Accessed: 04/07/2015 Time: 1:15 PM

9. Rilka Dragnera and Kataryna Wolczuk (August 2012) 'Russia, the Eurasian Customs Union and the EU: Cooperation, Stagnation or Rivalry?' Chnatham House-Briefing Paper (REP BP 2012/01) Russia and Eurasia Programme. Visit: www.Chathamhouse.org/sites/files/chathamhouse/public/Research/Russia%20 and %20 Eurasia / 0812bp. Accessed: 05/07/2015. Time: 10:05AM

10. The Economic Times (July9, 2015) 'India to be made permanent member of Shanghai Cooperation Organisation: Valadimir Putin to PM Modi'. Visit: articles.economictimes.indiatimes.com. Accessed: 07/08/2015 Time: 09:35.

11. Richarde Walace (August18, 2014) 'India's Quest for energy in Centre Asia'. The Diplomat. Visit : The diplomat.com/2015/08/indias-quest-for-energy-in-

central-asia. Accessed: 10/07/2015. Time: 08:45 AM.

12. P Stobdan (July 14, 2014) 'Shanghai Cooperation Organisation and India'. IDSA-Policy Brief. www.idsa.in/policy/brief/shanghaicooperation organisationandindia_PStobdan _14 0714.hml.

13. William Piekos (July 8, 2015) 'The Risks and Rewards of SCO Expansion '. Council on Foreign Relations – Expert Brief. http://www.cfr.org/international-organizations-and-alliances/risks-rewards-sco-expansion/p36761. Accessed: 03/08/2015. Time: 02:25 PM.

14. Op. Cit.5.

15. Farkhod Tolipov . (July 2011) 'Micro-Geo Politics of Central Asia: A Uzbekistan Perspective'. Strategic Analysis, Vol.35, Issue.4. Visit:http://www.tandfonline.com/doi/abs/10.1080/09700161.2011.576098#. VcmUcvmqqko. Accessed: 8/08/2015. Time: 11:15 AM.

16. Uzbekistan National News Agency (July 7, 2015) 'President Islam Karimov Attends SCO Summit in Ufa'. Visit: http://uza.uz/en/politics/president-islam-karimov-attends-sco-summit-in-ufa-11-07-2015. Accessed: 31/07/2015. Time: 5:25 PM.

17. The Guardian (Dec 21, 2006) 'The personality cult of Turkmenbashi' Visit: http://www.theguardian.com/world/2006/dec/21/1. Accessed: 10/07/2015. Time: 03:15PM.

18. Joseph Dobbs (Sept 12, 2014) 'The Shanghai Cooperation Organisation: A non – Western G10 in the making'. European Leadership Network. Visit: http://www.europeanleadershipnetwork.org/the-shanghai-cooperation-organisation-a-non-western-g10-in-the-making_1891.html. Accessed: 07/08/2015. Time: 01:25 PM.

19. Ministry of Foreign Affairs of the People's Republic of China (May 21, 2014) 'The 4th Conference on Interaction and Confidence Building Measures in Asia (CICA) Summit'. http://www.fmprc.gov.cn/mfa_eng/topics_665678/yzxhxzyxrcshydscfh/t1162057. shtml. Accessed: 06/08/2015. Time: 02:25 PM.

† **Major General GG Dwivedi, SM, VSM and Bar (Retd), PhD** was commissioned into 14th Battalion, the Jat Regiment (14 JAT) on 14 Nov 1971. A veteran of Bangladesh War, he later commanded 16 JAT in Siachen and a Mountain Division in the Eastern Sector. He was India's Defence Attaché in China from Jan 1997 to Aug 1999 and retired as Assistant Chief of Integrated Defence Staff, HQ IDS in 2009. Currently, he is a Professor and Chairman, Faculty of International Studies, Aligarh Muslim University.

China's Military Strategy: Will the Rise of China be Peaceful?*

Mr Claude Arpi

Introduction

On May 27, 2015 Xinhua announced the publication of its Ninth White Paper on National Defence. Since 1998, every two years or so, the State Council (the Chinese Cabinet) releases a White Paper (WP) on defence; 'over the years, each of them has distinctive characteristics', noted the news agency. The theme of the latest edition, titled 'China's Military Strategy', is 'active defence'. It should be mentioned that the new WP is the shortest, with 9,000 **Chinese characters** only.[1]

China Military Online, a website affiliated to the PLA, explained: "This is the first time that the Chinese government published a WP specialised in China's military strategy. The WP systematically expounded on the Chinese military's missions and strategic tasks in the new era, pointed out that the basic point in making preparation for military struggle (PMS) shall be focussed on winning local wars in conditions of modern technology, and highlighted maritime military struggle and maritime PMS."[2]

The PLA website acknowledges that the WPs never earlier mentioned that "PLA Navy (PLAN) shall be in line with the strategic requirement of offshore waters defence and open seas protection". Open sea protection has been an addition compared to the previous WPs, similarly, "the PLA Air Force (PLAAF) shall be in line with the strategic requirement of building air-space capabilities and conducting offensive and defensive operations."[3]

* This article was first published in the *Journal of the United Service Institution of India*, Vol. CXLV, No. 600, April-June 2015.

As importantly, it says "the traditional mentality that land outweighs sea must be abandoned," while China should expedite the development of a cyber force. Mao's old view of 'an Army of peasants' is dead and gone. In the years to come, the Chinese Navy and the Air Force are bound to take a more preponderant place in Beijing's defence strategy.

There is certainly a lot for India to learn from these 'strategic' statements; in fact, it is not a phenomenon restricted to the Middle Kingdom, it is a planetary evolution.

The Evolution of the White Papers

Let us have a look at the earlier eight WPs.[4] Released in July 1998, the first WP was entitled 'China's National Defence'. Xinhua explained that it "created the first complete and systemic framework on national defence that was consistent with not only the international practices, but also the Chinese characteristics. For the first time, China systematically expounded on its defence policies and explicitly expressed its new outlook on security."

Two years later, the second WP pointed out a 'serious security situation' in the world; it emphasised that in the present world "factors that may cause instability and uncertainty have markedly increased and the world is far from peaceful". It further stressed that China always prioritised safeguarding its sovereignty, unity and territorial integrity and safety. It also dealt at length with the Taiwan issue, stating that "creating splittism [between the Mainland and the Island] means giving up peace across the Taiwan Straits".

In December 2002, another WP on 'China's National Defence' was released. It brought out five national 'core' interests "as the fundamental basis for defence policy and systematically expounded on the military strategy and guideline in the new era." The composition of the People's Liberation Army (PLA), the Chinese People's Armed Police Force (PAPF) and the Chinese militia was for the first time revealed. The 2004 WP developed the idea of 'dual historical missions of mechanisation and informatisation'. One chapter dealt with the concept of revolution in military affairs (RMA) …with Chinese characteristics. The public was informed about the decision of Beijing (or the Central Military Commission) to promote 'informatisation' and to 'reduce the military staffs by 200,000'. That was an important reorientation.

Two years later, the 2006 WP dealt with the 'critical period of multi-polarisation' and spoke of the concept of national security strategy. A special chapter dealt with the Chinese PAPF and provided information about border defence and coastal defence. It was a time when Zhou Yongkang, the 'security czar' was all-powerful and the PAPF was given a larger budget than the PLA. The 2008 WP on China's National Defence provided a strategic blueprint for national defence development and talked about the basic mission of China's strategic missile troops and the specific tasks of its nuclear missile forces.

The 2010 WP introduced the military security mechanism of mutual trust across the Taiwan Straits and comprehensively expounded on the diversified employment of China's armed forces in peacetime. It mentioned the military modernisation drive and spoke of China's efforts to establish a joint operation system; it also pointed out the development of a military legal system and elaborated on the objectives and principles of building military 'mutual trust under new circumstances', by giving an all-round introduction to what China had done to promote military mutual trust in recent years (for example humanitarian or UN-mandated missions).

The 2013 WP had a different title; it was called 'Diversified Employment of China's Armed Forces'. According to China Military Online, the 2013 paper "illustrated the principles for diversified employment of China's armed forces and officially publicised the designations of the 18 Group Armies in the PLA Army." It provided information on the size of the PLA Army's operational troops, the PLAN, the PLAAF as well as the types of missiles equipping the Second Artillery Force (SAF). According to Beijing, the objective was to make China's armed forces more transparent.

There is definitively an effort at transparency, though there is still a gap between the 'theory' professed in the WPs and the ground scenario on China's extended frontiers (on land, in space and on seas). We shall come to this later.

The 2015 White Paper

As mentioned earlier, the latest WP is titled China's Military Strategy. Xinhua, quoting Chinese analysts, says that the WP attaches more significance to maritime interests and marine power in open seas 'amid increasing reported maritime threats'. There is a clear evolution, not to say revolution, giving prominence to the seas and the Navy, over the ground forces and the PLAAF. According to a press release of the Ministry of National Defence (MND), it is the first WP 'on strategic defence and operation and tactical offence'. It reiterated the principle of 'active defence', which means that 'China will not attack unless under attack itself'. The WP states that a world war is unlikely in the foreseeable future and China remains in a period of strategic opportunities for development.

However, China's maritime rights and interests are strongly highlighted: "Some of [China's] offshore neighbours take provocative actions and reinforce their military presence on China's reefs and islands that they have illegally occupied." Beijing warned "some external countries are also busy meddling in South China Sea affairs [and] a tiny few maintain constant, close-in-air and sea surveillance and reconnaissance against China."[5] The WP admitted that China generally enjoys a favourable environment for development, but external challenges were increasing; and though only briefly mentioned, Beijing also admits the existence of several internal threats. The WP spoke of many multiple and complex security risks, "leaving China an arduous task to safeguard its national unification, territorial integrity and development interests."

In Beijing's eyes, the 'bad guy', of course, remained Washington; Beijing does not appreciate the US 'rebalancing' strategy' and its 'enhanced' military presence in the region. Then, there is Japan, Mao would have probably called Tokyo, a US lackey; the WP affirmed that Japan is "sparing no effort to dodge the post-war mechanism, overhauling its military and security policies."

As a result of these threats, Beijing believes that China now "faces a long-standing task to safeguard its maritime rights and interests."[6] Other nations certainly do not share the same perception about peace and stability in the region; this does not bother Beijing as the WP affirmed. Then, the WP listed the Korean Peninsula and Northeast Asia as being 'shrouded in instability and uncertainty'; but perhaps more importantly for Beijing, the 'Taiwan independence separatist forces' were termed by Beijing as the biggest threat to the peaceful development of cross-Straits relations.

That is not all, and here come the 'internal' threats: "Separatist forces for 'East Turkistan independence' [Xinjiang] and 'Tibet independence' have inflicted serious damage, particularly with escalating violent terrorist activities by 'East Turkistan independence' forces." Beijing should seriously consider this particular menace at a time when China is financing the Pakistan Economic Corridor. It is also an open admission that Beijing is more bothered by a 'terrorist' Xinjiang than a non-violent 'Tibet'.

One of the WP's conclusions was that "China's national security is more vulnerable to international and regional turmoil, terrorism, piracy, serious natural disasters and epidemics, and the security of overseas interests concerning energy and resources, strategic sea lines of communication."[7] In the years to come, this will practically translate in an important enhancement of the capacity of the PLAN. The future belongs to those who will control the Sea, believes China.

Has the message been received in Delhi?

Some Comments on the WP

According to some Chinese analysts quoted by the nationalist Global Times, the new WP contrasted with others, including the 2013 version, which had only mentioned that 'some neighbouring countries' were making moves which 'complicated' the situation. At that time, Japan was singled out for 'making trouble' over the Diaoyu Islands in East China Sea.

The US is now the main villain as China wanted "to mark out its bottom line regarding its maritime rights and interests as the country needs enhanced capabilities to protect its increasing number of overseas interests." In the past, WPs used to focus more on the ground forces instead of the Navy; it has resulted in 'a lack of maritime technology and experience' for China, believe those who drafted the WP.

The most important information contained in the WP was the confirmation that the PLAN is 'gradually' shifting its focus from 'offshore waters defence' to a combined strategy of 'offshore waters defence and open seas protection'. Wen Bing, an associate research fellow at the Academy of Military Sciences (AMS), who participated in previous WP compilations, told The Global Times "It is also a win-win when our protective measures can safeguard regional stability. It should be noted that China always abides by the law and respects the safety concerns of countries involved. ...According to international conventions, we often protect our overseas interests through cooperation."[8] One could call it 'regional stability' with Chinese characteristics.

Soon after the release of the WP, Real Admiral Guan Youfei, director of the Foreign Affairs Office (FAO) briefed more than 80 foreign military attachés based in Beijing. He explained that the WP expounded the missions and strategic tasks of the Chinese Armed Forces in the new historical period and interpreted the strategic guidelines of 'active defence'. He spoke of the Chinese Armed Forces' steadfast determination and strong will to safeguard national sovereignty, security and development interests, as well as regional and world peace.[9]

Four Critical Security Domains

Interestingly, the WP speaks of four 'critical security domains':-

(a) Oceans - Shifting focus to the combined one of "offshore waters defence and open seas protection."

(b) Outer space - Opposing an arms race in outer space while vowing to secure its space assets.

(c) Cyberspace - Expediting the cyber force development to tackle "grave security threats" within the digital realm.

(d) Nuclear force - Stating China will never enter into a nuclear arms race.[10]

It is a qualitative shift as the ground forces and the PLAAF are not even mentioned.

A Historical Background of the PLAN

The WP gives an historical background on the PLAN: "The Chinese Navy kept troops close to land from the 1950s to the end of the 1970s under the strategy of inshore defence. Since the 1980s, the navy has realised a strategic transformation to offshore defensive operations." Today, says the WP, the Navy will continue "to perform regular combat readiness patrols and maintain a military presence in relevant sea areas" while the Chinese armed forces: "will also strengthen international security cooperation in areas considered especially important to China's overseas interests."

In a recently-published paper, the US Office of Naval Intelligence (ONI) argued that since 2009, the PLAN "has made significant strides in operationalising as well as modernising its force. Although the PLAN's primary focus remains in the East Asia region, where China faces multiple disputes over the sovereignty of various maritime features and associated maritime rights, in recent years, the PLAN has increased its focus on developing blue-water naval capabilities. Over the long term, Beijing aspires to sustain naval missions far from China's shores."[11]

The 2015 WP definitively marks a trend in this direction. As we shall see, it translated in reclaiming reefs in the South China Sea and continuously building new infrastructures.

In a chapter on the Evolution of a (Chinese) Naval Strategy, the ONI paper explained that the launching of the Liaoning, the country's first aircraft carrier was a turning point "although Liaoning remains several years from becoming fully operational, and even then will offer relatively limited combat capability." The ONI affirmed: "China's leaders have embraced the idea that maritime power is essential to achieving great power status. Since the 1980s, China's naval strategy has evolved from a limited, coastal orientation, to one that is mission-focussed and becoming increasingly unconstrained by geography."[12]

It mentioned China's shifting threat perceptions and growing economic interests which "have catalysed a major shift in strategic orientation and the perceived utility of naval forces." Today, Chinese naval strategists have expanded "the bounds of China's maritime capabilities and defences beyond coastal waters." Since 1987, PLAN has a strategy referred to as 'offshore defence', which focusses on regional goals and deterring a modern adversary from intervening in a regional conflict.

Offshore defence is usually associated with operations in the Yellow Sea, East China Sea, and South China Sea—China's Near Seas.

The 'Joint Sea-2015' drills between China and Russia should be seen in this light. Held between May 11 and 21, 2015 in the Mediterranean Sea, it involved nine surface ships from both navies. Geng Yansheng, the spokesman for the Chinese Defence Ministry explained that the exercises "will deepen friendly and pragmatic cooperation between China and Russia, and boost response operation capabilities in the event of security threats at sea."

Peaceful or not, it is a fact that the PLAN is spreading further and further from its bases.

Some Other Points

China promises not to join nuclear arms race. China reiterates it will never enter into a nuclear arms race with any other country. It promises to keep its nuclear capability at the minimum level required for maintaining its national security. The PLA will however "optimise its nuclear force structure, improve strategic early warning, command and control, missile penetration, rapid reaction, survivability and protection."[13] China will also deter others from using nuclear weapons against China, says the WP. There is nothing new on the above.

Cyber security. As we have seen, Beijing considers cyberspace as 'grave security threats within the digital realm'; therefore, according to Xinhua, China will speed up the development of a cyber force. The WP noted: "International strategic competition in cyberspace has become increasingly fiercer and quite a few countries have developed their cyber military forces." It further points out that China is one of the major victims of hacker attacks: "China will enhance its capabilities of cyberspace situation awareness, cyber defence, support for the country's endeavours in cyberspace and participation in international cyber cooperation, so as to stem major cyber crises, ensure national network and information security, and maintain national security and social stability."[14]

No Naval Bases. Quite surprising, at least seen from an Indian perspective, the Defence Ministry spokesperson Yang Yujun asserted that China has not built any military bases overseas, as China 'seeks no hegemony or military expansion'.[15] All the more astonishing as a few days earlier, it was reported that China was negotiating a military base in the strategic port of Djibouti. Djibouti President Ismail Omar Guelleh openly stated: "Discussions are ongoing".

Already last year, Geng Yansheng, the Chinese Defence spokesman, defended a Chinese submarine's docking at Colombo port and calling 'utterly groundless' reports that China was setting up 18 naval bases in Sri Lanka, Pakistan, Myanmar and several other nations in the western and southern Indian Ocean. He was commenting on an article in a Namibian newspaper[16], citing a report which had appeared on the Internet in China; Geng said: "The report also exaggerated and twisted the content of that commentary. Therefore the report is utterly groundless".

They may not be called 'bases' in Putonghua, but they are 'bases' in English.

The Other Side of the Coin: Chinese Aggressive Posture in the South China Sea

During the recently-held Shangri-La Dialogue in Singapore, the US Defence Secretary Ashton Carter, in his keynote address, affirmed that the US would continue to fly, sail, and operate in the region wherever international law allows. Carter also demanded "an immediate and lasting halt to land reclamation by all claimants" in the South China Sea.

The latest move by China was to build man-made islands in the South China Sea to impose its sovereignty over the area. The American Admiral Harry Harris called this a 'great wall of sand' in strategically important waterways. Steve Tsang explains in The Guardian: "The Chinese are dredging the seabed to transform a few reefs and rocks in the Spratly group of islands and atolls – which they claim – into man-made islands with a runway that can support military flights. This has caused great concern among their neighbours. The Chinese government rejects international criticisms, asserts its sovereign right to build on the islands, and demands that American naval surveillance aircraft overflying the new islands leave the Chinese air control zone immediately. There are also reports that China has begun to put heavy weapons on one of them."[17] China immediately dismissed the US views as 'incomplete and lacking of jurisprudential evidence'.

Rear Admiral Guan Youfei, director of Foreign Affairs Office of China's National Defence Ministry, told the Shangri-La Dialogue: "Freedom of navigation should be for the benefits of economic development, rather than sending military aircraft and vessels everywhere". He justified the lighthouses built by Beijing on Huayang and Chigua Reefs (also known as Cuarteron and Johnson South Reefs). These sites have recently witnessed massive reclamation work: it was just 'to improve navigation safety in the South China Sea'. Guan added: "China has been exercising restraint on the South China Sea issue and the United States should treat the South China Sea issue in a more objective way."[18]

Observers believe that Beijing will use the reef reclamation as bases in order to extend its naval reach. A few days before the 'dialogue', a US spy plane flew over a disputed region, taking the fever to a scale higher. As the

P-8A Poseidon aircraft went over the islands, the Chinese navy sent eight warnings before the plane flew away. The US announced that it had decided to publicise the incident "to raise awareness of China's massive land reclamation activities in the disputed waters."

Beijing's answer came a few days later: "it would not tolerate any party violating its overseas interests and would expand its naval power as part of a military strategy that aims to extend its offshore reach."[19]

These few incidents show that though the China speaks of its peaceful rise in the WP, it is not always the case on the ground (or more correctly on the Seas). There is however no doubt that the publication of the new WP marks a change in Beijing's strategy and in the future, the PLAN is bound to play a more preponderant place in China's defence strategy.

The Chinese Navy

How does this manifest on the Seas? During a two-day conference held by the US Naval War College's China Maritime Studies Institute in Newport, Rhode Island, James Fanell, the former director of the US Pacific Fleet's intelligence and information, declared that China will soon have some 415 warships including four aircraft carriers and 100 submarines. This was reported by the Defence News.

A Taiwan publication Want ChinaTimes says: "A lot of the anti-ship missiles equipped by the Chinese warships or submarines have ranges far in excess of similar missiles in service with the US Navy. With such a large number of long-range surface-to-surface missiles in hand, the PLA Navy is altering politics and strategies throughout the Asian theater."[20]

The already-quoted report of the US ONI confirms: "During 2014 alone, more than 60 naval ships and craft were laid down, launched, or commissioned, with a similar number expected through the end of 2015. Major qualitative improvements are occurring within naval aviation and the submarine force, which are increasingly capable of striking targets hundreds of miles from the Chinese mainland. Although the PLAN faces capability gaps in some key areas, it is emerging as a well-equipped and competent force."[21]

It is a fact that India can't ignore.

Some Conclusions

Though the new Chinese 'transparency' is welcome, the situation on the ground is quite different from what it is professed in the WP, whether one looks at the situation in the South China Sea or on the LAC with India, in the high Himalayas.

Beijing believes that 'nobody can tell China what to do'. The South China Morning Post noted: "Beijing has hit back at the US criticism of its land reclamation operations around the Nansha Islands in the South China Sea, saying, "No one has the right to instruct China on what to do."[22] The China Daily quotes a Chinese 'expert' who warned: "Washington is playing with fire as it has adopted an increasingly high profile over the South China Sea situation in recent months."

Beijing does not seem to be in a mood to relent on any front. A few days ago, it turned down the Indian proposal to clarify the Line of Actual Control (LAC), a move which seems most reasonable and logical.

At the same time, it is clear that, on the seas, India can't match China's fast paced development of its Navy, whether it is in terms of speed and quantity, but a smaller, disciplined and well-equipped Indian naval force could be a deterrent factor. The Indian Government probably realises that it can't stop the rise of the Middle Kingdom, neither on land, nor on seas, but in the years to come, a professional and well-trained Indian Navy could indeed 'balance' the fast growing Chinese Navy and its expanding aspirations beyond its shores.

Endnotes

1   The full text of the 2015 White Paper (China's Military Strategy') is available on different Chinese official websites; for example, China Daily, May 26, 2015; see: http://www.chinadaily.com.cn/china/2015-05/26/content_20820628.htm

2   Overview of all China's white papers on national defence, China Military Online, May 27, 2015; see: http://eng.mod.gov.cn/TopNews/2015-05/27/content_4587121.htm

3   See reference for note 1.

4   Overview of all China's white papers on national defence, China Military Online, May 27, 2015; see: http://eng.mod.gov.cn/TopNews/2015-05/27/content_4587121.htm

5   Ibid.

6   Op.Cit 1.

7   Ibid.

8   Ibid.

9   Defence Ministry briefs foreign military attaches on white paper, China Military Online, May 27, 2015; see http://eng.mod.gov.cn/Press/2015-05/27/content_4587116.htm

10 MoD unveils military strategy, op.cit.

11 The PLA Navy: New Capabilities and Missions for the 21st Century, Office of Naval Intelligence, April 10, 2015; see: www.oni.navy.mil/.../china.../2015_PLA_NAVY_PUB_Interactive.pdf.

12 Ibid.

13 China promises not to join nuclear arms race, Xinhua, May 26, 2015; see: news.xinhuanet.com/english/2015-05/26/c_134271147.htm

14 China to speed up building a cyber force, english.news.cn, May 26, 2105; see: http://english.gov.cn/news/top_news/2015/05/26/content_281475115069380.htm

15 China hasn't any overseas military bases: Spokesperson, Xinhua, May 26, 2015; see http://www.globaltimes.cn/content/923615.shtml

16 China Mulls Building Naval Base in Namibia, Namibian Times Says, Bloomberg, November 27, 2014; see: http://www.bloomberg.com/news/articles/2014-11-27/china-mulls-building-naval-base-in-namibia-namibian-times-says

17 China cares little for other countries' territorial claims, The Guardian, May 30,2015; see: http://www.theguardian.com/world/commentisfree/2015/may/30/beijing-policy-south-china-sea

18 China dismisses U.S. views on South China Sea as incomplete, lack of jurisprudential evidence, Xinhua, May 30, 2015; see: http://news.xinhuanet.com/english/2015-05/30/c_134283714.htm

19 China's foothold in South China Sea: analysts reveal endgame to Beijing's reclamation efforts, South China Morning Post, May 30, 2015; see: http://www.scmp.com/news/china/diplomacy-defence/article/1813082/chinas-foothold-troubled-waters?page=all

20 PLA Navy will have 415 warships in near future: US expert, WantChinaTimes, May 26, 2015; see: http://www.wantchinatimes.com/news-subclass-cnt. aspx?id=20150526000161&cid=1101

21 The PLA Navy: New Capabilities and Missions for the 21st Century, op. cit.

22 No one tells us what to do, Beijing says, China Daily, May 29, 2105; see: http:// www.chinadaily.com.cn/china/2015-05/29/content_20851774.htm

† **Mr Claude Arpi** was born in Angouleme, France and graduated as Dental Surgeon from Bordeaux University in June 1974. Soon after, he decided to come and live in India. He has authored several books on Tibet, China, and French India. Recently, he published 1962 : The McMahon Saga (Lancer Publishers) and Glimpse of Tibetan History (Tibet Museum, Dharamsala). He regularly writes on Tibet, China and Indo-French relations for Indian publications. Presently, he is the Director of the Tibetan Pavilion at Auroville, India.

One Belt One Road: A Strategic Challenge[*]

Lieutenant Colonel K Nishant Nair, SC

Introduction

The origin of the "One Belt and One road" initiative dates back to September 2013, when Chinese President Mr Xi Jingping during his visit to Kazakhstan and Indonesia, invited the countries to join the Silk Road Economic Belt (SREB)[1] and the 21st century Maritime Silk Road (MSR) respectively[2]. Together, they form the "One Belt and One road" (OBOR) initiative, which has been touted as an economic initiative presenting a win-win situation for all the countries participating in it. Undoubtedly, a land and maritime silk route stretching across the heartland of Eurasia and the rimland of the Indian and Pacific ocean will facilitate trade and provide impetus to economy but it will also provide China with an unprecedented foothold in these areas, making it a big stakeholder in the affairs of management of sea lanes of communication (SLOCs), provide it with a springboard to exert influence across the Asian, African and Eurasian continents. Hence, the OBOR presents both an economic opportunity and a strategic challenge of unprecedented proportions to countries like India. This article explores the geostrategic dimensions of the OBOR initiative, highlights the Indian concerns and provides policy recommendations on the same.

OBOR Initiative

Please refer to Map 1. The initiative as mentioned earlier comprises of the land based SREB and the MSR. According to the available data the SREB will begin in Xi'an in central China pass through Lanzhou (Gansu province),

---

[*] This article was first published in the *Journal of the United Service Institution of India*, Vol. CXLV, No. 600, April-June 2015.

Urumqi (Xinjiang), and Khorgas (Xinjiang) to the West near Kazakhstan. Thereafter, run southwest from Central Asia to Northern Iran before swinging to West through Iraq, Syria, and Turkey. From Istanbul, the Silk Road crosses the Bosporus Strait and heads northwest through Europe, including Bulgaria, Romania, the Czech Republic and Germany. Reaching Duisburg in Germany, it swings North to Rotterdam in the Netherlands. From Rotterdam, the path runs to the South to Venice, Italy — where it meets up with the MSR.[3]

Map 1

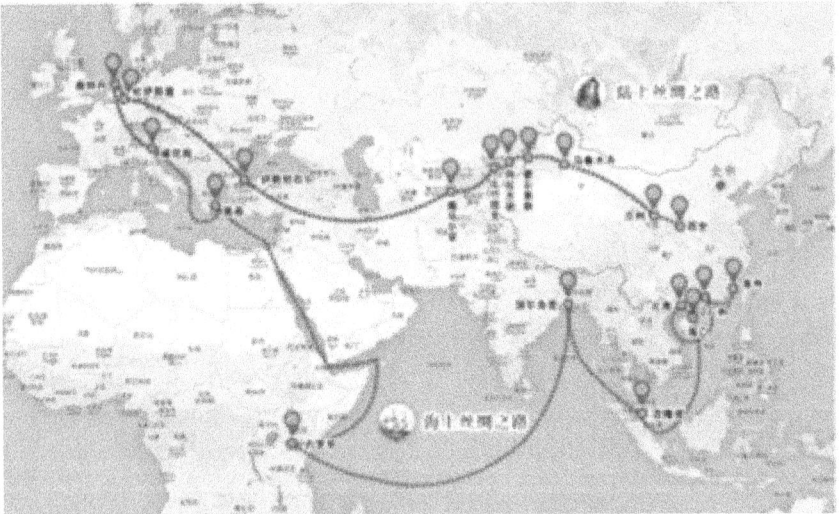

China: Proposed Land and Maritime Silk Roads
Source : http://www.xinhuanet.com/world/newsilkway/index.htm.

A recently published vision document by Chinese Government identifies specific gateways that will connect China with other Silk Road economies, like Xinjiang province for connecting Central, South and West Asian countries including Pakistan. Similarly, China's Heilongjiang will become the gateway for Mongolia and Russia's Far East. Eurasian high-speed transport corridor linking Beijing with Moscow will also be developed through the area. China also plans to leverage Tibet's geographic location for extending a Silk Road node to Nepal. Two areas in southwest China: Guangxi Zhuang Autonomous Region and the Yunnan province will be used to establish links with the Association of South East Asian Nations (ASEAN). Yunnan, which borders Vietnam, Laos and Myanmar will connect with the Greater Mekong sub-region, and serve as a pivot to link China with South and South East Asia. Yunnan's provincial capital, Kunming, is the end-point of the proposed Bangladesh-China-India-Myanmar (BCIM) economic corridor, which starts in Kolkata.[4] Thus, the SREB will comprise the main artery and a number of hubs and spoke networks connecting the hubs or gateways to other areas of economic interest. The document also mentions developing of China-Mongolia-Russia, China-Central Asia-West Asia and China-Indochina Peninsula economic corridors.[5] However, the details of the same have not been elaborated upon.

The MSR will stretch from the western Pacific to the Baltic Sea beginning in Quanzhou in Fujian province then connecting Guangzhou (Guangdong province), Beihai (Guangxi), and Haikou (Hainan) before heading south to the Malacca Strait. From Kuala Lumpur, the MSR heads to Kolkata in India then crosses the rest of the Indian Ocean to Nairobi, Kenya. From Nairobi, the MSR goes North around the Horn of Africa and moves through the Red Sea into the Mediterranean, with a stop in Athens before meeting the land-based Silk Road in Venice (Italy).[6] The vision document published by the Chinese Government also visualises a route from China's coast through the South China Sea to the South Pacific.[7]

Geostrategic Dimensions of OBOR

Overt Objectives

The OBOR has been overtly touted as an economic initiative with potential to bring unprecedented economic growth to the participating nations. It will also provide means to achieve the security of SLOCs and help mitigate security concerns. The integration of all existing cooperation in the neighbourhood and the region will create trade networks, boost economic activity and productivity through infrastructural linkages like port facilities and development of continental arteries.[8] This will provide accessibility to the China's hinterland and allow it to capitalise on vast manufacturing infrastructure that it has created. China has also created a 10 billion Yuan fund ($ 1.6 billion) for neighbouring countries which are part of MSR and has plans to create a $16.3 billion fund to build and expand railways, roads and pipelines in Chinese provinces that are part of SREB.[9] It also plans to promote policies that encourage Chinese banks to lend money to other countries along the planned route. This is in addition to the funds which it has already committed (Sri Lanka - $1.4 billion for developing port infrastructure; Central Asia - $50 billion for infrastructure and energy deals; Afghanistan -$327 million). With the establishment of China's new Asian Infrastructure Investment Bank (AIIB) more money is likely to flow into the region to shore up infrastructure capabilities. Thus, the idea is not just to create an economic trade route but also increase its political influence by creating a community with "common interests, dependencies and responsibilities."[10]

Covert Intentions

An analysis of OBOR reveals a deeper strategy, a strategy which has the ingredients to turn the 21st century as the Chinese century. The strategy once implemented has the potential to establish China as the predominant maritime power in Asia-Pacific, apart from a continental power with political and economic influence across Eurasia. It would provide China an uninterrupted access to the various ports which are part of the project along the SLOCs through which its energy and other resources flow and at the same time reduce the concerns of the 'Malacca dilemma'.[11] Thus the project has the potential to bind the participating nations in a collective security framework. The economic potential of the project will attract many countries which are not part of the framework to join it, while China will take the centre stage with its economic might and investments. The initiative has the potential to further tilt the skewed balance of power in Asia in favour of China and establish her as the predominant power in the Asia-Pacific. To that extent, it is indeed a response to the US strategic rebalance to Asia.[12]

In India the echoes of Booz Hamilton's 'String of Pearls' theory are becoming louder.[13] As the scope of the project is yet to be defined, the gamut of security concerns it will bring about are still being debated. The fact that it was initially proposed specifically in relation to ASEAN and later extended to Sri Lanka (February 2014)[14] and Maldives (Signed a Memorandum of Understanding (MOU) with China to join the MSR in December 2014)[15] while the initial maps did not include Gwadar (Pakistan) and Hambantota (Sri Lanka), all point to a plan which is still unfolding. Hence, it can be argued that MSR is a manifestation of the 'String of Pearls' strategy albeit with a different name serving the same purpose. In the same vein the 'String of Pearls' may manifest in terms of access to ports and bases for People's Liberation of Army Navy (PLAN) for logistic support like refuelling etc. rather than having permanent bases as envisaged by Hamilton.

Militarily, the MSR initiative is part of its attempt to breakout of its maritime isolation, constrained by the US led alliance domination of the first and second island chains, which have effectively restricted Chinese maritime space.[16] The implementation of the initiative would be in sync with the PLAN programme of expansion which might make it one-third larger than the US Navy by 2020. The development of the carrier groups which is likely to be increased to four by 2020 with their likely area of operations in Indian Ocean Region (IOR) will also facilitate PLAN to play larger role in security of MSR operations, thereby facilitating the PLAN to secure a foothold in the IOR.[17]

As China uses its economic strength to secure foreign policy goals, the OBOR initiative has also been compared to the 'Marshall Plan' enacted by the US after World War II. The US implemented the plan to establish itself as a bona fide super power; Beijing is also betting its twin Silk Roads can do the same.[18]

India's Concerns

The sheer magnitude of the project itself is overwhelming. As the project unfolds the participating countries would be intertwined with each other in more complex ways than can be imagined at present in terms of trade agreements, visa regimes, logistics agreements, customs regulations etc. to facilitate trade and business. The OBOR initiative has the potential to drive affected nations to enter into agreements with each other to derive economic benefits, thereby pushing countries more closely into the Chinese fold. Needless to say, China with its investments in the OBOR will hold the centre stage in the geo-economics. The integration of all the existing cooperation with neighbouring and regional countries will result in a group of polarised nations which are economically interdependent, share the common trade and security concerns, look up to China to be the common arbiter thereby; creating a regional and international geo-economic, geopolitical and collective security framework. This may result in reduced Indian influence in the subcontinent and effectively restrict Indian importance to its periphery.[19]

Though Chinese analysts have been insisting that OBOR is a geo-economical initiative and not a geopolitical one, India has all the reasons to be sceptical. The impact of infrastructure development of the magnitude as envisaged in the OBOR initiative has increased the fear of being encircled by China, physically and geo-politically.[20] The possible manifestation of the 'String of Pearls' has already been delved upon earlier in the article. Even if the

China does not have a 'String of Pearls' strategy, the project will undoubtedly facilitate the Chinese to establish a foothold in the Indian Ocean thereby contesting India's position as the security provider to countries in the region.[21]

The project also has military implications for India; the unresolved border dispute with China and the trust deficit which exists after the 1962 War between the two countries further complicate the issue in India's neighbourhood. India is also wary of growing Sino-Pak nexus. Pakistan and China are already in the process of developing the Karakoram Highway which forms part of the Xinjiang Gateway. India also has unresolved border issues with Nepal, Myanmar, Bangladesh. thus the initiative has the potential to further complicate the resolution of outstanding border issues between India and its neighbours, if part of the project is implemented through the disputed areas. The possibility of the infrastructure created under the initiative to be used in case of a military conflict by Indian adversaries is also a matter of concern.

Recommendations

As China engages regional powers and India's neighbours proactively to prepare the groundwork for implementation of OBOR, India finds itself in a dilemma to cooperate or compete. Cooperation as mentioned earlier will entail a long term geopolitical price and India by itself may not be in a position to compete. Hence, India must engage multilaterally to safeguard its interests in the IOR and Asia-Pacific. The broad Indian strategy must aim at safeguarding Indian interests in immediate areas of interest in the short term to mid-term. India must deepen its relations through economic, diplomatic and military cooperation with important countries along the IOR to include Sri Lanka, Maldives, Iran, Mauritius, Seychelles, Madagascar and countries in the African continent and, South Asian countries like Nepal, Bhutan, Myanmar and Bangladesh.

The Project 'Mausam' and India's 'Spice Route' projects are steps in the right direction.[22] However, the scope of both should be restricted to immediate area of interest to ensure a focussed and sustained effort. India must strengthen the multilateral framework by drawing on its Strategic Partnership with the USA and, its deepening ties with Japan and Vietnam to ensure freedom of navigation and prevent domination of the IOR and Asia-Pacific by a single country. This will help India to safeguard its national interests while maintaining its strategic autonomy. India must also strengthen the existing mechanisms of Indian Ocean Rim Association (IORA) and South Asian Association for Regional Cooperation (SAARC) to implement 'Project Mausam' and the 'Spice Route' initiative.

India should be more proactive to resolve all its outstanding border and maritime issues in an earlier timeframe with its neighbouring countries, as without their resolution it will be difficult for India to win their complete trust in the implementation of the aforementioned projects. This will go a long way in bringing down the geopolitical concerns of its neighbours who look up to India for support. In South Asia, where most countries have suffered from colonialism, countries are more likely to be influenced by geopolitical considerations than geo-economical ones in their major policy decisions. Hence, resolution of border disputes and unresolved border issues will play an important role in the success of such initiatives in the region.

Conclusion

Since 2002, China's leaders have described the initial two decades of the 21st century as a 'period of strategic opportunity', a period during which the international conditions are conducive for growth of Comprehensive National Power. China's leaders have also routinely emphasised the goal of reaching critical economic and military benchmarks by 2020. These include successfully restructuring the economy, promoting internal stability, military modernisation in order to attain the capability to fight and win potential regional conflicts, protection of SLOCs, defence of territorial claims in the South China Sea and East China Sea, and defence of western borders.[23] Undoubtedly, China's OBOR initiative will go a long way towards meeting many of these objectives. However, the geopolitical concerns of the countries are likely to be the biggest impediment towards achieving the full potential of the initiative. The unprecedented scale of the project gives rise to associated geopolitical insecurities which may prevent wholehearted participation from at least some of the countries. Thus, geo-economics may initially prompt the countries to join the OBOR initiative; however, geopolitics may prevent it from achieving its full potential. Add to it, China's recent aggressiveness in dealing with disputes in South China Sea[24] and coercive economic practices[25] the challenge presented is indeed a grand one, not just for India but for other regional powers too. Timely implementation of 'Project Mausam' and the 'Ancient Spice Route' along with multilateral cooperation with other regional powers offers a way out for India to safeguard its national interests in the IOR and Asia-Pacific.

Endnotes

1 Ministry of Foreign Affairs, the People's Republic of China, "President Xi Jinping Delivers Important Speech and Proposes to Build a Silk Road Economic Belt with Central Asian Countries", September 7, 2013 at www.fmprc.gov.cn/ mfa_eng/topics_665678/.../t1076334.shtml (Accessed March 30, 2015)

2 Jiao Wu and Yunbi Zhang , "Xi in call for building of new 'maritime silk road" , China Daily, October 4, 2013 at http://www.chinadaily.com.cn/ china/2013xiapec/2013-10/04/content_17008913.htm (Accessed March 30, 2015)

3 Tiezzi Shanon, "China's 'New Silk Road' Vision Revealed", May 9, 2014, The Diplomat at http:// the diplomat.com/2014/05/chinas-new-silk-road-vision-revealed/ (Accessed March 30, 2015)

4 Aneja Atul, "China unveils details of ambitious Silk Road plans", March 30, 2015, The Hindu at http://www.thehindu.com/news/international/china-unveils-details-of-ambitious-silk-road-plans/article7048921.ece(Accessed March 30, 2015)

5 National Development and Reform Commission, Ministry of Foreign Affairs, and Ministry of Commerce of the People's Republic of China ,"Vision and Actions on Jointly Building Silk Road Economic Belt and 21st-Century Maritime Silk Road", March 28, 2015,at http://www.fmprc.gov.cn/mfa_eng/ zxxx_662805/t1249618.shtml (Accessed 07 April 2015)

6 Op cit. 3.

7 Op cit. 4.

8 Tiezzi Shanon, "The Maritime Silk Road vs. The String of pearls", 13 February 2014, The Diplomat at http://thediplomat.com/2014/02/the-maritime-silk-road-vs-the-string-of-pearls/ (accessed on 30 March 2015).

9 Ray Ranjan Dhriti, "Experts see big benefits from Silk Road Economic Belt", Economy Lead, 06 July 2014 at http://www.economylead.com/international/ experts-see-big-benefits-silk-road-economic-belt-20684 (accessed on 30 March 2015).

10 Brig (Retd) Sahgal Arun, "China's Proposed Maritime Silk Road (MSR): Impact on Indian Foreign and Security Policies", July 2014, at http://ccasindia.org/ issue_policy.php?ipid=21 (accessed on 31 March 2015).

11 Ji You, "Dealing with the Malacca Dilemma: China's Effort to Protect its Energy' Supply", May 2007, Volume 31, Issue 3 athttp://www.idsa.in/strategicanalysis/ DealingwiththeMalaccaDilemma_yji_0507.html (Accessed March 30, 2015).

12 Mingjinag Li, "China's "One Belt, One Road" Initiative: New Round of Opening

Up?", March 11, 2015,RSIS Commentary No 050at http://www.rsis.edu.sg/wp-content/uploads/2015/03/CO15050.pdf(Accessed March 30, 2015).

13 Bo Zhou, "The String of Pearls and the Maritime Silk Road Keywords : Asia-Pacific, China-ASEAN Relations, One Belt One Road, Silk Road", February 11 2014 at http://www.chinausfocus.com/foreign-policy/the-string-of-pearls-and-the-maritime-silk-road/(Accessed March 30, 2015).

14 Zorawar Daulet Singh, "Indian Perceptions of China's Maritime Silk Road Idea", Journal of Defence Studies, Vol. 8, No. 4 ,October-December 2014, pp. 133-148 at .http://idsa.in/jds/8_4_2014_IndianPerceptions ofChinasMaritime SilkRoad.html(Accessed March 30, 2015).

15 Aruma Fathimath, "MSR deal sealed, Free Trade deal in the making", December 17 , 2014,Haveeru Online at http://www.haveeru.com.mv/news/58038 (Accessed March 30, 2015).

16 Ibid.

17 Mahadevan Prem , "China in the Indian Ocean: Part of a Larger PLAN", June 2014, CSS Analyses in Security Policy No 156 at http://www.css.ethz.ch/publications/pdfs/CSSAnalyse156-EN.pdf(Accessed April 7, 2015).

18 Tiezzi Shanon,"The New Silk Road: China's Marshall Plan?", November 06, 2014, The Diplomat, at http://thediplomat.com/2014/11/the-new-silk-road-chinas-marshall-plan/(Accessed April 7, 2015).

19 Ibid.

20 Sibal Kanwal, "Silk route to tie India in knots", February25, 2014, Mail Today, at http://indiatoday.intoday.in / story silk-route-to-tie-india-in-indian-ocean-indo-china/1/345394.html (Accessed March 30, 2015).

21 Singh Abhijit, "China's Maritime Silk Route: Implications for India", July 16,2014, IDSA Comment at http://www.idsa.in/idsacomments/ChinasMaritimeSilkRoute_AbhijitSingh_160714.html(Accessed March 30, 2015).

22 "Modi's 'Mausam' manoeuvre to check China's maritime might", TNN, September 16, 2015 at http://defencenews.in/defence-news-internal.aspx?id=rd4q5QSTg7Y=(Accessed March 30, 2015).

23 Annual Report to Congress, "Military and Security Developments Involving the People's Republic of China 2014", Department of Defence, USA , 24 April 2014, pp 15-16 , at http://www.defense.gov/pubs/2014_DoD_China_ Report .pdf on 13 April 2015 (Accessed April 13, 2015).

24 Bhattacharya Abanti , "South China Sea: China's Renewed Confrontation and ASEAN Option", May 28 2014,IPCS,China - Articles No 4469, at http://www.ipcs.org/article/china/south-china-sea-chinas-renewed-confrontation-and-

asean-options-4469.html(Accessed April 13, 2015).

25   Glaser S Bonnie, "China's Coercive Economic Diplomacy", July 25, 2012, The Diplomat, at http://thediplomat. com /2012/07/chinas-coercive-economic-diplomacy/(Accessed April 13, 2015).

---

†   **Lieutenant Colonel K Nishant Nair, SC** was commissioned into the 7th Battalion, The Bihar Regiment on 09 Dec 2000. He has served in counter-insurgency operations in Manipur and has been General Staff Officer Grade I (GSO1) of a mountain brigade and GSO1 (Operations) of a corps. Presently, he is posted with the Military Intelligence Directorate (Foreign Division) at the Integrated HQ of the Ministry of Defence (Army).

In My Eyes: India, Indians and India-China Relations*†

Mr Luo Zhaohui, Ambassador of the People's Republic of China in India

It's my great honour to come to the United Service Institution of India (USI) and meet with friends here. USI is one of the major, most influential Indian think tanks with the longest history. I want to thank General Singh for his invitation and gracious remarks.

Last month, I visited Assam and paid special homage to the Second World War cemetery of Chinese soldiers at Tinsukia district. Among the over 400 soldiers buried there, only one name can be found on the tombstones; and that cemetery is only one of many. From 1942 to 1945, Chinese soldiers fought side by side with the British and the Indian Army and more than 100,000 of them sacrificed their precious lives on foreign soil. Even today, their families, if any, don't know where they are buried. This is what being a soldier is all about.

Being a soldier means devotion, sacrifice and defence of peace. I am a career diplomat, and there is much in common between a diplomat and a soldier. Being a diplomat also means sacrifice, discipline and pursuit of peace. On this occasion, I want to salute all the soldiers.

I am from China, a neighbour of India. Our two countries have thousands of years of friendship and practical common interests, and sometimes, differences and grievances.

* This is the text of the talk delivered by His Excellency Mr Luo Zhaohui, Ambassador of the People's Republic of China in India at the USI on 05 May 2017, with Shri Kanwal Sibal, IFS (Retd), former Foreign Secretary of India, in the chair.

† This article was first published in the *Journal of the United Service Institution of India,* Vol. CXLVII, No. 608, April-June 2017.

First of all, let me share with you how the Chinese look at India and the Indians. First, speaking of India, people in China may immediately think of the long history of exchanges and profound integration of our two cultures. The Indus River civilization, Buddha and the ancient Silk Road will crop up in mind. In 67 AD, the Ming Emperor of China's Eastern Han Dynasty dreamed of a golden man and was told by his advisor that it was the Buddha. So the Emperor sent envoys to invite the Buddha to his land. On the way, the envoys met two Indian monks carrying Buddhist sutras on the back of a white horse. They returned to the capital city of Luoyang, and built the first Buddhist temple in China – the White Horse Temple. Of course, this episode was not the first record of historical contact between China and India. Our two countries had been in touch for hundreds of years before that.

In 2003, Indian Prime Minister Vajpayee visited the White Horse Temple and donated for the construction of an Indian style Buddhist Hall with good intention, which became a new symbol of China-India friendship. At the time when Golden Gupta Dynasty ruled India, there were Hindu temples in China's Quanzhou city, the starting point of the Maritime Silk Road. They attested to the large presence of Indian merchants in Quanzhou at that time as well as the prosperity Quanzhou enjoyed due to the Maritime Silk Road.

Not long ago, I visited Ajanta Caves, which inspired the Dunhuang Grottoes, Yungang Grottoes and Longmen Grottoes in China, and whose styles of caves, sculptures and frescos had great influence on China. China's history books are full of stories of eminent monks like Xuanzang, Faxian and Bodhidharma travelling through the Silk Road and serving as bridges between Chinese and Indian cultures. Our two countries have jointly produced the film *Kongfu Yoga*, and I'm facilitating the co-production of a new movie, the *Bodhidharma*. Monk Bodhidharma went to China at the beginning of the 6th Century A.D. and originated the Zen Buddhism and Shaolin martial arts. Before the 18th Century, no country had a larger impact on Chinese culture than India.

Secondly, there is a high degree of similarity between the history of China and India, signaling a special link between the two countries. Both are among the four ancient civilisations. Confucius lived during the Spring and Autumn Period of China, while Buddha emerged in India at about the same time, and Buddha was 10 years older than Confucius. The first Emperor who unified China was Qin Shi Huang, the First Emperor of Qin Dynasty, while the first Emperor that unified India was Ashoka. They also lived around the same period. When China was enjoying strength and prosperity under the rule of Tang Dynasty, India was experiencing the Golden Age of Gupta Dynasty. And, the Mughal period of Indian history ran in parallel with the heydays of Qing Dynasty. After that, China and India became semi-colony or colony, and then gained independence and liberation at almost the same time. This degree of similarity of history shows the similarity between our civilisations, and economic development level, as well as the closeness of our exchanges. That's why we put forward the "Panchsheel" together.

Thirdly, there is a well-known tourism promotion slogan about India – Incredible India. For the Chinese people, India is a country with long history and profound civilisation, wonderful landscapes and unique culture. Chinese people believe the Indian people are intelligent, good at math and logical analysis. They think everyone here is an IT genius, good singer and dancer. This is a tradition derived from the ancient *Upanishad*. Almost all the major religions, including Brahmanism, Buddhism, Hinduism, Islam, Jainism, Sikhism etc., can trace their origin back to India. There were also many prominent historical figures in India, like Rama, Buddha, Sankaracharya, Akbar, Mahatama Gandhi, Tagore, etc. In recent years, as India promotes Yoga across the world, Yoga is becoming highly popular among Chinese white collar workers. A Yoga college and many Yoga organisations have been established in China. There are many Yoga practitioners among Chinese diplomats in the Chinese Embassy in India. Indian cuisines are popular in China and famous for their spicy, hot and curry taste, particularly Tandoori chicken and Chapati. In a word, speaking of India, all that comes to mind of a Chinese are the good things.

For me, India is like my second hometown. Before joining the Foreign Service, I was doing research on India in a Chinese think tank. The opportunity to go to India was the only reason inspiring me to become a diplomat. Indeed, under the circumstances in the 1980s, becoming a diplomat seemed to be the only way to come to India. I was first posted in India in the late 1980s, and since then, I personally witnessed and took part in many major events in the China-India relations. My wife Dr. Jiang Yili was the first Chinese to get PhD from Delhi University.

Friends, I would like to share with you the Chinese perspective on India's development and China-India relationship.

The ecological environment is as good as what it was during my first posting in India more than 20 years ago. Delhi has become cleaner with wider streets and new high risings. The subway and highway impressed me with the rapid and tremendous changes taking place in India. I have visited Maharashtra, Assam, Rajasthan, West Bengal and Bihar, where I saw remarkable progress in local infrastructures. According to the latest statistics, India's GDP has reached 2.2 trillion US dollars, ranking the 6th largest economy in the world. India is also the fastest growing economy. I would like to congratulate you on what India has achieved.

I am also glad to see that China has contributed its share to India's development. The China-India bilateral trade volume is now over 70 billion US dollars. Cumulative Chinese investment in India was nearly 5 billion US dollars. Over 500 Chinese companies have established themselves in India. Over one million people travelled between our two countries last year. There are 80 flights between our two countries every week.

Today, China is the second largest economy in the world, with a GDP of 11 trillion US dollars. China's development also benefited from India's participation.

We sincerely hope that India can become more developed, as it not only benefits Indian people but also creates more opportunities for China's development. Some people in the West misread China and tend to think that the "Dragon" and the "Elephant" are inevitable rivals, and that China would not like to see India developing. This conception is wrong. We hope to see India develop well and we are more than happy to help India develop to achieve common development.

That is why we attach great importance to the China-India relations. Only with sound bilateral relations can we promote development, and create more facilities for our common development. Essentially, the growth of bilateral relations and common development are inseparable.

First, we need to synergise development strategies. As the two largest developing countries, China and India have similar visions and complementary strategies of development. We both support globalisation and free trade. China is at a crucial stage of comprehensively deepening reform and economic restructuring. We are implementing programmes such as "Made in China 2025", "Internet Plus". India is also at a critical juncture of reform and development, and Prime Minister Modi has put forward such initiatives as "Make in India", "Digital India", and "Smart Cities". We need to synergise our development strategies and pursue common development.

Second, we need to continue to deepen practical cooperation in the economic and trade area. We may actively explore building a China-India Free Trade Area or Regional Trading Arrangement, and encourage cooperation on major projects. We look forward to the new industrial cities to be built by Wanda Group and China Fortune Land Development Co. (CFLD) in India. These projects will help create local jobs and boost India's development. We can work together in new and renewable energy and foster new areas of cooperation.

Third, we need to continue the close exchanges in political, people-to-people and cultural fields. We should give full play to the role of high level exchanges in guiding bilateral relations. President Xi Jinping and Prime Minister Modi will have opportunities to meet each other on the sidelines of Shanghai Cooperation Organisation Summit, G20 Summit and Brazil, Russia, India, China and South Africa (BRICS) Summit this year. We may also further expand exchanges between youths and local governments. China will receive a 200-member youth delegation from India next month.

Fourth, we need to properly manage differences. As two large neighbours, it is natural that we have some differences. Even family members may have problems. What we need to do is to properly manage the existing issues while actively resolve newly emerged problems. We shall reduce differences by focusing on cooperation and work for a healthier bilateral relationship by addressing differences.

Fifth, we need to set a long term vision for the China-India relations. Here is my suggestion. Firstly, start negotiation on a *China-India Treaty of Good Neighborliness and Friendly Cooperation*. Secondly, restart negotiation of China-India Free Trade Agreement. Thirdly, strive for an early harvest on the border issue. Fourthly, actively explore the feasibility of aligning China's "One Belt One Road Initiative" (OBOR) and India's "Act East Policy".

The OBOR and regional connectivity could provide China and India with fresh opportunities and highlights for the bilateral cooperation. The OBOR is a major public product China has offered to the world. It is a strategic initiative aimed at promoting globalisation and economic integration.

India has initiated a host of attractive reforms and open-up policies, such as "Make in India". On the diplomatic front, India has put forward the "Act East Policy", "Spice Route" etc., and a number of regional connectivity initiatives, as well as vigorously pushed forward the Bay of Bengal Initiative for Multi-Sectoral Technical and Economic Cooperation (BIMSTEC). As close neighbours, China and India could be natural partners in connectivity and the OBOR.

Now the GDP of India is roughly that of China in 2004, some 13 years ago. China leads India by 13 years mainly because we started reforms and opening-up 13 years earlier. India has its advantages, such as a large number of English speaking population, the population dividend, a booming market, a sound legal system, as well as its leading role in IT, bio-pharmaceutics and Bollywood, to name just a few.

Compared with China, India has a few disadvantages. Globally, the current trend of anti-globalisation and anti-free trade is not in line with India's open-up efforts. India's neighbouring environment is different from that of China. China's reforms and opening-up benefited from its proximity to developed economies like Hong Kong, Japan and Singapore. Shenzhen grew into a major metropolis mainly thanks to its closeness to Hong Kong. China and India differ in political systems and China enjoys stronger policy consistency. India's political system has its own advantages but sometimes may cause fluctuations in its policies or at least in its pace of development. As soon as China set reforms and opening-up as its center task, the whole nation is in full sail. China's accession to the World Trade Organisation (WTO) is a typical example where domestic development and reform are boosted through external factors. After I came to India, one of my impressions was that some bureaucrats of India, to a certain extent, could not catch up with the pace of its politicians. Some policies are implemented too slowly. At the same time, Pradeshes are keener on attracting investments and expanding trade relations with foreign countries.

In this context, like the Indian initiatives, China's OBOR focuses on improving regional connectivity and economic cooperation, especially infrastructure building. It can meet the need of the countries along the OBOR and provide India and other regional countries with important opportunities. We have noted that India is relatively positive to the BCIM Economic Corridor, and hosted the third meeting of the BCIM Economic

Corridor Joint Study Group not long ago. As a founding member of Asian Infrastructure Investment Bank (AIIB), India has appointed the Vice President to the Bank. Just a few days ago, the AIIB granted funds for the projects under India's "Power for All" in Andhra Pradesh.

However, India still has reservations over the OBOR, saying that the China Pakistan Economic Corridor (CPEC) passes through the Pakistan-Controlled-Kashmir, raising sovereignty concerns. China has no intention to get involved in the sovereignty and territorial disputes between India and Pakistan. China supports the solution of the disputes through bilateral negotiations between the two countries. The CPEC is for promoting economic cooperation and connectivity. It has no connections to or impact on sovereignty issues. Even we can think about renaming the CPEC. China and India have had successful experience of delinking sovereignty disputes with bilateral relations before. In history, we have had close cooperation along the ancient Silk Road. Why shouldn't we support this kind of cooperation today? In a word, China is sincere in its intention to cooperate with India on the OBOR, as it is good for both of us.

Some Indian media say that China always puts Pakistan first when handling its relations with South Asian countries. I want to tell you this is not true. Simply put, we always put China first and we deal with problems based on their own merits. Take Kashmir issue for example, we supported the relevant UN resolutions before 1990s. Then we supported a settlement through bilateral negotiation in line with the *Simla Agreement*. This is an example of China taking care of India's concerns. Today few Indian friends remember this episode, or they have chosen to forget it. On Nuclear Suppliers Group (NSG) issue, we do not oppose any country's membership, believing that a standard for admission should be agreed upon first. On promoting India-Pakistan reconciliation, we hope that both sides could live together in peace, because this is conducive to regional stability and is in the interests of China. The development of China, India, Pakistan and the stability of the whole region call for a stable and friendly environment. Otherwise, how could we open up and develop? That's why we say we are willing to mediate when India and Pakistan have problems. But the precondition is that both India and Pakistan accept it. We do this only out of good will. We do hope that there is no problem at all. When the Mumbai terrorist attacks on November 26, 2008, took place, I was Chinese Ambassador to Pakistan, and I did a lot of mediation at that time.

Now I want to move on to the topic of China-India counter-terrorism cooperation. Last November, Mr Meng Jianzhu, Special Envoy of President Xi Jinping and Secretary of the Political and Legal Affairs Committee of the CPC Central Committee visited India. He met with Prime Minister Modi and Minister of Home Affairs, Rajnath Singh. The two sides had in-depth communications on counter-terrorism and security cooperation. Before that, the two sides held the High-level Security and Counter-terrorism Meeting, opening a new chapter in law enforcement and security cooperation between our two countries. I attended all the meetings and was greatly encouraged.

China has been a victim of terrorism. In the 1990s, Taliban trained the East Turkistan Islamic Movement (ETIM) elements. Then the ETIM elements took refuge along the Pakistan-Afghanistan border area, threatening security and stability of Xinjiang Uygur Autonomous Region of China. As a UN sanctioned terrorist group, ETIM is still creating trouble for us today, and we are ready to step up counter-terrorism cooperation with India and Pakistan. While I was Ambassador to Pakistan, I got to realise that Pakistan also suffered seriously from terrorism. Back then, my 9-year-old daughter was with me in Pakistan. Every time we returned to China for holiday, upon arriving at the Beijing Airport, she would let out a sigh of relief, saying that finally she could hang out freely. What I want to say is, first, China strongly opposes terrorism; second, China is ready to work with India, Pakistan, Afghanistan and the international community in fighting terrorism, and believes that terrorism knows no borders; third, countries need to have compatible policies, consensus and actions in fighting terrorism.

Thank you.

---

‡ **Mr Luo Zhaohui** has a Master's Degree in History and started his career as Attaché, then Third Secretary, Department of Asian Affairs, Ministry of Foreign Affairs of the People's Republic of China in 1985. He has been an Ambassador to Pakistan, Canada and presently, he is the Ambassador of PRC in India since September 2016.

China-Pakistan Economic Corridor: Connecting the Dots[*]

Lieutenant General PK Singh, PVSM, AVSM (Retd)

Introduction

Connectivity is an old game which great nations and empires have played since times immemorial. The Grand Trunk (GT) Road, with a length of over 1,600 miles (2500 km), which has existed from the reign of Chandragupta Maurya, is one of Asia's oldest and longest major roads.[1] It was extended westwards during the Mughal rule. Over two millennia old, the GT Road has linked India with Central and Western Asia and beyond. Today, it coincides with N1, N4 and N405 and N6 in Bangladesh; NH12, NH27, NH19 and NH44 in India; N45 in Pakistan and AH1 in Afghanistan. During the Mauryan Empire in 3rd Century BC, overland trade between India and Western Asia and the Hellenistic world went over this road. But what needs to be remembered is that all these connectivity projects always had commercial as well as strategic security connotations. It will not be any different today. As regards the strategic importance of these roads, it has been rightly stated that, "one can hardly over-estimate its importance from a commercial or military point of view. Troops could easily be moved from one place to another – even from the capital to the far confines of the frontier."[2] It is said that even Alexander the Great in 326 BC followed an almost identical track up to the Beas.[3] Rome too is supposed to have paved 55,000 miles of roads and built aqueducts across Europe. It is China's turn to play this game now.

---

[*]   The article has also been published as USI Occasional Paper NO 8-2017 and in the *Journal of the United Service Institution of India,* Vol. CXLVII, No. 608, April-June 2017.

The Belt and Road Forum for International Cooperation (BRF) held by China on 14-15 May 2017 brought its "One Belt, One Road (OBOR)" also called "Belt and Road Initiative" (BRI) and the China-Pakistan Economic Corridor (CPEC) into the limelight. What also caught the media glare was the fact that India chose not to participate in the event citing its strategic and sovereignty concerns, stating that "no country can accept a project that ignores its core concerns on sovereignty and territorial integrity." Many voices were heard criticising India's decision to stay away from OBOR/CPEC which were termed as connectivity projects. Nothing could be further from the truth, as India is all for connectivity – connectivity within the country, regionally and beyond. India also believes that connectivity projects should take the participating countries to higher levels of trust and diffuse national rivalries and not add to regional tensions, which OBOR/ CPEC seem to be doing at present. India further believes that international projects should evolve from a consultative process and not be based on unilateral decisions by any one party. It goes without saying that consultations achieve better results when done prior to launching any multilateral project. But the bottom line for any multi-national project to succeed would be that sovereignty issues cannot be ignored under any circumstances. Discussions on connectivity should address not only the physical infrastructure aspects but also the institutional, financial, commercial, legal and management issues. International collaborative projects demand statecraft and sagacity of a unique order to reconcile different points of view.[4]

As regards connectivity within the Indian sub-continent, attention needs to be drawn to the fact that before partition in 1947, the sub-continent was a single unit and its rail, road, canals, electricity/power were all connected. Partition not only broke this connectivity, but also cut off trade routes to Central and West Asia and beyond. Pakistan further went on to block rail and road connections between India and Pakistan. What needs to be taken note of is that CPEC does not address issues of connectivity in South Asia – on the contrary, it draws Pakistan further away from South Asia towards China.

Today, the China-Pakistan nexus is touted as an all-weather friendship which is deeper than the deepest ocean, so it may be instructive to step back in time and recall some statements made by leaders of Pakistan in the 1950s and 60s. It was on 16 July 1957 that Prime Minister Suhrawardy of Pakistan, declared in Los Angeles that, "We have thrown our lot with you (the you here refers to USA). We are very gravely apprehensive of communist domination, infiltration and aggression......... We have no difficulty in cooperating with you in helping keep the world safe from communist aggression."⁵ And on the seizure of Tibet by China in 1959, Field Marshal Ayub Khan on 23 October 1959 said, "Events and developments on the Tibet border and Afghanistan would make the sub-continent militarily vulnerable in about five years. This is to say that facilities have been created on either flank of the subcontinent whereby a major invasion could take place."⁶ And two months later Ayub Khan referred to the possibility that "Russia could move across West Pakistan down to the Sea and China towards the Malay peninsula. Not only Pakistan but the entire Indian Ocean littoral would be exposed."⁷ Pakistan's reaction to Chinese incursions into Jammu and Kashmir (J&K) was also very different then. When Chinese incursions into Ladakh in J&K were discovered and India took up the matter with the Chinese Government, Field Marshal Ayub Khan in an interview with the Daily Telegraph, London, on 27 November 1959 warned India that "without our concurrence any settlement between China and India will be something we will not recognise." So let us wait and see what the Pakistan narrative would be a decade down the line.

China-Pakistan Economic Corridor

The CPEC is a multi-billion dollar strategic project that connects the Maritime Silk Road and the Silk Road Economic Belt, also known as OBOR. It is an ambitious geo-strategic plan to carve out a combination of continental and maritime geo-strategic realm. The aim of the project is to link North West China with ports in the Arabian Sea via a road and rail corridor. It provides China the shortest and quickest access to the Arabian Sea and Persian Gulf. Through CPEC which includes the Gwadar Port, in the restive Balochistan province of Pakistan and construction in the illegally occupied Gilgit-Baltistan (GB) area of Pakistan Occupied Kashmir, China will project its power in the Indian Ocean Region (IOR). In an exhaustive report on China's BRI, the UN's Economic and Social Commission for Asia and the Pacific (ESCAP) has cautioned about the likely geo-political tensions that will be created by CPEC, stating that "the dispute over Kashmir is also of concern, since the crossing of the CPEC in the region might create geo-political tension with India and ignite further political instability."⁸

Before looking at CPEC in detail, it is desirable to have a broad understanding of the genesis of OBOR. China realised that when its Foreign Direct Investment (FDI)-Manufacture-Export driven growth model plateaus, it would have an over-capacity, especially in the infrastructure industry; an idle industrial and financial capacity available for deployment; and, an infrastructure hungry Asia waiting to build/upgrade this. This then was the genesis of OBOR.[9] From the projects announced and/or undertaken, it can be surmised that OBOR will help China upgrade its industry by gradually moving its low-end manufacturing to other countries and take pressure off from industries that suffer from an excess capacity problem, thereby, reducing the supply glut at home. In a nutshell, OBOR is less about boosting exports and more about moving excess production capacity out of China. China is very deftly converting its domestic economic liabilities into its foreign economic and diplomatic assets.[10] However, a recent article titled "Why China's One Belt, One Road plan is doomed to fail" states that, "If Beijing attempts to pursue projects at a pace and in a number sufficient to make a dent in its excess capacity, it will end up building white elephants, wasting money, and encouraging corruption on a scale never before seen."[11]

Now coming down to CPEC,[12] according to President Xi's statements, CPEC has four separate sections – energy, infrastructure, Gwadar and industrial cooperation. Surprisingly, Gwadar, which only constitutes about two percent of total investments, has found a mention in Xi's categorisation. The projects that form part of Gwadar include the port infrastructure, an airport, an expressway, a hospital, water treatment and supply projects etc. The breakdown of the financial allocation for the Gwadar Project, which is an interest free loan is – International airport – US$ 230 million, Hospital - US$ 100 million, East Bay Expressway - US$ 140 million, Water treatment and supply - US$ 130 million, Port infrastructure - US$ 32 million, Port dredging - US$ 27 million and Port breakwater - US$ 123 million.

It is to be noted that Gwadar, which was sold by Oman to Pakistan in 1958, probably at the behest of UK and/or USA, not only provides direct access to the Indian Ocean but it is also where the land and maritime network of OBOR converge. Although Gwadar's commercial viability as a transhipment port is suspect considering its distance from the circumequatorial navigation route, low depths and lack of rail connectivity, its administrative control was handed over to China for a period of 40 years in 2013. Is it mere coincidence that the operational control of Pakistan's Karachi Port is with China Overseas Port Holdings Company and that Sri Lanka's Colombo South Container Terminal is built, run and controlled by China Merchants Holding? Is it also a coincidence that Chinese naval submarines including a Ming-class, diesel-electric nuclear submarine are docked in Karachi and Colombo? The pointers are clear, Gwadar with its proximity to Hormuz, its suitability to accommodate naval warships and submarines, and its capability to serve as a hub for replenishment and weapon logistics make it an ideal naval base. With an airport, as part of the Gwadar Project, it becomes an ideal surveillance and interdiction hub. Recently there were reports that Pakistan has created a special force for the protection of Gwadar port and that two Chinese Warships were pressed into service to enhance Gwadar port's security. Does one use warships and naval security units to protect commercial ports in peace time? The answer is simple – Gwadar is a strategic naval port and that it may well turn out to be China's first overseas naval port, much sooner than expected.[13]

Now let us look at the other end of CPEC which is in Gilgit-Baltistan (GB), a part of the erstwhile princely state of Jammu and Kashmir (J&K) which legally joined India when its Ruler signed the instrument of accession in 1947. As per a report, the British Parliament recently passed a resolution stating that Gilgit-Baltistan is a part of J&K, which is under the illegal occupation of Pakistan.[14] It is not well known that Pakistan has no land borders with China. Its land borders with China are through its illegal occupation of GB. The local population of GB not only resents the forcible changing of its demography by Pakistan but have also opposed the CPEC as they fear exploitation. This does not portend well for China which wants legal cover for its billions of dollars investment in CPEC and is, therefore, pushing Pakistan to elevate the status of GB to that of a province. India objects not only to the illegal occupation of its territories by Pakistan and China but also objects to the construction activities undertaken by China in Pakistan Occupied Kashmir including GB and stationing of PLA personnel there.[15] Today, the strategic role played by GB during the Soviet occupation of Afghanistan is overlooked. It was through GB that China sent its arms and equipment to the Mujahideen, who were training in camps in GB. It is believed that not only did Chinese instructors train the Mujahideen but hundreds of Chinese muslims also joined the fight. It was also rumoured that the US and China had listening posts set up in GB and that the Soviets had even considered military options against the training camps and establishments in GB. So CPEC will remain mired in disputes and tension at its extremities in Gwadar and in Gilgit-Baltistan.[16] This has manifested itself in the form of internal security challenge for which Pakistan has already created and deployed a special force of 15,000 soldiers to protect CPEC in addition to the maritime force to protect Gwadar.[17] The moot question is, who poses the threat and who is being threatened? Obviously, the threat is from within Pakistan and the likely targets will be the Chinese personnel and projects.[18]

Energy projects under the CPEC will eventually add over 16 GW capacity in energy production at a cost of over US $ 34 bn, which amounts to approximately US $ 2 bn per GW generated. When completed, the CPEC energy mix will have about 75 per cent power generated by plants using coal. The environmental damage that this will cause in addition to the fact that Pakistan will have to import high grade coal needs to be factored in. Pakistan will be contractually obliged to buy power from Chinese companies building at a pre-negotiated high rate which can lead to a circular-debt problem. The coal fired projects will be a windfall for the Chinese as Pakistan has offered up to 34.5 per cent annual profit on equity invested in these projects.[19] It is often stated that once the energy projects are completed Pakistan will have approximately 11 to 12 GW surplus electricity to export to its neighbouring countries. The moot question is that if India, which was not invited to build these power plants, does not buy this surplus energy, who else will? Therein lies the rub and the invitation to India to join CPEC to make it economically profitable. There is no reason for India to do so.

The numerous Special Economic Zones (SEZ) are another contentious issue mainly because there is no transparency and that only Chinese industrialists will be allowed to set up industries in these SEZ.[20] There is already disquiet amongst the industrialists and trade chambers in Pakistan as the Chinese will be granted long-term leases at concessional rates along with 20-year tax holidays.[21] As an example, Balochistan has already signed a 43 years lease agreement in November 2015, handing over 2281 acres of land that it had acquired for US $ 62 million to the Chinese for developing a SEZ, near Gwadar Port. The fishing community in Gwadar fears that it will lose its livelihood because of the Port. This adds to the social tension too.

Presently there are around 19,000 Chinese personnel working on CPEC within Pakistan and this number will swell by thousands more once the projects and SEZ are set up. How will the presence of Chinese in large numbers be viewed specially by the radicalised, unemployed youth in Pakistan? Mohammed Ahsan Chaudhri had observed, "The heart of the matter is that Pakistan's alliances with the West cannot be supported ideologically."[22] So the question that arises is, "can Pakistan's alliances with Communist China be supported ideologically? Can ideological and religious friction be avoided?"

While strategic and other issues have been addressed above, the elephant in the room is the economic/financial implications of CPEC for Pakistan. Some estimates suggest a financial outflow ranging from US $ 3 to 5 billion per annum.[23] Pakistan is likely to end up paying US $ 90 billion to China over a span of 30 years against the loan and investment portfolio under CPEC.[24] The worrying question is, what will happen if Pakistan defaults on repayment, as we know that the Chinese are averse to rescheduling or forgiving debts owed by foreign governments?[25] Will Pakistan end up compromising its sovereignty at the projects in Gwadar, GB and in the SEZs by swapping its loan for equity? How will this impact the stability of Pakistan? Studying the Sri Lankan experience with the Chinese projects in Hambantota, where China used financial assistance to advance its strategic interests, may be instructive and also a pointer of things to come.

The Chinese Government is conscious of India's legitimate concerns about CPEC. They were very keen that India participates in the Belt and Road Forum in Beijing and to assuage India's concerns the Chinese Ambassador to India in a speech on 05 May 2017 even suggested that CPEC could be renamed.[26] This tokenism had no takers in India but Pakistan reacted to it and sought China's clarifications on it.[27]

In strategic discussions, when CPEC is discussed, the issue of Pakistan-China nexus invariably comes up. It may be of interest to note how China viewed the "two front challenge." On 16 May 1959, the Chinese Ambassador in Delhi, in a meeting with India's Foreign Secretary had said that, "China will not be so foolish as to antagonise the US in the East and again to antagonise India in the West. We cannot have two centres of attention......... It seems to us that you cannot have two fronts. Is it not so? If it is so, here lies the meeting point of the two sides." It is ironical that despite the slogans of *"Hindi-Chini Bhai Bhai"* (Indians and Chinese are brothers), the two sides that met turned out to be China and Pakistan, thereby, trying to create a two-front scenario for India. A hypothetical question that can be tossed around could be, "Is China with its allies and partners today prepared to face the US and its allies and partners in the Western Pacific and at the same time in the Strait of Hormuz and IOR? As China's economic footprints enlarge so will its security challenges grow and the two front dilemma can well become a multi-front dilemma.

CPEC Master Plan28

While the media was agog with the goings on at the BRI Forum in Beijing in mid-May 2017, the *Dawn* of Pakistan disclosed the details of the CPEC long term plan from the original documents, which highlights what the Chinese intentions and priorities are in Pakistan for the next decade and a half. The report states that the scope of CPEC "has no precedent in Pakistan's history" as it "envisages a deep and broad-based penetration of most sectors of Pakistan's economy as well as its society by Chinese enterprises and its culture.

Although President Xi had spelt out energy, infrastructure, Gwadar and industrial cooperation as the four separate sections of CPEC, the Master Plan shows that the main thrust of the plan actually lies in agriculture. The importance of the agriculture sector would be relevant as well as sensitive, because it would require millions of hectares of agricultural land to be handed over to the Chinese, across the length and breadth of the country, at subsidised rates, on which a large number of projects and plans will come up. It is worth nothing that the core areas for the agriculture projects include, "most of Islamabad's Capital territory, Punjab and Sindh, and some areas of GB, Khyber Pukhtunkhwa and Balochistan." One can well imagine how the feudal landowners and tribals would react when their land would be taken away for handing it to the Chinese. Land acquisition could well prove to be the Achilles Heel! The other aspects which merit attention in the Master Plan are:-

(a) The industrial plan for the western and north western zone, "covering most of Balochistan and KP province is marked for mineral extraction, with potential in chrome ore." The possibility of loan defaults being offset through mineral extraction cannot be ruled out though at this stage it is only a hypothetical proposition.

(b) As far as the textile industry is concerned, "China can make the most of the Pakistani market in cheap raw materials to develop the textiles and garments industry and help soak up surplus labour forces in Kashgar." The major beneficiaries would be the Chinese.

(c) Preferences need to be extended to Chinese enterprises in areas such as, "land, tax, logistics and services, as well as land price, enterprise income tax, tariff reduction and exemption and sales tax rate." This suggests a distortion of the level playing field to the disadvantage of

Pakistani entrepreneurs.

(d) The aspect of fibre optics and surveillance needs a detailed study, as "the link goes far beyond a simple fibre optic setup." The creation of electronic monitoring and control systems, as for Khunjerab, and how the full system of monitoring and surveillance in cities from Peshawar to Karachi will affect the society at large lies in the grey zone.

(e) The related issues of future cooperation between the media of China and Pakistan and how issues pertaining to dissemination of Chinese culture in Pakistan will play out, is a subject for study by itself. Will this bridge the ideological gap between the Pakistani and Chinese people or accentuate it, is any one's guess.

(f) The plans for developing coastal tourism are laid out in great detail and suggest visa-free entry to Chinese tourists into Pakistan, but are surprisingly silent on the issue of reciprocal visa-free entry for Pakistani nationals visiting China.

(g) The report is "at its most unsentimental when drawing up the risks faced by long term investments in Pakistan's economy." The report further goes on to suggest that "Pakistan's economy cannot absorb FDI much above US$ 2 billion per year without giving rise to stresses in its economy."

It further suggests that "China's maximum annual direct investment in Pakistan should be around US $ 1 billion." And as far as financial altruism suggested by many "experts" is concerned, the report unambiguously states, "The cooperation with Pakistan in the monetary and financial areas aims to serve China's diplomatic strategy." Does all this not suggest that the Chinese are aware of the financial risk involved in investing in Pakistan, yet are going ahead? Why? What is the hidden agenda, if any? After all CPEC is not a charity project.

The CPEC Master Plan appears to have avoided much mention of the Gwadar Port and projects, so as not to draw attention to its possibility of being a PLA Navy Base and surveillance-cum-interdiction hub. However, the *Dawn* report has flagged that Gwadar could "serve as a port of exit for minerals from Balochistan and Afghanistan". Importantly, the report also goes on to state that "There is no mention of China's external trade being routed through Gwadar." The strategic importance of the Gwadar project, which includes the port and an international airport, and its proximity to the Straits of Hormuz, needs detailed examination by experts looking at the maritime domain in this region. The Gwadar Port is not there to solve the Malacca dilemma, as some naively suggest. Gwadar will be a naval and surveillance base with commercial activity primarily restricted to taking away minerals extracted from Pakistan and Afghanistan.

The strategic importance of GB, though not spelt out in the Report for obvious reasons, needs a fresh look, more so as China has signed Memorandum of Understanding (MoU) with Pakistan to build two mega dams – Bunji and Bhasha, on the Indus River. How India reacts to the Chinese presence in PoK including Gilgit and Baltistan, as also how it proceeds with the Indus Water Treaty, is something that experts in "scenario building" could work on.

CPEC – Reading between the Lines

To get a somewhat better understanding of the CPEC, we need to create a mosaic that takes into account all that has been written and said about it. By doing so, the salient points of the picture that emerge are :-

(a) The Chinese and Pakistani establishments very cleverly kept away many details of the CPEC given out in the Master Plan from public scrutiny till the BRF commenced. Similarly, the details of the MoU regarding the five dams forming the North Indus River Cascade, for which an additional loan of US $ 50 billion was allocated but not revealed till the signing of the MoU at the BRF. Had an Indian delegation been present at the BRF the embarrassment that would have been caused to it can well be understood.

(b) The CPEC will provide China with a strategic gateway to the Indian Ocean through the Gwadar Port. To expand and safeguard its maritime interests in the IOR, Gwadar will be built into a PLA Naval and Surveillance and Interdiction Base. The Gwadar Port will not be a major commercial port to solve the Malacca dilemma, as erroneously suggested by some researchers, but commercially it will serve as an exit point for mineral resources extracted from Pakistan and Afghanistan. The land route from Afghanistan to China is unlikely to be used for this purpose due to cost and security considerations.

(c) GB is of the greatest strategic significance for Pakistan and China, as without this there will no border and land connectivity between these two countries. CPEC will unravel without GB being a part of it. It is thus imperative for Pakistan to hold on to GB and for China to develop it through various projects including those linked to CPEC. The five dams forming the North Indus River Cascade that China has promised to finance and build are not Run of River (RoR) projects and going ahead with them will be a Himalayas blunder and are likely to raise tensions in the region.[29] The construction of large dams for generation of electricity could lead to review of the Indus Water Treaty by India.

(d) The SEZ and/or industrial parks are crucial for China's plans for upgrading its industry by moving out its idle as well as low-end manufacturing and infrastructure industry. These SEZs and parks will also enable Pakistan to test the local population's reactions to sale of land to the Chinese at concessional rates with other facilities thrown in.

(e) The energy projects will be pushed through as these will not only provide the much needed electricity to Pakistan which will be welcomed by its population but will also cater for the needs of various industrial and agriculture projects which are part of CPEC. During the short to mid-term, there may not be any spare electricity to be exported out of Pakistan.

(f) Security of Chinese projects and personnel will remain a long term challenge. It could be accentuated by the religious-cum-ideological divide that exists. The political, tribal, religious and terrorist linked threats mentioned in the Master Plan need to be factored in.

(g) The agricultural projects mentioned in the Master Plan are ambitious and cover the length and breadth of Pakistan. However, the problems of land acquisition will have to be overcome for its success. One has to wait and watch.

(h) The fibre optics and surveillance projects are of strategic importance. The MoU for the fibre optic link was signed in July 2013 and precedes the ambitious plans for CPEC which have since emerged. This aspect needs further study.

(i)   While cooperation between the Pakistani and Chinese media should be welcomed, as it may enhance mutual understanding between people of the two countries involved, the aspect of cultural synergy between the two different ideologies will need deft handling.

(j)   The geo-strategic implications of Gwadar turning into a PLA Naval and Surveillance-cum-Interdiction Base, should it so happen, has far reaching consequences. The artificial islands created by China in the South China Sea, and ports such as Hambantota, Karachi, Gwadar and Djibouti need to be viewed as part of one continuum.

(k) So far it appears that the European Union has given the BRI/OBOR a somewhat cautious welcome and is still pondering over how to engage China strategically on this issue. The Western countries and their financial institutions appear to be concerned about commercial feasibility, transparency, sustainability, environmental issues etc. and are unlikely to finance projects in a hurry that haven't been suitably analysed and vetted.

(l)   The financial risks involved both for China and Pakistan are genuine and have not been analysed critically. While China will attempt to get other countries and international institutions to partner it for various OBOR projects, what appears worrying is the capacity of Pakistan to repay the loans it is contracting under CPEC. A World Bank Report titled, "Global Economic Prospects 2016", released in January 2016, had cautioned that "Sovereign guarantees associated with CPEC could pose substantial fiscal risks over the medium term." A default is very much on the cards and how this will play out will be crucial for Pakistan's stability. Instability in Pakistan will not only accentuate its internal troubles but will also affect its relations with India, Iran and Afghanistan.

(m) The Chinese would definitely be aware that while ports, power projects, dams, railways etc. can be built in a short span of time, building the human and institutional capacity that allows these projects to operate efficiently and contribute effectively to economic and social progress, takes a much longer time. This may lead to scaling down of some of the ambitions projects.

The *Dawn* has very aptly concluded by stating that, "In fact, CPEC is only the opening of the door. What comes through once that door has been opened is difficult to forecast."[30] This is indeed a very mature, visionary and cautionary statement which needs to be taken note of seriously by some experts, especially in India, who have been asking India to rush headlong into joining BRI/OBOR/CPEC, the future costs notwithstanding.

Conclusion

In conclusion, what Prime Minister Narendra Modi said during his interaction with Chinese media organisations is worth examining :-

> *"Successful revival of the ancient trade routes require not only physical connectivity and requisite infrastructure, but even more important, a climate of peace, support for mutual prosperity and free flow of commerce and ideas."[31]*

While CPEC may have a great effect in Pakistan and on Pakistan-China relations, it does not in any way address issues of connectivity in South Asia. On the contrary, it draws Pakistan further away from South Asia towards China. In Pakistan, there is a "tendency to treat CPEC like the proverbial gift horse. The gift horse may prove to be a Trojan Horse! There is a need for transparency."[32] One should also consider what might be the fate of CPEC if relations between Pakistan and China turn sour in the future. This may seem a far-fetched concern at this time but the evolution of the relationship with Iran should provide a reality check.[33]

The CPEC is a strategic project of China and not a silver bullet for Pakistan's economic woes. Right now it is just the rosy perception about the CPEC, the reality may prove to be quite different. The concerns that India may have succeeded in isolating itself by staying away from the BRF are unfounded, as many nations would have appreciated not just the principled stand but also the fact that India can stand up to China in open international fora. As they say, "the jury is still out". We have a long wait ahead!

Endnotes

1   KM Sarkar, "The Grand Trunk Road in the Punjab : 1849-1886".

2   Ibid.

3   Ibid.

4   From the Preface by Lt Gen PK Singh (Retd) to the book "China's One Belt One Road – Initiative, Challenges and Prospects, edited by Bal Kishan Sharma and Nivedita Das Kundu, Vij Books India Pvt Ltd, 2016. ISBN : 978-93-85563-59-1 (Hardback).

5   *Dawn,* Karachi, 18 July 1957.

6   *Pakistan Times,* Lahore, 24 Oct 1959.

7   *Morning News,* 21 Dec 1959.

8   Available at http://toi.in/2UI_tb/a18ag.

9   Peter Cai, *"Understanding China's Belt and Road Initiative",* Lowy Institute for International Policy, Sydney, Australia, March 2017.

10   Sara Hsu, *"How China's Asian Infrastructure Investment Bank Fared Its First Year",* Forbes, January 14, 2017. Available at http://www.forbes.com/sites/sarahsu/2017/01/14/how-chinas-asian-infrastructure-investment-bank-fared-its-first-year/#43b2eec2f4d1.

11   Available at http://m.scmp.com/week-asia/opinion/article/1999544/why-chinas-one-belt-one-road-plan-doomed-fail.

12   *Dawn,* "CPEC: Lessons from History", 17 Jan, 2017. Available at http://www.dawn.com/news/ptint/1308873.

13   Christopher Bodeen, 'Pakistan, China Set Sights on Arabian Sea Link', The Streets, 5 July 2013.

14   *Times of India,* "Gilgit-Baltistan Part of J&K, Pakistan in Illegal Occupation: Resolution in British Parliament", 27 Mar, 2017. Available at http://timesofindia.indiatimes.com/india/gilgit-baltistan-part-of-jk-pakistan-in- illegal-occupation-resolution-in-british-parliament/articleshowprint/57846246.cms.

15   The Indian Express, *"The Gilgit-Baltistan Feint",* Tilak Devasher, 19 Apr 2017. (www.indianexpress.com).

16   China Base Sparks, 'Very Significant Security Concerns', Colin Clark, 27 Mar, 2017. Available at breakingdefense.com.

17   Wang Qingyun, "Pakistan Military to Ensure Security for Economic Corridor". Available at http://www.chinadaily.com.cn/world/2017-03/15/content_28569141 .htm

18   Ibid.

19   *Express Tribune,* "Windfall for Chinese on Coal Fired Projects", 21 Feb 2017. Available at https://tribune.com.pk/story/1327172/windfall-chinese-coal-fired-projects/

20 *Dawn*, Khurram Husain, 09 Mar 2017. Available at http://www.dawn.com/news/ print/1319301.

21 *Dawn, Economic & Business*, "CPEC : Looking a Gift Horse in the Mouth", 27 Mar 2017. Available at https://www.dawn.com/news/print/1323124.

22 *Foreign Policy of Pakistan*, Karachi, pg 25.

23 Op. cit. *Dawn, Economic & Business*.

24 Express Tribune, "Pakistan will be Paying China US$ 90 bn Against CPEC Related Projects", 29 Mar 2017. Available at https://tribune.com.pk/ story/1352995/pakistan-will-paying-china-906-cpec-related-projects

25 Op. Cit. *Dawn*, Khurram Husain.

26 Available at https://thewire.in/133138/china-pakistan-india-obor.

27 Available at https://www.pakistantoday.com.pk/2017/05/08/pakistan-contacts-china-over-luos-delhi-address/.

28 Available at https://www.dawn.com/news/1333101

29 Available at https://thewire.in/139147/indus-cascade-himalayas-blunder

30 Op Cit. Note 28.

31 "Transcript of Prime Minister's interaction with Chinese Media Organisation", http://mea.gov.in/interviews. htm?dtt/24011/Transcript_of_Prime_Ministers_Interaction_with_Chinese_media organisations

32 Op. Cit. *Dawn, Economic & Business*.

33 Op. Cit. *Dawn*, "CPEC: Lessons from History".

† **Lieutenant General PK Singh, PVSM, AVSM (Retd)**, a former General Officer Commanding-in-Chief, of the Indian Army, is the Director of the United Service Institution of India, New Delhi. The views expressed are his personal views, and draw from his participation on discussions held at the international workshop hosted by SIPRI and FES at Tutzing, Germany in February 2017 and at the CSIS, Washington DC and Georgetown University, Washington DC in April 2017. The author would also like to specially thank Commander MH Rajesh, Research Fellow at the USI of India for his valuable suggestions and inputs.

The Undeclared Power Play behind Belt and Road Forum[*]

Major General SB Asthana, SM, VSM (Retd)

Introduction

President Xi Jinping's dream summit to "Transform the Eurasian and African infrastructure landscape as never before" and "defend and develop an open world economy against threats of trade protectionism emanating from the West"[1] on May 14-15, 2017 may not have as many takers as he expected, but was a mega event with delegates from over 100 countries. In 2013 President Xi Jinping coined the word 'One Belt One Road' (OBOR) to showcase China driven global connectivity model. It was projected as the biggest foreign policy initiative for global connectivity and inclusive growth of everyone partnering it. In Mar 2015, the text of 'Belt and Road Initiative' (BRI) action plan was released by China, followed by release of full text of China's Military Strategy in May 2015,[2] and a comparison of the two clearly indicates that the OBOR/ BRI is not purely for inclusive growth and not as benign as it is made out to be. In fact it marks the beginning of a major global strategic power play in the affected regions through connectivity initiatives.

China's OBOR Summit of May 14-15, was to showcase its diplomatic might and ambitious globalisation plan, presuming that the US will still be settling down with new President with 'Protectionist' outlook, and Xi Jinping will be able to project himself as the tallest global leader, with attendance of most global leaders to the Summit. When it became evident that all leaders may not turn up and many countries may send some officials of varying status, it was named as 'Belt and Road Forum' (BRF). Finally out of delegates from

* This article was first published in the *Journal of the United Service Institution of India*, Vol. CXLVII, No. 608, April-June 2017.

over 100 countries, only 29 Heads of States turned up, who were looking for Chinese infrastructure/trade investments for varying reasons on bilateral/multilateral basis. These facts are well known to everyone, as large number of articles have been written on the subject so far. This article attempts to analyse and speculate the type and extent of power play, behind these facts, which the affected countries have not commonly spoken/declared with respect to OBOR in general, and BRF in particular.

Who Really Needs OBOR?

While China would like the world to believe that its efforts like OBOR and BRI are purely developmental, initiating inclusive growth in participating regions, seeking common destiny, but the largest beneficiary of OBOR projects is China itself. Some of the Chinese domestic compulsions/stakes are:–

(a) Politically, to ensure that democratic wind does not flow from Taiwan and Hong Kong to mainland China, Chinese Communist Party (CCP) Government has to continue delivering well economically to keep domestic population dreaming of becoming superpower by 2049. With global and Chinese slowdown, it has to innovate methods to continue the same pace of growth to achieve its global ambition.

(b) President Xi Jinping is a strong and undisputed leader of China, and despite being 64 years old there is hardly any doubt that he will continue to hold all current appointments in 19th National People's Congress (NPC) (meeting scheduled later this year), but his anti-corruption drive, and perceived over-centralisation of power, may create some rivals within domestic political community and people who need to be mesmerised before 19th NPC Session so that he gets a comfortable hierarchical composition. OBOR Summit was one such occasion, where he has attempted to project himself as tallest leader in the world. This was the right time as President Trump was still settling down, grappling with protectionist agenda, having annoyed a number of allies and leaders of other countries who do not have that kind of economic muscle.

(c) To refuel/reignite economic growth at the desired pace, China is looking at promoting investments, creating demands, offloading trade surpluses, overcapacities, exploiting resources and integrating itself into world economic system further.

(d) The Chinese desire to put into effect its 'Western Area Development Plan' dating 2000, and the need to connect globally is not new, but it now needs to seek new areas of investments and infrastructure development. It, therefore, has to explore neighbourhood as well as global opportunities for infrastructure development.

(e) Chinese infrastructure growth within the country aims to rectify the developmental asymmetry between highly developed Eastern seaboard and Western areas including restive Xinjiang and Tibet. The BRI action plan lays substantive emphasis on this aspect, as part of accelerating 'Western Development Plan' and 'Go West' Strategy.

(f) By creating an infrastructure demand internally, regionally and globally, China can help its major construction companies, create jobs and earn more revenue. Chinese efforts are in sync with its economic, logistics and domestic compulsions, shortened lines of communication, warm water access, and smooth flow of oil, raw materials and goods, to improve its economic might as part of its development of 'Comprehensive National Power' (CNP). While this infrastructure development is justified for China's economic, trade and sectoral development, its potential of playing a dual role (civil and military) in future cannot be ruled out.

(g) It is a Chinese model of global connectivity, which will help them in increasing strategic footprints by getting the global deployment capability of PLA to secure her Sea Lanes of Communication (SLOC), commercial and strategic interests, as infrastructure is a dual use facility. If the model is globally accepted, China gets a licence to deploy its military to protect its lines of communication, and deploy Chinese labour (including security personnel in the garb of labour) outside China, at crucial strategic points.

(h) China on numerous occasions has been talking about multi-polar world order with a view to emerge as one of the strong poles, especially in Asia. The Chinese Military Strategy lays down protection of its SLOC, and ensuring world peace as role of PLA.[3] To achieve that PLA must have regional and global deployability which needs continental and maritime connectivity, and BRI is a significant step in this direction.

Why did 30 Countries Sign-up for it?

An analysis of countries that have signed-up for OBOR reveals a definite pattern. There are countries, that are falling prey to China's 'Infrastructure Diplomacy' and 'Purse Diplomacy' by allowing the Chinese to invest in their infrastructure, despite knowing that it is pushing them into a debt trap or exploitation of their natural resources, or some strategic compromises. They actually have no choice because they themselves do not have economic resources and technology to deliver it to their population, necessary for their leaders to remain in power in next election even if it amounts to a long term disadvantage. There is another set of countries, mainly in neighbourhood, who just cannot stand up to economic, strategic and military might of China, hence have no choice but to sign for it. The case of Russia is slightly different, because to bear the economic sanctions from the West, and fast changing diplomacy of President Trump, a convergence of interest with China has taken place. Russia has decided to link the initiative with its own regional economic framework of the Eurasian Economic Union. Russian President's attendance symbolises its current economic linkage with China, besides protecting their interests in Central Asian Republics (CAR).

In this era of economic cooperation together with strategic competition, it is significant to note that China is putting together a policy of engaging its periphery exercising 'Neighbourhood Diplomacy' through a series of infrastructural development projects, that provide China easy access to energy sources, shorter trade routes, and warm waters access from its landlocked part of western region. The development of land and strategic energy corridors through Pakistan, Myanmar, Bangladesh, and its desire to get into the Bay of Bengal avoiding maritime choke points, are part of the above strategy.

What Signal has the US and the EU Sent by Sudden Attendance?

The last day surprise entry by the US could be attributed to the sudden realisation by the US, that President Donald Trump's protectionist trade agenda and isolationist diplomacy may push the global fulcrum of trade and globalisation in China's favour. Some commercial and economic *quid pro quo,* intense Chinese diplomatic efforts and need to understand Beijing's grand plan for geopolitical domination may have prompted the US to send

Matthew Pottinger, the Senior Director for Asia at the National Security Council in the White House.

The attendance also included senior officials from European Union like Christine Lagarde, Managing Director of the International Monetary Fund and UN Secretary General António Guterres. The European Union officials did attend the BRF, but not buy Chinese narrative of 'Win-Win Situation', because the one sided advantage to Chinese construction companies, and their financial institutions was easily discernible; hence, they did not sign-up for it, and asked for level playing field.

Japan and South Korea, despite serious differences with China on security matters, have strong economic linkages and may have come looking for opportunity for financial investment.[4] Their other intention may have been to understand the plan to work out the counter strategy, if it did not suit them.

What does OBOR Encompass in Real Terms?

OBOR may well be a future blueprint of China-centric infrastructure connectivity model, encompassing variety of infrastructure initiatives, but there is nothing very new in it. These initiatives were earlier being taken up in bits and pieces, on bilateral and multilateral basis, to improve and secure its external connectivity, warm water accessibility, security of its SLOC and to get economic advantages. In connecting the Continental Belt, in most places the road and rail network already exists, although in poor state, which is proposed to be improved through this initiative to meet the specifications required by China to transit its commercial goods to farthest destination. The promises of Special Economic Zones (SEZs) along the route are by-products/fringe benefits to woo the host nations. The mining and energy projects also need to be studied with care, more so after not so good experience of Myitsone Dam in Myanmar and Hambantota Port in Sri Lanka. Many writers in Pakistan are also concerned about getting into debt trap. Production of energy is too costly to be purchased by locals, leading to other economic and strategic compromises.

This also has concealed strategic intentions of extending its strategic space. Besides looking at Chinese intention of leveraging its soft power, there is also need to analyse the hidden intention of improving its hard power through this Chinese model of regional infrastructure development.

Regarding 'Maritime Road', the global shipping is already happening in international waters along the same routes, hence, it basically amounts to China being permitted to develop ports and maritime bases to facilitate its shipping, which can be suitably used as military bases, whenever the strategic situation so demands.

Has BRF Succeeded?

Despite dream-selling speeches by China about 'inclusive' globalisation, no worthwhile framework or common plan could be arrived at. Attractive packaging of BRI included Chinese pledge of investing US $113 billion in extra funding to kick-start the initiative, to build a new network of transcontinental railways, ports and highways. President Xi Jinping announced an import expo to take place next year, at which China will open up its domestic markets.

There is also a long-term plan as revealed by the announcement that Beijing will host another summit in 2019 to promote its globalisation strategy.[5] Beijing also promised to import US $2 trillion worth of products from "Belt and Road" countries over the next five years. Xi promised a major funding boost for his new Silk Road, with an additional 100 billion Yuan (US $14.5 billion) going into the Silk Road Fund. The China Development Bank and Export-Import Bank of China will set up special lending schemes, worth 250 billion Yuan and 130 billion Yuan respectively to support infrastructure projects. In addition, China will provide 60 billion Yuan over the next three years for poverty alleviation in developing countries along the new Silk Road. More than 270 cooperation projects or agreements had been signed during the summit.[6]

China was looking for more capital by selling the inclusive growth benefits of OBOR, as some of its OBOR projects got delayed because of strict capital control by Beijing due to capital shortage; but was possibly disappointed, as no worthwhile commitments were made by most countries. Even the financial institutions are not too sure of funding such costly projects. The excitement and urge of private companies to utilise their over-capacities, and make their trade surpluses commercially profitable is understandable but they will also be doing their cost-benefit analysis.

The much publicised success of Asian Infrastructure Investment Bank (AIIB) can also be attributed to the fact that a number of countries joined it to get an alternative/additional source of funding other than IMF and World

Bank, on which some economic powers have monopoly, and not because of BRI.

Many countries besides the US, Japan, Australia, several European countries, including Germany, France and Britain also declined to sign a trade statement at the Summit, citing lack of clarity on a level playing field for private companies in tendering against state-owned enterprises for government contracts, or on social and environmental standards. Scepticism remains among Western countries and many other countries, who may not have expressed it.[7]

Chinese reassurances to its neighbours to dispel the fear of assertiveness, strategic dominance, and its strategic intentions among most industrialised nations did not cut ice with most of them. It left China to rethink that its actions for globalisation and world leadership role are perhaps too premature. China is yet to become a developed nation before thinking of such role.

Why India's Non-Participation is not a Case of Missed Opportunities?

A number of articles have appeared in Indian and Chinese media criticising India's non-participation at the event, without analysing it in the context of India's national interest. The analysis is as under:-

(a) No other country is confronted with an issue as serious as "sovereignty issue" in context of OBOR as India, with China-Pakistan-Economic-Corridor (CPEC) passing through Pakistan occupied Kashmir (PoK), which is sovereign territory of India, hence, India is well justified in skipping the event.

(b) India has been able to drive home the point that the 'sovereignty issue' of PoK, is extremely sensitive, and cannot be compromised. The 'sovereignty issue' of PoK overrides the isolation threats, commercial concerns, opportunity cost (if any) of skipping it. The Foreign and Defence Ministers of India have already clarified the same many times. This has been well-understood by global community, as well as China, which has indicated its willingness to welcome India even at a later stage. Germany has supported Indian action of skipping it.

(c) It proves that India follows an independent foreign policy, to protect its core interests, even if it amounts to being absent/insignificant

146

representation in a large summit like OBOR. Participation by Indian scholars (as mentioned by Chinese Foreign Ministry Spokesman Mr Geng Shuang) cannot be assumed as Indian participation, unless delegated to represent by Ministry of External Affairs of India.

(d) In case of Bangladesh-China-India-Myanmar (BCIM), India has already negotiated connectivity through Bangladesh and work is in progress. The roads in Northeastern states are being developed by India, and connectivity to Myanmar is being negotiated bilaterally, hence China driven BCIM has very little to charm India.

Where do India-China Relations go from here?

India and China are two neighbours (a geographical fact which no one can change) and have to deal with each other. Both are fast growing economies, housing largest consumer markets. To maintain their pace of growth, they have to tap each other's consumer market, hence, would continue to do commercial business. The economic cooperation alongside strategic competition is unavoidable, and will continue.

CPEC is going to be a reality even if it amounts to Pakistan becoming an economic colony of China. We thus need to be ready to face a different Pakistan, whose strategic choices are hostage to China. At the same time, the US will not dump Pakistan, because they still feel that for controlling some of the terrorist groups, which may threaten their mainland, they may require help from Pakistan.

Strategically, CPEC, Gwadar, infrastructure development near Indian borders in Tibet, and Indian Ocean will continue to be a strategic and security challenge to India, and there is no alternative but to create military capacity to face it. CPEC and Gwadar will not only bring PLA to Indian backyard, but will also impact our military and strategic options, should proxy war by Pakistan become unbearable to India. Diplomacy and strategic partnerships with other global powers have their benefits, but our own 'Comprehensive National Power', especially the hard power needs to be further developed to address the security concerns. So far in history no country has become a big power without a strong military.

Conclusion

BRF could not showcase a convincing and clear vision of OBOR for global growth, and ended with dream-selling speeches, without worthwhile achievements from global perspective. It could not convince the Western countries to sign-up for it. The main signatories to the communiqué are regional countries, that in any case are dependent on China. Even if Trump Administration with protective outlook may have lost some ground, China could not convince the world to be the architect of globalisation as yet. However, OBOR will continue to draw attention in the context of connectivity and globalisation. In Indian context, CPEC will go through and keep India concerned about its security. India will have to look for alternatives, especially for connectivity to CAR.

The idea of grouping Chinese investments in Africa and Latin America, under the umbrella of OBOR, indicates China's dream of global dominance, and BRI seems to be the strategy to support it. BRI, therefore, is going to be the centre stage of Chinese strategy and foreign policy for the 21st Century. BRI has some potential of inclusive growth to help some needy countries, but it also has the potential to further destabilise fragile states. Its Chinese commercial bias also adds to the concerns/scepticism of large number of countries. The BRI may well be Xi Jinping's landmark strategy, similar to Hu Jintao's "peaceful rise".[8]

Endnotes

1   Heydarian Richard, *China at the vanguard of globalisation and the great paradox of our age,* South China Morning Post, May 16, 2017. Avaiolable at http://www.scmp.com/news/china/diplomacy-defence/article/2094539/opinion-china-vanguard-globalisation-and-great-paradox. Accessed on 28 May 2017.

2   Information Office of the State Council of the People's Republic of China, Beijing (2015), Government White Paper, 26 May 2015, Full Text: *China Military Strategy,* CHINADAILY.COM.CN, Accessed on 28 May 2015.

3   Asthana SB, *Skipping OBOR Summit would reflect 'India First' Policy,* Indian Defence Review, May 16, 2017. Available at http://www.indiandefencereview.com/news/skipping-obor-summit-would-reflect-india-first-policy/. Accessed on 17 May 2017.

4   Ibid.

5   South China Morning Post, *Significance of the 'Belt and Road Initiative' goes beyond trade,* 17 May, 2017. Available at http://www.scmp.com/comment/insight-opinion/article/2094585/significance-belt-and-road-initiative-goes-beyond-trade. Accessed on 17 May 2017.

6   Wong Catherine, *Five things to watch as China's belt and road plan unfolds,* South China Morning Post, 17 May, 2017. Available at http://www.scmp.com/news/china/diplomacy-defence/article/2094578/five-things-watch-chinas-belt-and-road-plan-unfolds. Accessed on 17 May 2017.

7   Bhattacharjee Subhomoy, *Race for supremacy: India, Japan plan alternative to counter China's OBOR,* Business Standard, May 16, 2017. Available at http://www.business-standard.com/article/economy-policy/race-for-supremacy-india-japan-plan-alternative-to-china-s-obor-1170515012731.html. Accessed on 28 May 2017.

8   Brînza Andreea, *Is China's belt and road ready to be the new face of globalisation?* May 15, 2017. Available at http://www.scmp.com/comment/insight-opinion/article/2094368/chinas-belt-and-road-ready-be-new-face-globalisation. Accessed on 29 May 2017.

---

†   **Major General SB Asthana, SM, VSM (Retd)** was commissioned into 7 ASSAM on 16 Dec 1978 and retired as Additional Director General Infantry on 01 Jun 2014. He is a security analyst and participates at various forums related to strategic issues and international relations. Presently, he is the Chief Instructor at United Service Institution of India since 16 Mar 2015.

The China Dream, *Tianxia* and Belt and Road Initiative: *'Pax Sinica'* or Middle Power Coalition for Asia-Pacific?[*]

Major General Rajiv Narayanan, AVSM, VSM
(Retd)

China, today sits on the cusp of a unique position amongst the comity of nations – feared by the small nations, yet needed for its financial muscle (that it has no compunctions in providing to gain long term 'strategic equity' in lieu of short term financial 'gains' for the ruling elites of these nations) while the developed countries are stuck proverbially between the 'Devil and the Deep Sea'. Having financed the economic rise of China through much of the last three decades, thereby converting China into their manufacturing hub, any economic counter to a 'Rising, Revanchist' China thus has its blowback on their own economies.

With the US in a 'strategic retrenchment', first under Obama and now the unpredictable Trump Presidency, the West is in a dilemma as the European Union does not have the heft to fill the rising vacuum in Asia.[1] Neither do the other middle powers of Asia, be it Japan, South Korea or India, on their own. Xi Jinping appears to view the coming decades as a 'strategic opportunity' for China to fill this vacuum and establish a *'Pax Sinica'*2 in Asia – the fruition of phase one of the China Dream and the great rejuvenation of the nation.

This article analyses the China Dream within the Chinese view of *Tianxia,* and the role that the Belt and Road Initiative (BRI) is likely to play in furthering China's domination and control on Asia – a modern version of *'Pax Sinica'* in Asia, thereby enhancing Xi Jinping's legacy. It looks at a

---

[*] This article was first published in the *Journal of the United Service Institution of India*, Vol. CXLVII, No. 608, April-June 2017.

'Middle Powers Coalition' for the Asia-Pacific to provide stability and counter this cynical push by China for domination, and provide multi-polarity in Asia.

The China Dream

The term 'China or Chinese Dream' has ancient origins in Chinese literary and intellectual history and has had a revival of sorts in the West[3]. To name a recent few from the West, in 2008 architect Neville Mars, Adrian Hornsby and the Dynamic City Foundation published "The Chinese Dream – a society under construction"[4] and the 2010 book by author Helen H Wang *The Chinese Dream.*[5] Both the books looked more at the society than the geo-political and geo-economic spheres that the term Chinese Dream now connotes[6].

Just after becoming General Secretary of the Communist Party of China in late 2012, Xi announced what would become the hallmark of his administration. "The Chinese Dream", he said, is "the great rejuvenation of the Chinese nation." Xi's Chinese Dream is described as achieving the "Two 100s":-

(a) The material goal of China becoming a "moderately well-off society" by 2021, the 100th anniversary of the Chinese Communist Party.

(b) The modernisation goal of China becoming a fully developed nation by about 2049, the 100th anniversary of the founding of the People's Republic.[7]

The Chinese scholars have spoken of overcoming 100 years of humiliation and the great renewal of the nation, alluding to the 18th Century 'Opium Wars' with the West that greatly debilitated the nation and the subsequent subjugation during the Japanese War in the 20th Century. It is universally agreed that a 'Rising China' flexing its muscles and appearing to be stridently revanchist, revisionist or revolutionist to its neighbours and the world at large, coupled with a growing perception of a 'retreating West' is leading to, what the many thinkers term as, 'a Strategic Age of Uncertainties'.

Xi Jinping is the first Chinese leader who has not hesitated in using terms that the Chinese hardliners, have been proposing - 'strong nation dream' (*qiangzhongquomeng*),[8] and the road to renewal or rejuvenation (*fuxingzhilu*), a factor that also underlines the rise of an aggressive Chinese posture under his leadership.

Michael Pillsbury, in his book 'The Hundred Years Marathon', opines that the marathon strategy that China's leaders are pursuing today, and have been pursuing for decades, is largely a product of lessons derived from the Warring States period by these Hawks. These have never been translated in English and are very popular and extensively studied in China.[9] It is no small wonder that there is such a rise of jingoistic nationalism within the Chinese society.

Xi Jinping perceives the current flux in the global order as an opportunity for China to take the lead. This is a strategic foreign policy goal, almost officially announced by Xi in his statement that the PRC should establish "great power diplomacy with Chinese characteristics,"[10] while Deng's 24 character principle is being replaced by phrases such as "active and pressing on"[11] or "forging ahead."[12] It also serves as an effective tool for diverting attention from its internal instabilities.

The push currently is for gaining geopolitical space in Asia with 'Neighbourhood Diplomacy', which appears to be centred on commercial penetration through infrastructure projects and selling a short term' 'economic dream' to the underprivileged nations on its periphery. Commercial penetration is the precursor to the 'strategic equity' squeezed out from these nations due to the debt trap caused by these unviable projects, thereby, gaining political, diplomatic and geopolitical space needed to achieve the China Dream of becoming a 'Great Power' by 2049 – a Unipolar Asia centred around China. This appears to be the Phase One of the China Dream – to be the sole Super Power of the World.

Tianxia

To achieve this Dream, China seems to be assiduously following the concept of 'Tianxia', as articulated by the philosopher Zhao Tingyang in 2005[13]. The term 'Tianxia' opens itself to different interpretations since Mandarin has no alphabets but characters and thus the meaning changes based on pronunciation and intonation. Thus, the word could be interpreted as – 'Under-Heaven' or 'Empire' or 'China', thereby implying a 'Unified Global System with China's superior characteristics on top'.[14]

Although Zhao does not clearly or logically lay out its elements, his views in his book, '*Investigations of the Bad World: Political Philosophy as the First Philosophy*', published in 2009 by China Renmin University Press, throws disconcerting light on the Chinese view of securing such a system, which transcends the nation-state. It builds on the ancient system of the vassal/tributary states 'kowtowing' to the 'Celestial Emperor' of China ' and paying tribute to be able to trade with it.

This new system has the two ideas - 'the Strategy of Common Imitation' and 'Confucian Improvement'. The strategy of common imitation is regarded in Game Theory as the key to the formation of a stable institution, since it is argued that a common imitation of the best strategy given by the leader and abided by the players will lead to a stable equilibrium.[15] It implies that these small under-developed nations in the neighbourhood would perforce abide by the 'Strategy of Common Imitation', i.e. follow China's lead and abide by its decisions.

To foster understanding of Confucius, China has embarked on creating Confucius Institutes (CI) all over the world, since 2004, overseen by Hanban (officially the Office of Chinese Language Council International). As of 2014 it had 480 such institutes in dozens of countries in all continents,[16] with the stated aim of establishing 1000 Confucius Institutes by 2020[17].

While the West has been able to voice its concerns on this issue, the smaller nations on China's periphery do not have the same capacity. Funded and staffed entirely by China, these nations welcome the money and do not interfere in the alleged activities of these teachers. Many foreign scholars have characterised the CI programme as an exercise in soft power, expanding China's economic, cultural, and diplomatic reach through the promotion of Chinese language and culture, while others have suggested a possible role in intelligence collection. The soft power goals also include assuaging concerns of a "China threat" in the context of the country's increasingly powerful economy and military.[18]

China appears to be moving towards 'an integration of the Comprehensive National Power (CNP)' of the 'Neighbourhood' with itself, in a step by step approach – an umbilical connect that would not be easily disrupted, a reshaping of the regional economic and security architecture with 'Chinese Characteristics'. The Belt and Road Initiative (BRI) appears to be a part of this strategy. It would be a phased peripheral expansion, akin to '*salami slicing*' – a carefully crafted economic push that does not appear provocative, but the accumulated gain would radically alter the geo-economic and geo-commerce balance in its favour.

The Belt and Road Initiative

Much has been written and discussed on the poor economics and viability of this initiative. The BRI itself is not a new construct, but connecting the old, ongoing and some future projects under one narrative. According to a *People's Daily* commentary by Zhou Hanmin, the BRI is not only an effort to "tell the China story well and spread China's message properly" but also an attempt to build up a "community of destiny" with nations, particularly those in the developing world. The commentator also noted that the BRI was intimately connected with President Xi's Chinese Dream, one of whose key goals is that the country would emerge as a superpower by 2049, the centenary of the establishment of the People's Republic of China.[19] This further underlines the fears of a modern version of *'Pax Sinica'*, since economic viability seems to be the least concern for Xi Jinping as compared to China's visualised geo-strategic gains in the 'Neighbourhood'.

However, the smaller neighbours are now realising the pitfalls of doing such business with China. Sri Lanka, Myanmar, Bangladesh and Cambodia in Asia and Venezuela in South America are facing a severe debt crisis with China. China provides loans with an interest rate of 6.3 per cent, while the interest rates on soft loans from the World Bank and the Asian Development Bank are only 0.25–3 per cent,[20]. further the projects have no economic viability, thereby leading to a resource crunch in these small countries and the current debt crisis.

China has also made major economic inroads into Central Asia. It currently holds major stakes in Kazakhstan's energy industry and Turkmenistan's gas fields. While Russia continues to pump oil and gas out of these countries, China has diversified its interests by building power plants, refineries and transmission lines, in addition to gas and other infrastructure projects all over Central Asia to the detriment of Russian companies.[21] The Central Asian markets are also flooded with cheap Chinese products, thereby, increasing their dependency on China. It is the Eurasian Economic Union that has held China back till now from sweeping away Russia from Central Asia, but the question is for how long?

While these peripheral smaller nations have resisted mortgaging their sovereignty to the Chinese geo-economic push to establish the modern version of the *'Tianxia* System' – a new *'Pax Sinica'*, the economic cost of such continued resistance would be prohibitive. The size of Chinese loans given/planned is more than 20-25 per cent of the GDP of these countries, which cannot be sustained by them, thus leading to a debt crisis. The 'Middle Powers' in Asia need to step forward and be a 'net security provider to maintain and sustain the CNP' of these and other countries in the Asia-Pacific.

Pax Sinica and Middle Power Coalition

The term *'Pax Sinica'* has been used for the periods of Chinese hegemonic domination of East Asia during the periods that China was the dominant civilisation in the region, due to its political, economic, military and cultural power. Throughout most of its history, the 'Middle Kingdom', as China was known, was the regional hegemon in East Asia. It expressed its dominance in the region through a 'tribute' system that required regional states to acknowledge Chinese supremacy and accept their inferior status as 'vassals', which lasted till the Opium Wars of 1840s that resulted in 100 years of subjugation initially by the West and then by Japan.

The tribute system was the ultimate institution of regional order. It defined China's grand strategy, behaviour and its interaction with its neighbours. Asia today is witnessing a similar Chinese push for a *'Pax Sinica'*, especially in East Asia, South East Asia, South Asia and Central Asia. Beijing seeks to achieve the following to be able to establish its *Pax Sinica*:-

(a) Replace the United States as the primary power in Asia;

(b) Weaken the US alliance system in Asia, and create new security architecture;

(c) Undermine the confidence of Asian nations in US credibility, reliability, and staying power;

(d) Use China's economic power to tie smaller Asian nations closer to its geopolitical policy preferences; and

(e) Increase PRC military capability to strengthen deterrence against US military intervention in the region.[22]

However, this process may hit a road block, as the smaller nations of the region are becoming aware of China's ulterior motives and designs. This provides space for the 'Middle Powers' of the region – India, Japan, South Korea and Singapore to form a coalition of the like-minded. Such a coalition should provide an alternate geo-economic and geo-commerce model for the Asia-Pacific Region and facilitate economic activities, security, trade, intelligence exchanges, military capacity building, technology sharing, agenda setting for regional forums and coordinated diplomatic initiatives. It would be a truly 'win-win' situation for all countries of the Asia-Pacific region.

It should be a "South-South East-East Asia Forum" or a true Asia-Pacific Association. The reach to the Central Asian region and beyond could be worked out in conjunction with the Eurasian Economic Union, thereafter.

It would lead to multi-polarity within Asia, act as a succour to the smaller nations and ensure that rule of international law, good governance, equality, transparency and economic prosperity for all is ensured within the region. Such an association would be able to ensure stability, peace and prosperity within the region. The foundation of the association or coalition should not be based just on countering any country's rise but for stability and prosperity, only then would it be self sustaining and long lasting.

Conclusion

The rise of China can be viewed from different angles of perspectives, and is divided into three schools of thought. The 'Confident School' that asserts that China's rise is inevitable and its ascendancy will challenge the US preponderance both regionally and globally. The 'Pessimist School' that argues China is facing both domestic challenges and external constraints which perhaps make it unlikely to compete with or replace the US in this. The 'Not-Yet/Uncertain School', positing that although China has immense potential to be a great power or 'a challenger' to the US, its willingness to take the leadership role as a great power is uncertain or seemingly falls short of expectations.[23]

Xi Jinping sees the current geo-political flux as an opportunity for China to assert itself within Asia and occupy the vacuum due to US's strategic retrenchment. Towards that end, he has clubbed the existing infrastructure projects and added more under the much touted BRI – that started as the Silk Road Economic Belt in Kazakhstan and the Maritime Silk Road in Indonesia, which were then clubbed as the One Belt One Road to finally being christened as the BRI.

It aims to gain geopolitical space in Asia centred on a phased commercial penetration through infrastructure projects and selling a 'short term' economic 'dream' to the underprivileged nations on its periphery. Commercial penetration would be the precursor to the 'strategic equity', squeezed out from these nations due to the debt trap caused by these unviable projects, thereby gaining political, diplomatic and geopolitical space needed to achieve the China Dream of becoming a 'Great Power' by 2049 – a Unipolar Asia centred around China.

The penetration was supposed to be achieved by the BRI, a conglomeration of past, present and future infrastructure projects cobbled together – not considering economic viability but more to dump its excess capacity and labour, backed by financial muscle. However, the past seems to have come to haunt the Chinese. Having given loans to these small nations at market rates for unviable projects, the countries are facing debt crises and are not amenable to China's arm twisting as yet.

The Middle Powers of Asia must utilise this opportunity to form a 'Middle Power Coalition', an Asia-Pacific Association, to assist these small nations and ensure peace and stability within this region. The time is now for these Middle Powers of Asia to seize the initiative.

Endnotes

1   Colin Dueck, The Strategy of Retrenchment and Its Consequences, FPRI, 13 Apr 2015, http://www.fpri.org/article/2015/04/the-strategy-of-retrenchment-and-its-consequences/

2   PaxSinica, Wikipedia, https://en.wikipedia.org/wiki/Pax_Sinica

3   Ryan Mitchell, "Clearing Up Some Misconceptions About Xi Jinping's 'China Dream" (http://www.huffingtonpost.com/ryan-mitchell/clearing-up-some-misconce_b_8012152.html), The Huffington Post, August 20, 2015

4   Neville Mars, Adrian Hornsby (2008). *The Chinese Dream – a society under construction* (http://www.nai010.com/component/zoo/item/the-chinese-dream)

5   Helen H Wang (2010, 2012). *The Chinese Dream: The Rise of the World's Largest Middle Class* https://www.amazon.com/Chinese-Dream-Worlds-Largest-Middle/dp/1452898049

6 The China Dream, Wikipedia, ibid

7 Xi pledges 'great renewal of Chinese nation', English.news.cn, 29 Nov 2012

8 (*zhongguomeng*): Chinese Dream, ChinaDaily.com.cn, http://www.chinadaily. com.cn/opinion/2013-03/22/content_16333031.htm

9 Michael Pillsbury, The Hundred Year Marathon: China's Strategy to replace America as the Global Super Power, St. Martin's Griffin; Reprint edition (15 March 2016), pg 34

10 "Xi Jinpingchuxizhongyangwaishigongzuohuiyibingfabia ozhongyao jianghua" [Xi Jinping attended the Central Foreign Affairs Work Conference and delivered an important speech], Ministry of Foreign Affairs of the People's Republic of China, 29 November 2014. Chinese experts explain the specific meaning of the "great power," which they also call "leadership-type great power:" to take responsibility with confidence that the world needs China. This model differs from the traditional type of hegemonic power.

11 "Xi Jinpingzaizhoubianwaijiaogongzuozuotanhuishang fabiaozhongya ojianghua" [Xi Jinping at the Work Forum on Chinese Diplomacy towards its Neighbourhood delivered an important speech], Ministry of Foreign Affairs of the Peoples Republic of China, 25 October 2013.

12 Lei Mo, "Zhongguoxinwaijiao: yishiliqiuheping" [China's new diplomacy: seeking peace through strength], Nanfeng Chuang,no. 5, 25 February 2015.

13 Zhao Tingyangu, The Tianxia System: An Introduction to the Philosophy of a World Institution (TianxiaTixi: Shijiezhiduzhexuedaolun), 1 Nanjing: Jiangsu JiaoyuChubanshe, 2005, translated in English and republished by China Renmin University Press in Oct 2011.

14 Michael Pillsbury, op cit. pp. 17 - 30

15 Zhang Feng, ibid.

16 Confucius Institutes Worldwide, UCLA Confucius Institute, http://www. confucius.ucla.edu/about-us/confucius-institutes-worldwide

17 Confucius Institute: promoting language, culture and friendliness, Xinhua, 2 October 2006.

18 Confucius Institute, Wikipedia, https://en.wikipedia.org/wiki/Confucius_ Institute

19 China's Global Power Projection Hit With "Strategic Overdraft", Willy Wo-Lap Lam, China Brief Volume: 17 Issue: 7, https://jamestown.org/program/chinas-global-power-projection-hit-strategic-overdraft/

20 Dead ends on the new Silk Route: Why business with China is risky business,

The Economic Times, 17 Jun 2017

21 Tom Miller, China's Asian Dream, Zed Books, London, 2017, pp.73-75

22 Robert Blackwill, 'China's Strategy for Asia: Maximize Power, Replace America', http://nationalinterest.org/feature/chinas-strategy-asia-maximize-power-replace-america-16359, *(Editor's note: This article is adapted from a presentation to congressional staff, delivered on May 20, 2016. The presentation was drawn from two Council on Foreign Relations Special Reports, Revising U.S. Grand Strategy Toward China (March 2015), by Robert D. Blackwill and Ashley J. Tellis; and Xi Jinping on the Global Stage: Chinese Foreign Policy Under a Powerful but Exposed Leader (February 2016), by Robert D. Blackwill and Kurt M. Campbell.)*

23 Wuttikorn Chuwattananurak, 'China's Comprehensive National Power and Its Implications for the Rise of China: Reassessment and Challenges', http://web.isanet.org/Web/Conferences/CEEISA-ISA-LBJ2016/Archive/01043de7-0872-4ec4-ba80-7727c2758e53.pdf

---

† Major General Rajiv Narayanan, AVSM, VSM retired as the Additional Director General Military Operations (B) in 2016 and is closely involved with geopolitics, future strategy, force structures and force modernisation. He is also an avid follower of China issues, Asia-Pacific and the Af-Pak-CAR region.

Chinese Military's Perspective on the Indian Military Strategy*

Brigadier Iqbal Singh Samyal

Introduction

Since the 1990s, India and China have invested in a host of confidence building measures, including agreements and protocols, to maintain peace along the disputed borders. The Chinese military, as an important pillar of the Chinese political structure, has considerable influence on Chinese perceptions on India. This has been borne out by the recent developments along the India-China border. In this context, understanding the Chinese military's perspective of the Indian military strategy is an important constituent of interpreting Chinese outlook towards India.

The Science of Military Strategy or *Zhanlue Xue* is an influential military publication periodically published by the PLA's Academy of Military Science (AMS) since 1987. This article is primarily based on the review of Indian military strategy carried out in the *Zhanlue Xue 2013* (hereafter referred to as ZX 2013), available, as of now, only in Chinese language.

The Overall Context

The Chinese military's perspectives of the Indian military strategy is not divorced from the overall strategic environment. Historical biases and contemporary issues, often termed as six "Ts"[1] by Chinese analysts, coalesce with the Chinese strategic assessment, in which Comprehensive National Power (CNP) plays a major role, to influence Chinese views on India.

---

* This articles was first published in the *Journal of the United Service Institution of India*, Vol. CXLVII, No. 609, July-September 2017.

Though dated, Pillsbury (2000)[2] contains a short review of Chinese views on India at the turn of the century. In 1990, while comparatively India figured low on the CNP index, Indian military strength was considered significant in comparison to other elements of national power. This is echoed in more contemporary analyses, with one Chinese analyst terming it as India's "unusual enthusiasm for strengthening and upgrading its military capability"[3] particularly in the naval and strategic fields. Apprehensions related to India being part of an Asian balance of power system to 'contain' China also play on the Chinese mind.

Even amongst the Chinese analysts, the defence related community is more likely to assume a hard line viewpoint[4] (probably applicable to all countries) and in some opinions, in comparison the military has a greater say in the policy towards India.[5] Lastly under the current leadership, Chinese assertiveness and self-perceptions have undergone a sharp change buoyed by the rapid economic rise and the pace of military modernisation. The Chinese perspective on Indian military strategy reflected in the ZX 2013 has to be viewed in this context.

The Science of Strategy (ZX 2013) and Indian Military Strategy

The ZX 2013 briefly analyses the military strategy of the 'contemporary world's big countries' namely USA, Russia, Japan and India.[6] It traces the evolution of Indian military strategy since independence and then gives out the prominent characteristics of the strategy.

The ZX 2013 reviews the development of Indian military strategy in three phases from Independence till the end of the Cold War. [7] It analyses that in the first phase (1947-1960), due to the 'economy first' policy, the military strategy was 'limited offensive' (*youxian jingong*) towards Pakistan, as it was viewed as a direct threat, and 'territorial expansion' (*lingtu kuozhang*) towards the India–China border. The second phase (1960–1970), after the 1962 conflict, led to defence being given priority. the inflow of aid and support from both the US and USSR and improved military capability led to 'military expansion thought'. This phase witnessed the formulation of the 'two front expansion' (*liang xian kuozhang*) policy and 'West offensive North defensive' (*xi gong bei fang*) guideline. The third phase (1970s and 1980s), after the 1971 Indo-Pak War led to the 'pattern of Indian hegemony in South Asia becoming established'. Changes in the international situation, withdrawal of some powers from the Indian Ocean Region and with the land strategic intent being realised, the strategic orientation increased towards the Indian Ocean leading to the formulation of the military strategy of 'defend land control sea' (*bao lu zhi hai*).

The period after the Cold War, in Chinese perception, witnessed change to 'regional deterrence' (*diqu weishe*) from 'regional offensive' (*diqu jingong*) strategy, implying that from aiming to capture territory or destroying enemy forces, a region covering area from the Himalayas to the Indian Ocean and Myanmar to Iran, was sought as a circle of deterrence from outside interference or influence.

According to the ZX 2013, the 21st Century has seen an increase in India's CNP with military strength surpassing the South Asian nations. The ZX 2013 analysis of this period, somewhat mirror images, the Chinese theoretical military strategic structure on the Indian military strategy.[8] It states that a large scale total war *(da guimo quanmian zhanzheng)* with either China or Pakistan is less probable and with growing terrorism, separatism and military operations other than war (MOOTW) threats, the possibility of 'mid to small scale limited boundary conventional war' becomes more probable. This perception has led to the strategy of 'regional deterrence' acquiring a new offensive intent of 'punitive deterrence' *(chengjie weishe).* In their view, the Indian strategic intent is to 'win high tech limited conventional war under conditions of nuclear deterrence' *(da yinghe weishe tiao jinxia de youxian zhanzheng).* Under this intent, the strategic objectives for India (zhanlue mubiao), in their perception are – primacy of politics, flexible military employment and influencing enemy's anti-India policies facilitating compromise on favourable terms. This strategy *(zhanlue zhidao)* requires adopting a form of preemption or active initiative *(jiji zhudong)* to gain initiative by striking first *(xian fa zhiren),* and not waiting for the enemy to enter borders, thereby seizing favourable position and preventing large scale offensive by the enemy. The operational guidance *(zuozhan zhidao),* in their view, is of joint operations by three services and the strategic deterrence guidance *(weishe zhidao)* is combined nuclear and conventional deterrence with conventional military strength as the offensive 'spear' and nuclear strength as the defensive 'shield'.

The ZX 2013 summarises four main characteristics of Indian military strategy[9]; strong regionalism *(diyuanxing)* or geopolitics, comprehensive inheritance *(jichengxing),* limited offensive intent and all round deterrence. The first characteristic reflects the Indian geostrategic outlook of being the center of the South Asian sub-continent, and using it as a strategic base for controlling the Indian Ocean. The second characteristic reflects not only the inheritance of British territory but also the British 'expansionist military thought'[10] with the "India centric theory" *(yindu zhongxin lun)* having Kashmir, Nepal, Sikkim, Bhutan and Assam as "Inner line of Indian defence" and Tibet as 'buffer state' in its sphere of influence. In present context, the ZX 2013 cites the Nehruvian policy of having a 'security inner circle' encompassing the sub continent and Indian Ocean. The third characteristic is based on the premise that Indian national strategic aims are – dominating South Asia, controlling Indian Ocean and striving to be a world class powerful nation *(zhipei nanya, kongzhi yinduyang, zheng dang shijie yiliu qiangguo;* a phrase commonly found in Chinese writings to describe Indian strategy). This makes the Indian military strategy offensive in intent even though it is claimed to be defensive. The past wars and other developments in the sub-continent, including 'provoking' the 1962 India-China conflict, are quoted to substantiate this intent. Further, in their perception, the Indian offensive intent is increasing with increase in national power and military strength. The fourth characteristic of overall deterrence refers to the use of deterrence in every sphere to compensate for the contradiction between hegemonic ambitions and limited national power. India, it states, has strengthened ties with big powers like the USA and Japan after the Cold War. India in their view adopts a 'dissuasive' *(quanzu)* deterrence towards China and 'punitive' *(chengfa)* deterrence towards other South Asian nations.

Table I summarises the Chinese military perspective on Indian military strategy in various time periods as stated in the ZX 2013. Though the latest doctrinal developments are quoted more often, contemporary Chinese writings when convenient often cite the strategy of previous periods. There are shared viewpoints and phrases in the ZX 2013 analysis and other Chinese military articles reflecting a common military thought process about the Indian military strategy.

Table I : Summary of Chinese Perspective

Time Period	National Strategy	Military Strategy	Strategic Guidance	Operational Guidance/ Pattern
1947-60		Limited Offensive (West) Territorial Expansion		
1960-70		Two Front Expansion	West Offensive North Defensive	
1970s & 80s After Cold War 21st Century	Dominate South Asian Subcontinent, Control Indian Ocean, and Strive to be a world class power	Defend Land Control Sea Regional Deterrence Regional Deterrence with Dissuasive and Punitive Intent Combined Nuclear and Conventional Deterrence	Active Initiative (Strike first to gain initiative) Offensive Defence	Joint operations, Manoeuvre Warfare and Information operations

Other Chinese Military Viewpoints

The ZX 2013 is a publication of the PLA's Academy of Military Science. At least two other articles by researchers from the PLA's National Defence University (NDU), an influential military institution, reflect similar viewpoints and phrases indicating a common thread in the military's perceptions about Indian military strategy. Similar to the ZX 2013, the first article mentions Indian hegemonic designs in South Asia and Indian Ocean while tracing the evolution of Indian military strategy using similar phrases, 'limited offensive', 'two front offensive', 'defend land control sea', 'regional deterrence' and 'punitive deterrence'[11]. The second article by a Professor in the Research Department of the PLA's National Defence University[12] reflects some additional concerns while sharing viewpoints with the ZX 2013. It commences with the same phrases, as in the ZX 2013, to describe Indian strategy "based in South Asia, controlling Indian Ocean and striving to be a world class powerful nation".[13] It reiterates the formulation of aiming to 'win high tech limited conventional war under conditions of nuclear deterrence', 'punitive deterrence', active initiative and gaining initiative by striking first. The offensive intent of Indian military strategy is even more pronounced in the second article quoting the 'Cold Start' *(leng qidong)* doctrine. It covers in fair amount of detail the strengthening of strategic deterrence in the nuclear and space domains, the modernisation of the armed forces, developments in the individual services and the ever increasing military diplomacy between India and other advanced armed forces. The key aspects highlighted in the article are that in recent years, India is expanding influence towards the Asia Pacific region and the formulation of a combined land sea strategy which includes; strong deterrence and deployment towards Pakistan, active involvement in Central Asia, 'infiltrating military strength' towards South West Asia, and striving to get an acknowledged place among big powers. It states that India using the 'Towards East Ocean Strategy' *(dongfang haiyang zhanlue),* wants to control the Indian Ocean as well as have expeditionary capability towards the Asia-Pacific region thereby expanding 'forward defence'. This reflects the rising Chinese concern about Indian military strength in the Indian Ocean as the growing arc of Indian and Chinese interests intersect in the Indo-Pacific region.[14]

China's rise has changed its self-perception and more significantly its interests, which are expanding outwards bringing new dimensions to the fore including the maritime, network and space domains.[15] Developments in the Indian military are closely monitored particularly in the strategic and maritime domains. Recurring themes in contemporary Chinese articles on Indian military are about increases in defence budget outlay, major defence acquisitions and the fact that India is the largest arms importer in the world, advances in strategically important defence technology fields like missiles and space, military diplomacy and training with other armed forces across the world. Chinese media highlights that India, with comparative ease has access to advanced weaponry and technology and diverse arms/weapons from the USA and Russia.[16] While acknowledging some strengths, the weaknesses highlighted are the defence industry, heavy reliance on imports from various countries and related logistics difficulties, and the inferior infrastructure along India's northern borders.[17]

Views on the Chinese Perspectives

The Chinese views on the Indian military strategy are coloured in historical and other biases, hence, do not objectively address Indian security concerns. It is not surprising that growing Chinese military power and its implications in the region are underplayed. The Chinese belief of Indian regional hegemony and expansionism, especially in the light of historical Chinese expansionism and unfolding events in the Asia-Pacific, should be taken as national narrative. ZX 2013 mirror images the Chinese strategic construct on the Indian military strategy, particularly in light of the developments in the 21st Century period. However this approach is not particularly unique to Chinese military writings.

In the 1950s, Chinese concerns were based on Tibet and the India-China border. Currently with growing maritime interests, China is becoming preoccupied with the Indo-Pacific and efforts to 'contain' China's rise. The Chinese concerns are accentuated by Chinese vulnerabilities in the region.[18] The Chinese military's apprehension of India aiming to 'control the Indian Ocean' plays into these fears. So much so that, while considering it a contemporary challenge, Chinese analysts trace India's ambitions in the Indian Ocean far back, ascribing them to Nehru's vision and KM Panikkar's writings.[19]

The overall analysis in the ZX 2013, looking at the likely future conflict scenarios, classifies border disputes and maritime conflicts at par, as middle to small scale and medium level intensity conflicts.[20] However, on the land borders, at the operational level, two important aspects of the Chinese views are highlighted. The ZX 2013 states that though Indian military posture towards China is overall defensive, but at the same time "is offensive for defence, actively strives for dominance in a part (area), combines continuous nibbling *(canshi;* at the border) during peace and by defence create conditions for offensive during war"[21]. The nibbling *(canshi)* or anti-nibbling *(fan canshi)* of borders is an old term which can be traced to Mao Zedong's time.[22] It finds currency even now as articulated by President Xi Jinping[23] and finds mention in the *PLA Military Terms* definition of the Border Defence Forces.[24] The second aspect is the marked 'offensive defence' intent attributed to the Indian military strategy in the contemporary period. This outlook has been also echoed in other commentaries[25] as some Chinese analysts posit that 'Indian military could occupy unoccupied areas' to gain favourable negotiating position post conflict. While on land, Chinese views acknowledge that strategically the military outlook towards China is defensive; at the operational and tactical level the view is that the offensive intent is increasing with growing military strength.

Conclusion

The salience of the ZX 2013 analysis is that it reflects a common military framework within the PLA looking at Indian military strategy. Despite its shortcomings, it provides a vital window into the PLA's outlook towards the Indian military. Aside from the strategic and operational implications, the framework provides a basis for identifying aspects which need to be addressed by military diplomacy in order to improve the efficacy of the confidence building measures between the two countries. It also underscores the need for faster military modernisation, both at sea and on land, to balance growing Chinese influence in the region.

Endnotes

1 "Territorial disputes, Tibet, threat perceptions, trilateral relationships (implying India China Pakistan, India China USA and India China Russia), trade, India's accession to NPT" in Jing Dongyuan, *India's Rise after Pokhran II: Chinese Analyses and Assessments,* Asian Survey, Vol.41, No.6 (Nov-Dec 2001), pp.978-1001.

2 Michael Pillsbury, *China Debates the Future Security Environment,* National Defence University Press, Washington D.C., 2000.

3 Maj Gen Pan Zhenqiang (Retd), *The Rise of India and China-India Relations,* in Dipankar Banerjee & Jabin T. Jacob, eds., *Military Confidence-Building and India-China Relations: Fighting Distrust,* Pentagon Press, New Delhi, 2013, p.31.

4 Jing Dongyuan, *op cit.*

5 Linda Jakobson and Dean Knox. *New Foreign Policy Actors in China.* SIPRI Policy Paper No 26. p.13. Accessed at http://books.sipri.org/product_info?c_product_id=410 on 07 Oct 2016.

6 Shou Xiaosong, ed., *Zhanlue Xue (The Science of Military Strategy),* 3rd ed., Academy of Military Science of the People's Liberation Army, Military Science Publishing House, Beijing, 2013, p. 50.

7   *Ibid.* pp.64-66.

8   As per the *Zhanlue Xue* 2013, the Chinese strategic system, though not fully implemented, consists of three levels and five categories: national strategy-military strategy- service strategy, theatre strategy, significant domain strategy (nuclear, space & network). The theoretical strategic structure varies from text to text but commonly involves some or all of these terms: strategic purpose/aim(*mudi*), strategic tasks (*renwu*), strategic guidelines (*fangzhen*), strategic direction (*fangxiang*), strategic guidance (*zhidao*), strategic means (*shouduan*), strategic layout/deployment(*buju/bushu*).*Ibid.* pp.5-8 & *Zhongguo Renmin Jiefangjun Junyu (PLA Military Terms)*, Military Science Publishing House, Beijing, 2011, pp.52-62.

9   *Ibid.* pp.66-68.

10   A point also made before in Michael Pillsbury, *op cit.*, p.147.

11   Abstract of Xiang Ruisheng, *Yinduxiandaijunshizhanluedeyanbian* (Development of Contemporary Indian Military Strategy), Journal of NDU, No.5, 2006 accessed at http://wenku.baidu.com/view/1aec3fa865ce0508763213b1.html on 07 Oct 2016.

12   Xinhua Wang, *"guofang daxue jiaoshou: yindu quanfangwei tiaozheng junshi zhanlue* (NDU Professor: India All-Around Adjusts Military Strategy)", accessed at http://news.xinhuanet.com/mil/2008-11/13/content_10351945. htm on 07 Oct 2016.

13   The phrase commonly used is *zhipei nanya, kongzhi yindu yang, zheng dang shijie yiliu qiangguo.* Often the term *zhipei nanya* (dominate South Asia) is replaced by lizu nanya (based on South Asia).

14   Toshi Yoshihara, *Chinese Views of India in the Indian Ocean: A Geopolitical Perspective,* Strategic Analysis, 36:3, 2012, pp.489-500.

15   Information Office of the State Council, The People's Republic of China. *China's Military Strategy (National Defence White Paper) 2015.* Accessed at http://eng.mod.gov.cn/Database/WhitePapers/ on 08 Aug 2015.

16   Zhongguo Junwang, *"yindujun gou: zuo-you feng yuan zhong zai pingheng",* 21 November 2015, Accessed at http://www.81.cn/bqtd/2015-11/21/content_6779354.htm on 07 Oct 2016.

17   Xinhua Wang, *"zhuanjia touxi:yindu junshi shili daodi you duo qiang,* (Expert Analysis: Indian Military Power Finally has many Strengths)"accessed at http://news.xinhuanet.com/mil/2010-03/31/content_13272946.htm on 07 Oct 2016.

18   Michael Pillsbury, *The Sixteen Fears: China's Strategic Psychology,* Survival: Global Politics and Strategy, 54:5, pp. 149-182.

19 Toshi Yoshihara, *op, cit.*

20 Shou Xiaosong, ed., *op. cit.,* p.99.

21 *Ibid.* p.67.

22 Wang Qitian, Tian Dongliang & Gong Xiaogang, *Mao Zhuxi Bianfang Sixiang Yanjiu* (Research on Chairman Mao's Border Defence Thought), Mao Zedong Thought Study, Vol 30 No 1, November 2013,pp.71-74.

23 Zhongguo Junwang, *"Xi Jinping: jiaqiang fan canshi, fan fenlie, fan kongbu douzheng* (Xi Jinping : Strengthen Anti-Nibbling, anti-Separatism, Anti-Terrorism Struggle)",02 January 2014,   Accessed at http://www.81.cn/ jwgd/2014-01/02/content_5717070.htm   on 07 Oct 2016.

24 *PLA Military Terms 2011,* op.cit., p.334.

25 Jing Dongyuan, *op cit.* p.990.

---

† **Brigadier Iqbal Singh Samyal** was commissioned into the KUMAON Regiment in December 1990. He has served as India's Defence Attaché in the Embassy of India, Beijing from October 2011 to November 2014. Presently, he is commanding an Infantry Brigade.

China's Energy Diplomacy and Changing Contours of Security Structure in the Indian Ocean: New Scramble for Sea Power[*]

Ms Dhanwati Yadav

Introduction

Architecting international economy through global trade, competitiveness to expand sphere of influence and military posturing have consequently heightened the strategic value of the Indian Ocean. As a result, the security structure in the Indian Ocean is reaching at the brink of sharp transformation with the proliferating demand for Sea Power. By turning words of 19th Century American naval strategist Alfred Mahan into reality, the Indian Ocean has come on the forefront on the geopolitical map of the world as a major 'game changer' in allotting power to different contestants.[1] The Indian Ocean Region (IOR), world's third largest water body has garnered mounted importance from the geopolitical and economic point of view for the last two decades.[2] The tectonic shift in the race for wielding power from the Atlantic Ocean to the Asia-Pacific, more certainly to the Indian Ocean involving emerging actors besides the traditional ones has vivified this scenario. The Indian Ocean has emerged as a centre theatre for the challenges of the 21st Century.[3] The existing interest of the traditional powers in the region exhibits the continual geo-strategic vitality of the region for the world. It provides critical sea trade routes that connect the Middle East, Africa, and South Asia with the broader Asian continent to the east and Europe to the west. Some most important strategic chokepoints of the world that drives more than 50 per cent of the world's maritime oil trade figure in this region.[4] Some 36

---

[*] This article was first published in the *Journal of the United Service Institution of India*, Vol. CXLVII, No. 609, July-September 2017.

million barrels per day – equivalent to about 40 per cent of the world's oil supply and 64 per cent of oil trade travel through the entryways into and out of the Indian Ocean, including the Straits of Malacca, Hormuz and the Bab-el-Mandeb.[5] Today, almost 90,000 vessels in the world's commercial fleet transport 9.84 billion tonnes per year. This represents an almost four-fold increase in the volume of commercial shipping since 1970.[6]

On the security realm, the non-traditional security challenges like terrorism, piracy, smuggling activities, possession of weapons of mass destruction, environmental crisis etc. are some matters of stern concern which draw collective attention of the major powers. There are seven key chokepoints in the IOR: the Lombok Strait, the Sunda Strait, the Malacca Straits, the Strait of Hormuz, the Suez Canal, Mozambique Channel, and the Bab-el-Mandeb. If these strategically vital key points fall under wrong hands, the future of the IOR will be encountering uncertainty having a crippling effect on dependent economies.[7]

The present Sino-Indian neo-rivalry on the Ocean waters has triggered various questions marking new contours of power equations. The strategic dynamic is changing with the emergence of China and India rising as naval powers at a moment of relative American decline.[8] Undoubtedly, a powerful China in any manner can potentially jeopardise India's strategic interests and national security. To abate China's growing influence, India strictly needs to revive its maritime policy while introducing slight modifications in its foreign policy as well with the aim of consolidating its alignment with the littoral states.

India's Historical Maritime Imperatives and Policy

Our present is unconditionally attached with the remnants of our history. Historical archives unveil that the inception of the golden phase of Indian seafaring is marked with the very dawn of the Indus Valley civilization. India was much affluent and secure when she was chiefly connected to the world through 'Sea'. India has evolved as a vibrant and rich maritime culture over the centuries. Indian maritime performance has traditionally been extended from Gujarat's coastline (*Lothal*) in the west to the *Kalinga* in the east. Ancient Indian civilisation had recorded activities like building ships, navigating the sea and monopolising international trade both by sea and land. The unfortunate fact is that our maritime history is not documented in a requisite manner. The available literature pertaining to maritime records is largely written by western historians. Admiral Arun Prakash, former Chief of the Indian Navy summarises this phenomenon as "one of the reasons for our maritime blindness is that as a nation we have been indifferent to the reading as well as writing of history; both our own and that of others. Whatever little history we do study, has been recorded by western historians who have made full use of the literary license to give it the slant that they wished to".[9]

Pandit Jawaharlal Nehru, India's first Prime Minister had concluded – owing to the history, *We cannot afford to be weak at sea. History has shown that whoever controls the Indian Ocean has, in the first instance, India's sea-borne trade at her mercy and in the second, India's very independence itself*".[10] India has since claimed the Indian Ocean as India's ocean and considers its legitimate role in the security of the Ocean region. Following its *Monroe Doctrine,* it strictly discourages the ingression of the external powers in the Indian Ocean.11 India has played a much active role in the Indian Ocean since the mid-1980s. When it is a matter of security in the Indian Ocean, India considers no 'ifs and buts'.

During 1983 political crisis in Mauritius, India although didn't intervene militarily to prevent a feared coup but on the contour of security facilitated a political solution to the crisis favouring large numbers of Indo-Mauritians that was termed as *'Operation Lal Dora'.* This had validated India's special role in the region.[12] India's security role in Seychelles in 1986 crystallised over its response during a series of coup attempts made against President Rene led by the Seychelles Minister of Defence, Ogilvy Berlouis. Proving its might and intent to establish peace, India had executed *'Operation Flowers are Blooming'* in Seychelles, when on a request by then-President Rene, Indian Prime minister Rajiv Gandhi instructed the then Indian Chief of Naval Staff, Admiral Tahiliani, to dispatch the frigate INS *Vindhyagiri* to avert a coup.

Under the Prime Ministership of Rajiv Gandhi in 1988, the Indian forces were despatched to the Maldives following *'Operation Cactus'* to foil a coup targeting the then President of Maldives, Maumoon Abdul Gayoom sponsored by Sri Lankan Tamil militants on behalf of the Maldivian businessman Abdulla Luthufi. That was possibly the first time when India learnt what 'out-of-area contingencies' were all about and secured itself as a predominant regional power.

During *'Operation Rahat'* in 2015, India showed exemplary bravery and magnanimity. The Indian Government spared no efforts in evacuating

Indians from Yemen as fighting raged between the Houthi rebels and the Yemeni government supported by aerial bombardment from the Saudi-led coalition. India's effort was so effective that over 26 countries including the US and UK had requested for Indian assistance in evacuating their citizens from Yemen. Operations undertaken by India to establish peace in the IOR are tabulated below:-

Classical Attempts by India to Establish Peace in the Indian Ocean Region (IOR)

Peace Maker Country	Country in Crisis	Year of Operations	Operation
India	Mauritius	1983	Operation Lal Dora
India	Seychelles	1986	Operation Flowers are Blooming
India	Sri Lanka	1987	Operation Pawan
India	Maldives	1988	Operation Cactus
India	Yemen	2015	Operation Rahat

What Fuels Sino-Indian Tension

The ascent of two continental powers, India and China following their swelled economies and military modernisation has triggered a new wave of power projection in the modern history of the Indian Ocean.[13] Discord and tension between India and China has been registered traditionally beyond the borders and the existing confrontation doesn't manifest any new episode of anonymity in the history of Sino-Indian relations. Importantly, their augmented competition is redefining the old power equations in the Indian Ocean while expressing their huge strategic interests. According to James Holmes and Toshi Yoshihara, India and China's quests for energy security, as well as their great-power aspirations have somehow obligated the two countries "to redirect their gazes from land to the seas".

As India claims the Indian Ocean as India's Ocean, an overriding China in the IOR is predictably becoming a futuristic threat for India. In 2015, Prime Minister Narendra Modi had pronounced that Indian Ocean is at the top policy priorities of India. Chinese Peoples' Liberation Army Navy (PLAN) signals the landing of a serious naval power in the world by launching the Shandong or CV-001A, the first 70,000-tonne indigenously produced aircraft carrier likely to be operational by 2020. Notably, President Xi Jinping has launched defence reforms which are taking away resources from land to air and naval power. Chinese naval presence in the Indian Ocean and the larger Pacific is on the increase in an unprecedented way and a blue water navy is seemingly a prerequisite for Chinese ambitions.[14] The PLAN is emerging as a serious challenger and, therefore, forcing India to re-build its naval muscle. It is not a matter of surprise that India is investing in ramping up its naval power. Indian Navy has drawn explicit aspirations for the Indian Ocean with the support of the Government. Unlike China, India has been operating an aircraft carrier since 1961, but delays and shoddy planning continue to mar Indian aspirations to be a prominent power in the region. India's first indigenous aircraft carrier, the 40,000-tonne INS *Vikrant,* was launched in 2013, but its commissioning has been delayed to 2020.[15]

INDIA VS THE REST

GLOBAL POWER PROJECTION

➤ US has **10 Nimitz-class nuclear-powered 'super carriers'.** Each over **108,000-tonne** & capable of carrying **80-90 fighters**

➤ China building **2 more** carriers after inducting the first **65,000-tonne** Liaoning in **Sept 2012,** & launching the second on Wednesday

➤ Italy has **two** carriers, while **UK, France, Russia, Spain, Brazil** & **Thailand** have **1 each**

THE INDIAN STORY

INS VIKRANT
Commissioning delayed to beyond 2020
Displacement | 40,000 tonne
Cost | Over ₹ 20,000 crore allocated for carrier being built at Cochin Shipyard
Crew | 160 officers and 1,400 sailors
Capacity | 20 fighters (MiG-29Ks & others) & 10 helicopters
Endurance | 7,500 nautical miles at 18 knots speed

INS VIKRAMADITYA
Commissioned in Nov 2013
Displacement | 44,400 tonne
Cost | Refitted Russian Admiral Gorshkov cost $2.33bn (45 MiG-29Ks cost another $2 billion)
Crew | 110 officers, 1500 sailors
Capacity | 34 aircraft (24 MiG-29Ks, plus helicopters)
Endurance | 7,000 nautical miles at 18 knots speed

INS VISHAL
In initial planning stage. Will take over 10 years to build carrier once project kicks off
Displacement | 65,000 tonne
Cost | Only ₹ 2-3 crore allocated as seed money
➤ Will be **nuclear-powered**
➤ Will have **CATOBAR** (catapult assisted take-off but arrested recovery) configuration for launching fighters as well as heavier aircraft from deck

Source: The Economic Times, April 2017

India has so far ripened its geographical dividends by constructing traditional proximity with other nations in the IOR. India enjoys cordial and progressive relations with the littoral states of the Indian Ocean; primarily with Mauritius, that is also known as 'Little India' because of the substantive presence of Indian diaspora (nearly 68 percent) and considerably a closest ally of India in the Indian Ocean.[16] Above all, India is geographically located at the Ocean's centre and privileged by having island territories. Despite this geo-strategic advantage, India is feeling the heat of China's naval expansionism.

Containment of India has been "China's Great Game".[17] It is a considered view that strategically, China retains interest in the IOR for geo-economic (energy security) and geopolitical (restraining India) objectives. After executing its 'String of Pearls' strategy through ports development projects in Gwadar, Hambantota, Myanmar and Bangladesh, it is further planning to encircle India by wooing other littoral states in the region.[18] In case of Sri Lanka, Chinese Foreign Direct Investment (FDI) is roughly five times that of India's investment. Other island nations like Mauritius and Seychelles are setting new instances of receiving affluent Line of Credits (LoCs) from China. Seychelles and Mauritius are regarded as ideal locations for China as a lot of its oil shipments from the Gulf region and its containers containing manufactured goods destined for Europe and America passes through this region.

India's maritime strategy fundamentally stresses over the build-up of its naval-infrastructure which includes a six fold strategy of increasing its naval spending, strengthening its infrastructure, increasing its naval capabilities, active maritime diplomacy, naval exercises in the Indian Ocean and keeping open the choke points. To materialise its maritime objectives, India had introduced the "Maritime Agenda 2010-2020" (MA-20) that has limited impact because of its singular emphasis on ports and harbours leaving behind entire arrangement of infrastructure in the 'maritime domain'.[19] According to *Stockholm International Peace Research Institute (SIPRI)* report, whereas China's military expenditure figure for 2002–11 increased by 170 per cent, India's increased by 59 per cent merely. India does not appear to be capable of advocating a 'containment-cum-counter-encirclement' policy against China in the Asia-Pacific or in the Indian Ocean. Indian Navy has to be made capable of ensuring India's strategic interests in the IOR and for this a sound national security strategy has to be enumerated.

China's maritime strategy, 'Maritime Silk Road (MSR)' founded by President Xi Jinping demonstrates China's Indian Ocean strategy of building an empire of Chinese built ports, initially as economic projects leading gradually to achieving strategic and military ends. Beyond that China is striving to gain mining rights in the central IOR which will eventually became an excuse for its naval presence in the area.

China is extremely vulnerable owing to dependence upon IOR sea lanes of communication (SLOCs) that are straddled by India and pass through narrow choke points at the northwest and northeast corners.[20] Since 2014, Chinese intelligence-gathering ships and submersibles have begun making regular forays into the Indian Ocean. Notably, China has also held its first military exercise encompassing the eastern Indian Ocean - until now such exercises have been only in the Pacific.[21] According to a Pentagon report China initiated the building up of Djibouti base in early 2016, near the US special-operations outpost, Camp Lemonnier. In the similar vein, Marine General Thomas Waldhauser, Chief of US Africa Command, said "you would have to characterise it as a military base. It's a first for them and they've never had an overseas base".[22] C Raja Mohan, the Director of Carnegie India states, "Bases is going to be the name of the game in the Indian Ocean, and that game is going to be pretty attractive." Experts believe that whether or not China is willing to show its intent to secure its permanent presence in the IOR so far, a semi-permanent presence of China in the region is not a matter of denial, counting on its extraordinary power projection and renewed ties with the littorals in the region.[23] In turn, India will have to brace up for a new era of rivalry in the Indian Ocean.

GREAT POWER COMPETITION IN THE INDIAN OCEAN

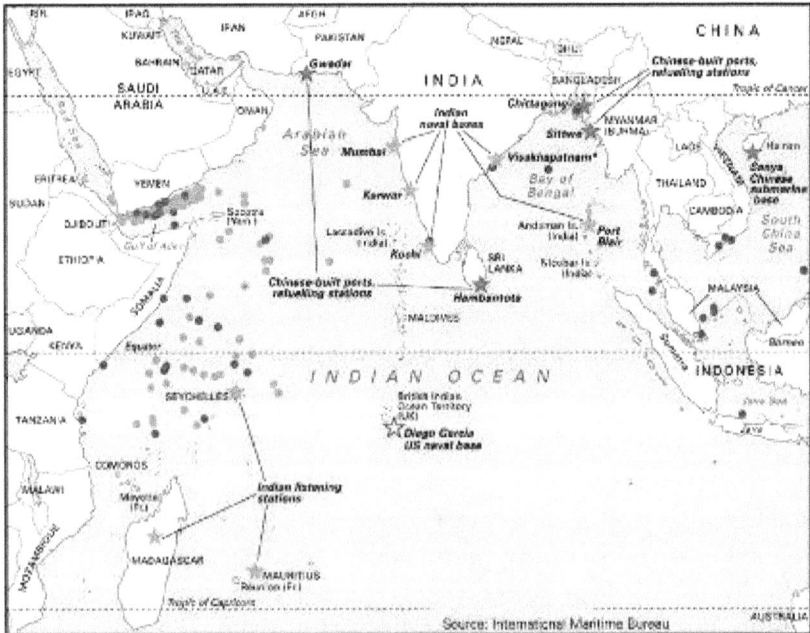

Source: International Maritime Bureau

Source: International Maritime Bureau

Strategic Matrix Positioning US as a Chief Defender

China is seen as a collective threat to India and the US especially when it is found denouncing the United Nations Convention on the Law of the Sea (UNCLOS) in the South China Sea. Traditional dominance of the US, regular claim of India over the Indian Ocean and atop overarching influence of China in the Indian Ocean in the 21st Century has formed a strategic triangle in the region. In a meeting of Indo-US Defence Joint Working Group held in 2007 at New Delhi, it was reported that both sides discussed the rapidly increasing Chinese naval presence in the Indian Ocean. During former US President Barack Obama's visit to India in 2015, a joint statement was issued, where particular attention was drawn to peaceful resolution of maritime territorial disputes and "freedom of navigation", with specific reference to the South China Sea.[24] The US appears incoherent in this context as the policy is missing and so far it has been unwilling in determining the extent of importance it needs to give to the IOR.[25]

On 13 Dec 2011, Chinese Defence Minister had officially announced that Seychelles had welcomed the Chinese Navy to establish facilities in order to resupply and recuperate international ships during escort missions. This had undoubtedly attracted worldwide media attention. As Diego Garcia is merely 600 km away from Seychelles in terms of geography, the US also expressed its deep concerns over this development besides India. However, it has been observed that the US is becoming less interested in policing the Indian Ocean.

The US warships are being transferred to the Pacific region. The most startling evidence that the US is out of the on-going game was the emergence of the Somali pirates between 2005 and 2011. Notably, a superpower like the US could be expected to handle it with a flick of the wrist. Instead, it was Indian and other navies that had to beat the pirates back.[26]

This sort of reluctant attitude can contribute to fostering power of China while boosting its strategic intents. A collective and active approach involving the US and India is desirable and urgently needed rather than undertaking indigenous actions to defeat the growing footprints of China. Constant and close surveillance over the footprints of China in the region is necessary to check its strategic psyche. Interestingly, the US had recently sent a naval warship near an artificial island in the South China Sea as part of the first "freedom of navigation" operation under President Trump, a move China has denounced in the name of challenging its sovereignty in the region.

The US appears to be showing its inclination for India to emerge as a 'Net Security Provider' in the region. Such a move turning into reality can possibly give India an unparalleled leverage and somehow may prove fruitful for the interest of the US as well by shrinking the existing role of China in the IOR. In the backdrop of gradual wane of the power of the US Navy, India seems well positioned to be the principal net security provider in the region.[27] But, to attain this objective India solemnly needs to walk further. India, who regards the Indian Ocean as its 'backyard' or major 'sphere of influence' is imbibed by large geo-strategic interests. However, India at the moment is not capable of staging its requisite potential against China's 'containment-cum-counter-encirclement' policy directed towards India in the Asia-Pacific or in the Indian Ocean.[28] India needs to strategically reconstruct its internal and external might for ensuring her strategic interests.

Conclusion

The US Quadrennial Defense Review wrote about India's emerging role as a 'net provider of security in the Indian Ocean'. India's desired role of being the net provider of security in the IOR can only be sustained by growth in India's maritime capability. A strong shipbuilding (both warship and commercial ships) and shipping infrastructure is imperative for enhancing the maritime capacity of any country. If India strategically aims to exercise predominant influence in the IOR it needs to adopt an aggressive policy of engagement with the island nations of the region on an urgent basis. With regard to China, India wants to maintain (and not lose) its privileged diplomatic-security links with Indian Ocean States. It should seek to maintain clear military superiority over the Chinese Navy in the IOR. As Raja Menon puts it; 'just because we cannot [globally] compete with China does not mean we do not defend our interests in the Indian Ocean where we wish to attain naval supremacy'. Therefore, to secure its long-term strategic and national interests India should consolidate its position through internal balancing in terms of further upgrading its naval assets and external balancing by deepening ties with the island nations and in other sense with the US. By undertaking such mechanisms India can affirm the security of its strategic interests while attaining grand objective of establishing peace, tranquility and stability in the region.

Endnotes

1   Kumar Ranjit, Island Nations: High stakes on high SEAS, (Africa Quarterly 2012)

2   Albert Eleanor, 'Competition in the Indian Ocean' at https://www.cfr.org/backgrounder/competition-indian-ocean (2016) (accessed on 11 June 2017)

3   Kaplan Robert, Center Stage for the Twenty-first Century: Power Plays in the Indian Ocean, Foreign Affairs, Vol. 88, No. 2, (2009) pp. 16-29, 31-32

4   Jaishankar Dhruva, Indian Ocean region: A Pivot for India's growth. Brookings India (2016)

5   "World Oil Transit Chokepoints," U.S. Energy Information Administration, (Nov 2014)

6   Amit A Pandya, Rupert Herbert-Burns, and Junko Kobayashi, "Maritime Commerce and Security: The Indian Ocean," The Henry L. Stimson Center, (February 2011), p. 36.

7   Singh Siddhartha, Security Outlook of Indian Ocean and India's Geostrategic interest in the IOR, India Foundation, New Delhi (2016)

8   Mohan C Raja, "India's rise as an Asia-Pacific Power: Rhetoric and Reality", Australian Strategic Pacific institute, (2012)

9   A Prakash, "At Sea about Naval History," http://www.bharat-rakshak.com/NAVY/History/ 1600s/Prakash.html (accessed August 3, 2011). Also see, A Prakash, From the Crow's Nest (New Delhi: Lancer Publishers, 2007).

10 Menon Shiv Shankar (Foreign Secretary), 'Maritime Imperatives of Indian Foreign Policy', Maritime Affairs 5/2 (Winter 2009), 15

11 Brewster David, India's Ocean: The Story of India's Bid for Regional Leadership (Abingdon: Routledge, 2014)

12 Brewster David & Ranjit Rai: Operation Lal Dora: India's Aborted Military Intervention in Mauritius, Asian Security, 9:1, (2013), 62-74

13 Albert Eleanor, Op. Cit.

14 (https://swarajyamag.com/magazine/the-dragon-in-the-indian-ocean-is-shaping-local-geopolitics-does-india-have-a-counter)

15 (http://economictimes.indiatimes.com/articleshow/58390869.cms)

16 (http://cf.orfonline.org/wpcontent/uploads/2015/03/Occasional   Paper_60.pdf)

17 M Nalapat, 'China's Great Game', Also M. Malik, 'China's Strategy of Containing

India', *Power and Interest News Report* (6 Feb. 2006), available at http://www. pinr.com/report.php?ac=view_ printable&report_id=434& language_id=1>; C. Griffin, 'Containment with Chinese Characteristics, Beijing Hedges against the Rise of India', Asian Outlook 3 (Sept. 2006)

18 Kumar Ranjit, (2012), Op. Cit.

19 Ghosh, PK and Naryan, Sripathy, Maritime Capacity of India: Strength and Challenges, Observer Research Foundation, (2012)

20 Pathak Vidhan, China and Francophone Western Indian Ocean Region, Journal of Defence Studiesw,Vol 3. (2009) No 4

21 Chaudhuri Pramit Pal, Making Waves in Indian Ocean: Modi building bridges to island states, available at http://www.hindustantimes.com/india/making-waves-in-indian-ocean-modi-building-bridges-to-island-states/story-kPGjODlHJO2 vlwgaaGhEdL.html (2015)

22 'The U.S military is worried about China building overseas bases right next to their own' at http://www.businessinsider.in/the-us-military-is worried-about-china-building-overseas-bases-right-next-to-their-own/articleshow/59042831. cms, (accessed on 2 June 2017)

23 Bhaskar Uday, Strategic Sustainment? China's Ships, silk roads, and Indian Ocean presence, IHS Jane's Navy International, Vol. 119, (2014), Issue 10

24 Choudhury Avinandan, India-US Naval Alliance: Chinese threat in Indian Ocean, available at http://www.dailyo.in/politics/india-us-naval-alliance-chinese-threat-indian-ocean/story/1/17780.html (2017)

25 Brewster, David (2014), Op. Cit.

26 Chaudhuri, Pramit Pal (2015), Op. Cit.

27 Choudhury, Avinandan (2017), Op. Cit.

28 Brewster, David (2014), Op. Cit.

† **Ms Dhanwati Yadav** is a PhD Research Scholar at Jawaharlal Nehru University. Her research concentrates on Mauritius Security Engagements with India and China.

China's Strategic Behaviour and Its Impact on India *

Shri R S Kalha, IFS (Retd)

Introduction

Soon after Xi Jinping took over as the new Chinese President and Chinese Communist Party [CCP] leader in 2012, he initiated a review of China's strategic and foreign policies. A signed article authored by State Councilor Yang Jiechi entitled *'New Type of Relations Between Great Powers'* was published in the CCP journal *Qiushi* [Seeking Truth] on 16 August 2013; clearly indicating that it had the approval of the Standing Committee of the CCP Politburo. This article succinctly reflected the new thinking of the Chinese leadership and outlined the policies to be followed in the coming decade.

The primacy of place in this article was on China's relations with the US. Chinese policies would be entirely conciliatory and based on three basic principles. Firstly, non-conflict and non-confrontation that required both sides to view each other's strategic intentions objectively *and stay as partners instead of adversaries [emphasis added]*. Secondly, mutual respect that required both sides to respect each other's choice of social system and development path and respect each other's core interests and major concerns. Thirdly, win-win cooperation *that required both sides to accommodate the others interests [emphasis added]*. It follows therefore that China seeks a position of a *co-equal* great power [emphasis added]. Since then the Chinese leadership, particularly President Xi Jinping, have continually emphasised that with the US:

---

* This articles was first published in the *USI Strategic Year Book 2016.*

> *There are now over 90 mechanisms for dialogue, and last year, the bilateral trade volume exceeded $520 billion, bilateral investment accounted for over $100 billion. There are over 41 pairs of friendly provinces or states from both sides, and 202 sister cities. People-to-people exchanges exceeded 4 million every year. China-U.S. cooperation not only benefits our peoples, but also promotes peace, stability and prosperity in the Asia-Pacific region and the world as a whole.*[1]

The Chinese leadership is thus confident that because of the vast and extensive relationship that they have developed with the US; *that the US would not easily 'sacrifice' this relationship, should a confrontation develop between China and any other country on its periphery [emphasis added]*, with the possible exception of Japan and that too only if the provocation is extreme. That being so where does India stand in the Chinese power calculus and strategic thought? There was no mention of India in Yang Jiechi's article, but at the end it contained a general warning against provoking China and perhaps was intended for countries on China's periphery that have disputes with it. Yang Jiechi categorically emphasised that:

> *No country should expect China to swallow the bitter fruit that undermines the country's sovereignty, security and development interests. In its diplomatic work, China will not dodge disputes or problems. China must not forsake its legitimate interests or compromise its core national interests.*[2]

In this context China has defined Tibet as a core national interest and continues to refer to Arunachal Pradesh as *Southern Tibet*. Therefore, apart from Tibet, Chinese strategic behavior in three critical areas significantly impacts on India. These are [a] the boundary issue, [b] the Sino-Pak nexus and [c] the Indo-Pacific region.

Tibet

China regards Tibet to be its core interest [He Xin Li Yi/核心利益]. This first appeared in an official document, as an explicit reference in April 2006, in a statement issued after a meeting between the Sri Lankan PM and the then Chinese Vice - Premier Zeng Qinghong. As a core interest, China will do nothing to even remotely lessen it's strangle- hold on Tibet, even while sometimes going through the motions of negotiations with the Dalai Lama's representatives.

The Dalai Lama continues to live in exile in Dharamsala [India] along with thousands of his followers. There are about 120,000 Tibetan refugees living in India. The Dalai Lama is the center of the Tibetan community, the person to whom the Tibetans look for guidance in all things. They give to him a faith and a belief and a trust unparalleled in other relationships.[3] China watches the Dalai Lama's every move with anxiety. The Dalai Lama can still initiate sufficient turmoil in Tibet to cause the Chinese anxious moments. The Chinese are aware of the moderation exercised by the present Dalai Lama, although they will never admit it, but are acutely embarrassed by the rise of the militant Tibetan Youth Congress [TYC] whom they equate with al-Qaeda.[4] What irked the Chinese was that elections were held for the Tibetan 'government-in exile' in India in 2011 and that India did nothing to stop holding of such elections.

Despite enormous efforts put in over the years China has still not been able to pacify Tibetan aspirations for complete autonomy or even independence. China has tried everything from brutal crackdowns to economic sops and yet the Tibetan yearning for independence has just not died down to China's utter exasperation. China faces a crisis of credibility in Tibet even after a half century of so-called 'democratic reforms.'[5] Since 2009 nearly 126 Tibetans have self- immolated in protest against Chinese rule. Most have left a record of their intentions, call for the return of the Dalai Lama to Tibet, of the independence of Tibet and of their frustrations as oppressed people.[6] Chinese suspicions and paranoia about Indian attitudes remain.

Sino-Indian Boundary Issue

The Sino-Indian boundary issue is a long standing one. Within the Indian leadership it was Indira Gandhi who first realised that it would be an 'over-simplification' to regard poor relations with China as a result of the border question. Indira Gandhi correctly surmised that Chinese policy on the Sino-Indian boundary dispute was a result of a more 'complex policy' that in turn required a much more sophisticated approach. She was conscious that poor relations with China limited India's foreign policy options. Since then Indian policy has been largely pragmatic. From denying that a dispute existed under Nehru, to stating that till the dispute was settled that there could be no full normalization of relations, to Rajiv Gandhi's assertion that normalization of relations could take place side by side with the boundary negotiations; the Indian position has moved quite significantly over the years. PM Vajpayee went even further and agreed with his Chinese counterpart that the boundary settlement could be explored '*from a political perspective*;' thus abandoning Nehru's oft stated position that the Sino-Indian boundary was established by '*treaty, custom and usage.*' Finally, in Article III of the '*Political Parameters and Guiding Principles Agreement*' signed in April 2005; PM Manmohan Singh accepted a '*package settlement*' and '*adjustment of its position*' on the boundary issue. So with India having moved so far, why then does China not agree to settle the boundary issue on the basis of a package deal? Apart from a boundary settlement, China also refuses to come to an understanding on a mutually agreed '*Line of Actual Control*' to avoid border incidents.

Present day Chinese strategists while referring to the boundary dispute also make it a point to emphasise that China-Pakistan, Tibet and the Dalai Lama and India's propensity to seek enhanced strategic and security links with countries of East Asia, under the aegis of US 're-balancing' towards Asia, are important factors that China takes into account while determining its policy. What worries them is that India may abandon its strategic autonomy and ally with the US to 'contain' China. They discern that a growing number of Indian strategists, as well as large sections of influential Indian media, are promoting the case for alignment with the US. [7] In the Chinese mind the link between a boundary settlement and these strategic factors is therefore well established. On each of these issues; China first seeks satisfaction. Being able to put pressure on India on the boundary issue is too valuable a coercive diplomatic asset to give up. As an article in the Hong Kong based newspaper *Wen Wei Po* put it, 'while New Delhi was quick to express hope to see both sides try harder to resolve their border dispute....China has implemented a policy of good neighborliness and incessantly extended its hand of friendship to India...India has adopted a policy a mega-strategy of restraining China with the United States on the one hand and imposing economic and trade restrictions on the other. In this situation *China does not need to rush for a quick solution to its boundary dispute with India*' *[emphasis added]*.

Sino-Pak Nexus

A Chinese diplomat once famously described Pakistan as 'China's Israel'. Superlatives have been used in the past and are still used with increasing frequency by both Pakistan and China to describe the depth and range of their relationship; the latest one being the Chinese President Xi Jinping who described both countries as 'Iron Friends'. There is no doubt that the bilateral relations are firm and deep, but the cement that holds it; is the anti-India syndrome that still retains its lustre. In the context of the burgeoning Sino-Pak nexus there are three issues that have an impact not only on Indian security, but also shape to an extent, the strategic landscape of South Asia. These are the situation in Xinjiang, leading to ethnic unrest and Chinese strong arm methods to control it. *The Chinese fear that this unrest has been fuelled by insurgents moving across the border from the northern areas of Pakistan to Xinjiang* [emphasis added]. The second is the nuclear nexus between China and Pakistan and the third issue is the continuing large scale arming and the military supply relationship between China and Pakistan. For India these are issues that adversely impact its national security and therefore it cannot but take cognizance of the developing situation.

The Chinese are miffed that Pakistan has not done enough to control jihadi elements, from entering Xinjiang some of whom presently reside in the Northern areas of Pakistan. During Xi Jinping's recent visit to Pakistan he promised an investment of US $46 billion, but insisted that more than adequate security steps be taken, not only to protect Chinese investments and personnel, but also to counter jihadi elements. Pakistani leaders promised to raise a new Special Security Division of the Pakistani Army, totalling some 10,000 men that will mainly come from the Special Services Group, an elite Pakistani Commando Force. In sharp contrast, the Pakistani leadership refused to commit troops to Yemen at the request of another 'all weather' friend Saudi Arabia.[8]

According to latest reports China's military exports saw a jump of 162% during the period 2008-2012 as compared to the previous five year period. Of this nearly 55% of China's exports went to Pakistan and China has replaced the UK as the world's fifth largest arms exporter.[9] China supplies almost every conceivable weapons system to Pakistan be it tanks, artillery guns, missiles, fighter aircraft and naval vessels.

Apart from a military supply relationship, China has also been instrumental in helping Pakistan build an indigenous arms industry of which the co-production of the JF-17 fighter aircraft in Pakistan is a prime example. The JF-17 is a single engine multiple role low cost fighter based on a design of the 1990s. Pakistan is the only country that has developed this weapons system jointly with China and recently Pakistan inducted the first indigenously built JF-17 Thunder Squadron into its Air Force.[10] Close collaboration between the two countries also extends to sharing intelligence. The wreckage of the stealth helicopter left behind by the US after the Osama raid was inspected by Chinese military engineers with Pakistani concurrence.[11]

However what worries Indian strategists even more is the clandestine nature and the extent of the Pak-China nuclear supply relationship. Recently de-classified CIA documents reveal information that though known but was perhaps not fully confirmed as follows:

> *On Pakistan specifically, the CIA had evidence suggesting close Chinese nuclear cooperation, of facilitating a nuclear weapons capability..... The estimate highlights some of the main developments, including "verbal consent [in 1974] to help Pakistan develop a 'nuclear blast' capability".... to provide nuclear weapons technology, and the "possibility that China has provided a fairly comprehensive package of proven nuclear weapon design information." The exchanges may not have been one-way and the reference to Chinese "involvement" in Pakistan's uranium enrichment program probably refers to gas centrifuge technology, which Pakistan shared with the Chinese.[12]*

The US was indeed apprehensive about the implications of the spread of nuclear capabilities and that China may have been aiding and abetting some potential proliferators, such as Pakistan, but for reasons of perceived national security interests was not willing to confront either China or Pakistan openly.

As far as civilian nuclear co-operation is concerned, the Chinese openly admit that they supplied the first nuclear power station in 1992 that was built at Chashma and became operational in 2001. The contract for the second nuclear power plant was signed on 5 May 2004 [Chashma-2] on the eve of China joining the Nuclear Suppliers Group [NSG]. As the contract per-existed China's date of joining the NSG, China insists that it was exempted from NSG requirements of full scope safeguards. In October 2008 China contracted to build two more nuclear power plants [Chashma-3 and Chashma-4]. In February 2010 China also agreed to finance these two nuclear power plants by providing a loan to Pakistan, but also acknowledged that these plants would be under IAEA safeguards. China, in what was seen as significant back-tracking, however claimed in September 2010 that these two plants were based on the 'contracts of 2003' and therefore not subject to full scope safe-guards that NSG membership mandated.[13] Further press reports indicated that China is expected to build two more nuclear power plants at Karachi for which it is expected to extend a loan of US $6.4 billion to Pakistan. Similarly other reports indicated that China and Pakistan are discussing building three new nuclear power plants at Muzaffargarh estimated to cost US $ 13 billion. [14] China does not accept that what was done for India under the Indo-US Civilian Nuclear Agreement cannot be done for Pakistan.

The Indo-Pacific Region

For China the perceived Indo-US strategic convergence in the Indo-Pacific region is a matter of concern. Although the PLA- N first began its forays into the Indian Ocean region as early as 1985, its presence there has increased considerably over the last five years. Since January 2009, the PLA-N has sustained counter piracy operations in the Gulf of Aden to protect Chinese commercial shipping interests. The inaugural counter piracy patrol represented China's first operational deployment of naval forces outside of China's regional waters.[15] In any event, given the immense help that China has provided for the infrastructure development it will be extremely difficult for Myanmar, Bangladesh, Sri Lanka and Pakistan to deny permission for Chinese naval port calls that could conceivably expand to base and repair facilities.[16] To be fair, all except Pakistan have denied the granting of such facilities. In 2012, the PLA- N, for the first time, began to deploy maritime intelligence collection ships to the Indian Ocean[17]. These ships are likely to have equipment enabling them to collect signals and electronic intelligence,[18] suggesting that the PLA- N may be planning for something more than mere routine naval operations in the Indian Ocean region in the near future. However one of the main hurdles that the PLA-N faces is the fact that it is operating far outside its base area.

China realises the strategic importance of the Indian Ocean area, as 75 per cent of oil imported by China traverses through this region, but considers this as a 'weak' link in its peripheral diplomacy. China 'understands' that the Indian Ocean region is vital to India's security. It does not grudge *for the present [emphasis added]*, the role of a security provider played by the US Navy. There are three influential platforms in the India Ocean region; IOR, SAARC and IONS and the Chinese feel that India should not object to China's membership of these organisations. On the other hand, India wishes to 'off-set' the negative effects of China's rise by enhancing co-operation with the US and countries around China. It is the Chinese hope that India would strike a careful balance between competition and co-operation with China.

Meanwhile Chinese strategists have keenly watched the development and direction of PM Modi's new policy of *'Act East'* as manifested by statements made during his recent visits to Japan, Myanmar, Australia and Fiji. The Chinese are confident that they can contain any rise of India's influence in the ASEAN region. The Chinese assessment is that the US combined with India and Japan, have all *intensified their input and involvement in the region to contain China' [emphasis added]*. The Chinese feel that these attempts may not be successful because 'China and the ASEAN countries are increasingly integrated in their economic interests and their interdependence has been increasingly expanded and deepened. Although India's relations with ASEAN countries are on the rise, yet it still lags far behind China.' Chinese analysts admit that although India can be classified as a South Asian power, yet it has gradually 'expanded and extended' its role to East Asia, thus 'squeezing into the rank of major powers in the Asia-Pacific region.' [19] That India has also 'accelerated its military modernization drive' is also admitted and it is this consolidation of military strength that has enabled India to 'march towards its strategic goal of becoming an Asia-Pacific military power.' In this endeavour, the US 'supports' not only India playing a larger role in South Asia, but in the entire Asia-Pacific region. The US also encourages India to 'jointly' participate in military exercises with other countries of the Asia-Pacific region such as Australia, Japan and South Korea. Chinese analysts are convinced that the US is firstly trying to incorporate India into the US led international and regional military system and secondly to exploit India-China conflicts so as to 'bring about a strategic situation that both India and the US jointly restrain China, thus landing China in an absolutely inferior position. [20]

However there are some elements in China who openly state that with the Maritime Silk Road, the AIIB, the China-Pak Economic Corridor, the surfacing of a Chinese nuclear submarine in Sri Lankan waters; Chinese 'strength' in the Indian Ocean Region has been demonstrated as never before.[21] Sober elements however feel that if the Indian Ocean is important for China, so is the Pacific Ocean for India. As a result of globalization, many believe that a broader Indo-Pacific era has arrived. Should this be the case, the Indo-Pacific has much larger room to accommodate a Sino-Indian rapprochement. The key question however remains that until there is a Sino-Indian 'understanding' on vital strategic issues; rivalry between the two emerging Asian powers will continue.

Endnotes

1   President Xi Jinping's speech at the opening of the sixth round of China-US Strategic and Economic Dialogue on 9 July 2014.

2   Xinhua, 16 August 2013

3   Ibid.

4   Beijing Review, 3 May 2008.

5   Dr. Dibyesh Anand. Interview to Zee Television (Delhi: zee.com), 19 November 2011.

6   Carole McGranahan. "Opinion," *The Outlook (Delhi)*, 22 October 2012.

7   Liu Zhongyi. Visiting Fellow at the Centre for Strategic and International Studies (CIIS). "Sino-Indian Border Dispute and their Competitive Symbiotic Relationship," *Future Directions International*, 28 May 2013.

8   Bruce Riedel, 'The Pakistani Pivot from Saudi Arabia to China' *Brookings*, 23 April 2015.

9   SIPRI, 18 March 2013

10   Zackery Keck. '*Pak Exporting JF-17 Thunder Jets*,' Diplomat, 30 October 2013.

11   Mark Mazetti. '*US aides believe China examined Stealth Helicopter*' NYT, 11 August 2011.

12   CHINA-PAK NUCLEAR NEXUS [National Security Archives Electronic Briefing Book No 423], 23 April 2013, Documents 3A-B.

13   Shirley Kan, Congressional Research Service [CRS], 'China and Proliferation of Weapons of Mass Destruction and Missiles: Policy Issues', 25 November 2014.

14   Saeed Shah. 'Pakistan in Talks to Acquire three Nuclear Plants from China.' Wall Street Journal, 20 January 2014.

15   U.S.-China Economic and Security Review Commission, *2013 Annual Report to Congress* (Washington, DC: November 2013), pp. 305-306.

16   Commodore [Retd] Lalit Kapur. 'China and the Indian Ocean' USI Commentary [Strategic Perspectives], 26 November 2014.

17   US Department of Defense, *Annual Report to Congress on Military and Security Developments Involving the People's Republic of China 2013* (Washington, DC: May 2013), p. 39; and Senate Armed Services Committee, *Hearing on U.S. Pacific Command Posture*, testimony of Admiral Samuel J. Locklear, 113th Cong., 5 March 2013.

18 Kyle Mizokami, 'These 5 Ships Are the Real Future of the Chinese Navy,' *Foreign Policy*, 16 December 2013. *http://complex.foreignpolicy.com/posts/2013/12/16/these_five_ships_are_the_real_future_of_the_chinese_navy*; See also *Zee News*, 'Chinese ship caught spying on India,' 31 August 2011

19 Shen Qiang. '*US New Strategies toward China, Russia and India.*' International Strategic Studies, 3rd Issue, 2012.

20 Shen Qiang. Op Cit.

21 Zhou Bo '*China Goes West and India Acts East*', Honorary Fellow, PLA Academy of Military Science, 21 April 2015.

---

† Shri Ranjit S Kalha, IFS (Retd) has been India's Ambassador to Indonesia and retired as the Secretary (West) in India's Ministry of External Affairs. He was also a member of the China study Group and led India at the 6th, 7th and 8th round of border talks with China. He has authored three books, the latest one being 'India – China Boundary Issues : Quest for Settlement'.

China and India: The Road Ahead[*]

Shri Mohan Guruswamy

There seems a misplaced notion prevalent in India, and it was much in evidence in the Prime Minister's interaction with Indian industrialists on September 15, 2016. It is that China's slowdown means an opportunity for India. Even the CEA (Chief Economic Adviser) Arvind Subramaniam, though somewhat circumspect, says: "Cheap oil will help our macro-economic indicators. The Chinese slowdown and massive excess capacity in sectors like steel will put pressure. But cost of building infrastructure has come down due to fall in commodity prices. This will boost infrastructure development. India will remain an attractive destination."

But there is little evidence that his government is investing more in infrastructure. The capital expenditure to budget, and capital expenditure to GDP ratios are both still pointed south. To expect foreign capital to build India's infrastructure is to be naïve. Foreign funds invariably come with a short term perspective, and as recent experience shows investment in India's infrastructure is neither easy nor does it offer attractive returns.

The two economies are now in two entirely different stages of development. For a start China's GDP is three and half times bigger than India's. Their GDP is in excess of $11 trillion and India has just scaled $2.2 trillion. How China moves and acts in the future will affect the developed economies enormously, as it has been the major provider of growth for the last two decades, and India's growth had little bearing or derived little benefit from it. They exist in different orbits of the world economy. A slowed down China now growing at 6 per cent still adds $660 billion to global growth, while a speeded up India now growing at 7 per cent adds a mere $144 billion.

---

[*] This articles was first published in the *USI Strategic Year Book 2017.*.

191

For India to pick up the Chinese slack, it needs to be posting a more frenetic 9-10 per cent over the next decade or more. There is not even a glimmer of that now. Hope is a good thing but wishful thinking leads to serious consequences. We must be careful and realistic, when we analyse our prospects and decide on our actions.

Although the Chinese economy does not compete directly with India's, the effect the former imposes on the global economy is likely to influence the Indian economy. In this regard, whether a slowing Chinese economy will really create more opportunities for the Indian economy? It needs, rethinking. If the global economy slows down further as part of the results of Chinese economic restructuring, it would be difficult to see why a sluggish world economy would help the Indian economy?

There are many factors that have hampered the Indian economy, and the most important reasons lie in exercising policy options and the level of domestic development, rather than external environment or international factors. The Indian economy is in a more favourable demographic transition, and how this will be translated into the kind of growth China experienced in the previous three decades depends on the sagacity, determination and vision of our leaders.

The success of the Indian economy in the years ahead depends on a number of crucial elements, and the most important ones are likely the leadership's policy options and internal interactions. Seeing how major policies relating to a common and nationwide tax regime (GST), and land acquisition have been stymied, do not present a very optimistic picture.

Let's therefore be clear about one important aspect - the present financial crisis in China does not affect its overall economic prospects one bit. Financial crises are inevitable, as greed and irrational expectations will always drive the market upwards till reality catches up and pulls it down.

But when some people lose money others make money. So to judge China's economic prospects by what happened to the stock market betrays an inability to separate issues pertaining to financial market behaviour and the economic reality. Also to think that the housing bubble is a crisis that will not be surmounted would be unwise. Most of the unoccupied housing units in China, as is in India, have been paid for. Those who speculated in the property market will inevitably get hurt in the process, but the economy has already gained from the investment. Future investment in the Chinese real estate market will inevitably be slow. But that is also inevitable as population is aging and new housing demand will reduce.

The real problems in China will get accentuated, as exports to the USA and EU will slowdown, as the USA in particular is determined to reduce its trade gap. Also low cost production is shifting to other low labour costs economies like Vietnam and Indonesia. China will naturally attempt to overcome this by stimulating domestic consumption, and can even finance it by slowly reducing its foreign reserves, as Saudi Arabia and others are doing now.

However much China may invest by running down its reserves, it will be irrational to expect near double-digit expansion when demographic trends are against it. The high growth period in China is petering off and that is the transition we must be wary off. Where will the world get its next growth engine? Demography favours India. But the Indian political discourse gives no inkling of any awareness of this or inclination to put immediate politics aside for a period to set course for the long term.

The transition from an export driven GDP to an internal consumption demand driven economy will be a daunting task. China's exports are mostly low labour cost exports, and hence skill levels will be low. Internal consumption will demand goods of higher sophistication and the retraining of labour will be a problem.

As demands rise and domestic standards of living rise, people will expect more from the system. As Abraham Maslow, the psychologist theorized, there is a hierarchy of needs, and so when one demand is satiated people will want more. This will increasingly take the form of demanding more political and social freedoms.

As China becomes upper middle class, dominating the challenge to the primacy of the Communist Party, will be from upper middle class values. These values are universal. Thus growth, that is the increase of choice for the consumer in goods and services, will be increasingly accompanied by demands for more choice in immediate governance issues.

Obviously China's interaction with the global economy and its size will only demand its greater participation in its organization. China also needs to invest more in other countries to create markets for itself. For instance if China invests in India, it will create a long and continued demand for Chinese goods. The current adverse trade situation will not be allowed to continue for very long.

China must invest more in rebalancing the international economic system. The world cannot only depend on western demand and consumption, financed by printing more money to finance it. China must team up with other large developing country economies like India, Brazil and Indonesia to restructure the IMF and World Bank. The BRICS is a great opportunity, but only if the discussions progresses to consider weightier issues than the usual cosmetics professional diplomats are habituated to post on the agenda. Chinese President Xi Jinping and Prime Minister Narendra Modi have the responsibility of looking well ahead and take a more cosmic view of how our world should look in the future. They can prepare China and India to assume the roles that beckons.

† **Shri Mohan Guruswamy** is a Distinguished Fellow at the United Service Institution of India, New Delhi, and a Visiting Professor at the Administrative Staff College of India, Hyderabad. He is the author of several books on policy issues, the latest being - Chasing the Dragon: Will India Catch-up with China? A Harvard graduate, he is a frequent commentator on matters of current interest in the print and electronic media and has held senior positions in government and industry.